Handbook of Japanese Grammar

HANDBOOK
OF
JAPANESE GRAMMAR

Masahiro Tanimori

CHARLES E. TUTTLE COMPANY
Rutland, Vermont & Tokyo, Japan

Published by the Charles E. Tuttle Company, Inc.
of Rutland, Vermont & Tokyo, Japan
with editorial offices at
2-6 Suido 1-chome, Bunkyo-ku, Tokyo 112

First edition, 1994
Second printing, 1995

LCC Card No. 94-60444
ISBN 0-8048-1940-8

Printed in Japan

Contents

Introduction

Language learners come with backgrounds and interests as varied as people come in shapes and sizes. To accommodate the burgeoning interest in Japanese-language study is an equal number of books and learning aids for all levels. One resource that anyone can use, no matter what their level of Japanese, is a thorough grammar reference. This one is designed for ease of use by the non-linguist—for the non-native *speaker* and *user* of Japanese rather than the *student* of Japanese.

Grammatical terminology is kept to a minimum, as are detailed explanations as to why words or phrases function as they do. Rather, example sentences show concretely how and where the key function words are used. It is hoped that this method will be immediately accessible (and useful) to a wide audience. Use of this reference book doesn't require extensive prior knowledge of grammatical terms, nor does it demand that the reader learn them, though of course one is not at a disadvantage for having that knowledge. To look up a word one simply need know how to say it—and be grateful that romanization of Japanese is easier than spelling in English.

Part One includes grammatical function words arranged alphabetically, with entries given first in romanized form, followed by Japanese characters. Each entry includes a brief grammatical description of the word or phrase, and several English equivalents. Below that follow sample sentences illustrating various positions within a sentence where the entry word or phrase may be used. In these sentences, the author treats the progressive (*te iru*) and *tai*-forms of verbs as dictionary forms, as these can be further conjugated.

The sample sentences illustrate a wide variety of everyday situations. While some of the English translations of the Japanese may seem a bit stilted, this has been done deliberately in the interest of clearly illustrating the grammatical pattern at hand. Other related or similar function words are cross-referenced at the end of each entry, and if the reference occurs in Part Two, a "II" in parentheses follows.

While Part One is for looking up specifics, Part Two takes a more traditional approach to grammar, examining parts of speech, their general usage, and conjugations. As such it can be used for further detailed study of a particular part of speech or grammatical usage. *Usage* is a key word throughout this book, as the author has made a concerted effort to show various nuances of particular Japanese forms. He has also included a detailed cross-reference with Part One. Thus if one looks up Verb Forms in Part Two, for example, a list of words and phrases in Part One that are commonly used with each of the verb forms is also provided.

A further word about verb forms is in order. Consistent with the minimal use of grammatical terminology, the author has not used the traditional terminology for verb forms. One will not find a listing for "conditional forms," for example, but rather the "*ba*-form" and the "*tara*-form." Once again, the user need only know how to say something in order to learn more about it. It is hoped that this approach will be found user-friendly. Like any systematic approach, however, one must allow time to become accustomed to it.

One final note in regard to the Prepositions entry in Part Two. While other sections list Japanese first, followed by English equivalents, this section alone lists English prepositions first, following them with example sentences illustrating how these may be expressed in Japanese. As these two, three, and four-letter English words function very differently in Japanese, the exceptional treatment of them here is not only justified but extremely helpful.

It is the author's hope that students using this book will make great progress in their study of the Japanese language. He has made every effort to include both everyday and exceptional usage in the example sentences presented here, for in grammar, there are no rules without exceptions.

Finally, special thanks go to Julie Iezzi and the staff of the Charles E. Tuttle Publishing Company for their hard and patient work in editing the English content.

PART ONE

Dictionary of
Grammatical Function Words

ageru あげる

VERB MEANING: give (something to a person who is either of equal or lower status), do (something for that kind of person)

Sashiageru is used with a person of higher status or to whom the speaker wishes to show respect. *Yaru* is very informally used instead of this verb. The 1st person cannot be the recipient.

1. After noun + *o*
   この本をあげます。
   *Kono **hon o agemasu**.*
   I give you this book.
   (*Kono **hon o sashiagemasu**.* [respectful])
2. After *te*-form of verb
   この自転車を貸してあげます。
   *Kono jitensha o kashi**te agemasu**.*
   I lend you this bicycle.
   (*Kono jitensha o kashi**te sashiagemasu**.* [respectful])
   彼女にネックレスを買ってあげました。
   *Kanojo ni nekkuresu o ka**tte agemashita**.*
   I bought a necklace for her.
→ See also *kureru, morau*

aida あいだ

NOUN MEANING: in between, between, during, from . . . through, among, while

1. Followed by *ni*
   間に立ってください。

Aida ni tatte kudasai.
Please stand in between.

2. After noun + *no*, followed by *ni*
留守の間に田中さんが訪ねてきました。
Rusu no aida ni tanaka-san ga tazunete kimashita.
Mr. Tanaka came to see you during your absence.

3. After noun + *to* + noun + *no,* followed by *ni*
郵便局は駅と学校の間にあります。
Yūbinkyoku wa eki to gakkō no aida ni arimasu.
The post office is between the station and the school.

4. After noun + *kara* + noun + *made no*
10日から15日までの間休みます。
Tōka kara jū go nichi made no aida yasumimasu.
I'll take holidays from the 10th through the 15th.

5. After verb in the progressive tense, followed by *ni*
本を読んでいる間に眠ってしまった。
Hon o yonde iru aida ni nemutte shimatta.
I fell asleep while I was reading a book.

6. After dictionary form of adjective, followed by *ni*
若い間にもっと勉強しなさい。
Wakai aida ni motto benkyō shinasai.
Study more while you are young.

amari あまり

ADVERB (used with a negative) MEANING: not much, not many, not enough, not well, not very

1. Used with negative verb
私はあまり食べません。

*Watashi wa **amari tabemasen**.*
I don't eat much.
彼のことはあまり知りません。
*Kare no koto wa **amari shirimasen**.*
I don't know much about him.
今あまりお金を持っていません。
*Ima **amari** o-kane o **motte imasen**.*
I don't have much money now.

2. Used with negative adjective
天気はあまりよくありません。
*Tenki wa **amari yoku arimasen**.*
The weather is not very good.
会社は家からあまり遠くありません。
*Kaisha wa ie kara **amari tōku arimasen**.*
The company is not very far from our house.

are あれ

DEMONSTRATIVE NOUN MEANING: that, those, it

It refers to an object or objects far from both the speaker and the hearer.

The polite form is *achira*, which also means "that person" or "that direction." *Are* becomes *ano* before a noun it modifies. Moreover, it becomes *asoko* when expressing "that place over there."

1. Followed by particle
「あれは何ですか。」「あれは日本のまつりです。」
*"**Are wa** nan desu ka." "**Are wa** nihon no matsuri desu."*

"What's that?" "It's a Japanese festival."

あちらに着いたら電話を下さい。

Achira ni *tsuitara denwa o kudasai.*

Please call me when you get there.

「あちらはどなたですか。」「山本さんです。」

"***Achira wa*** *donata desu ka.*" "*Yamamoto-san desu.*"

"Who is that person?" "She is Ms. Yamamoto."

銀行はあの建物の隣です。

*Ginkō wa **ano** tatemono no tonari desu.*

The bank is next to the building over there.

(*Are* becomes *ano* when used as an adjective.)

トイレはあそこにあります。

*Toire wa **asoko** ni arimasu.*

The restroom is over there.

(*Are* becomes *asoko* when meaning "that place over there.")

私の家はあそこです。

*Watashi no ie wa **asoko** desu.*

My house is over there.

→ See also *kore, sore*

arimasen　ありません

NEGATIVE VERB used for making the negative form of *desu, aru,* and adjectives

Note that the plain form is *nai*.

1. After (adjectival) noun + *dewa*

これは私のかばんではありません。

*Kore wa watashi no **kaban dewa arimasen**.*

This is not my bag.

その問題はあまり重要ではありません。

*Sono mondai wa amari **jūyō dewa arimasen***.

That problem is not very important.

2. After *ku*-form of adjective

この機械はどこも悪くありません。

*Kono kikai wa doko mo waru**ku arimasen***.

Nothing is wrong with this machine.

外は寒くありませんでした。

*Soto wa samu**ku arimasen deshita***.

It wasn't cold outside.

→ See also *aru, desu, nai, masu*, Verb Forms (II)

aru ある

VERB MEANING: be, there be, exist, have

1. After inanimate subject

銀行は駅の向こうにあります。

*Ginkō wa eki no mukō ni **arimasu***.

The bank is on the other side of the station.

2. After (object) noun + *ga*

「部屋にはシャワーがありますか。」「はい、あります。」

*"Heya ni wa **shawā ga arimasu** ka." "Hai, arimasu."*

"Does the room have a shower?" "Yes, it does."

3. After *ta*-form of verb + *koto* + *ga*

(used for expressing experiences)

東京に3回行ったことがあります。

*Tōkyō ni san kai it**ta koto ga arimasu***.

I've been to Tokyo three times.

4. After *te*-form of verb
   (used for expressing some continuing state caused by an action)
   ドアは閉めてあります。
   Doa wa shimete arimasu.
   The door is shut (because I shut it).
→ See also *arimasen, iru, koto ga aru, nai*

ato de あとで

PHRASE MEANING: after, later

1. After noun + *no*
   いつも食事の後でコーヒーを飲みます。
   Itsumo shokuji no ato de kōhii o nomimasu.
   I usually drink coffee after meals.
2. After *ta*-form of verb
   仕事が終わった後で話したいことがあります。
   Shigoto ga owatta ato de hanashitai koto ga arimasu.
   There is something I want to talk to you about after I finish work.
3. Used as adverb
   後で電話しましょうか。
   Ato de denwa shimashō ka.
   Shall I call you later?
→ See also *kara, mae*

au あう

VERB (added to other verbs) MEANING: each other, reciprocally

1. After conjunctive form of verb
   助けあうことが大切です。
   Tasukeau *koto ga taisetsu desu.*
   It is important to help each other.
   その問題について話しあえば解決できると思います。
   *Sono mondai ni tsuite **hanashiaeba** kaiketsu dekiru to omoi-*
   masu.
   If you talk with each other about the problem, I think you can
   solve it.

ba ば

PARTICLE MEANING: if, when

Note that *da* is irregular, becoming *naraba*. See Verb Forms
and Adjective Forms (II) for details about conjugation.

1. Used in *ba*-form of verb
   あそこに行けば山田さんに会えます。
   *Asoko ni **ikeba** Yamada-san ni aemasu.*
   If you go over there, you can see Mr. Yamada.
   もっと早く来ればよかった。
   *Motto hayaku **kureba** yokatta.*
   If I had come much earlier, it would have been better. (I should
   have come much earlier.)
   彼女が来れば教えてください。
   *Kanojo ga **kureba** oshiete kudasai.*
   When she comes, please tell me.
   (for a future condition, [*no*] *nara* is used instead of *ba* after
   dictionary form of verb)

東京に行くのなら新幹線がいいですよ。

*Tōkyō ni iku **no nara** shinkansen ga ii desu yo.*

If you're going to Tokyo, you should take the shinkansen.

2. After (adjectival) noun + *nara* (conditional form of *da*)

あした雨ならば行きません。

*Ashita **ame naraba** ikimasen.*

I won't go if it is rainy tomorrow.

3. Used in *ba*-form of adjective

よろしければどうぞ食べてください。

***Yoroshikereba** dōzo tabete kudasai.*

If it is all right (If you feel like it), please eat.

→ See also *nara*, *tara*, *to*, *to sureba*, Adjective Forms (II), Verb Forms (II)

ba . . . hodo　ば . . . ほど

PHRASE MEANING: the more . . . the more . . .

It follows the stem of *ba*-form of verb/adjective. The dictionary form of the same verb/adjective is repeated before *hodo*.

1. Used with verb

練習すればするほどうまくなります。

*Renshū **sureba suru hodo** umaku narimasu.*

The more you practice, the better you can do.

2. Used with adjective

早ければ早いほどいい。

***Hayakereba hayai hodo** ii.*

The sooner, the better.

→ See also *dake*

bakari　ばかり

PARTICLE MEANING: only, just, always, be ready to (do), have just (done), about

1. After *te*-form of verb, followed by *iru/imasu*
   彼は遊んでばかりいる。
   *Kare wa ason**de bakari iru**.*
   He is always playing.
2. After dictionary form of verb, followed by *da/desu*
   彼はいつも食べるばかりです。
   *Kare wa itsumo tabe**ru bakari desu**.*
   He is always ready to eat.
3. After *ta*-form of verb, followed by *da/desu*
   今ここに着いたばかりです。
   *Ima koko ni tsui**ta bakari desu**.*
   I've just arrived here.
4. After noun
   彼は勉強ばかりしている。
   *Kare wa **benkyō bakari** shite iru.*
   He is always studying.
5. After particle
   彼女は図書館にばかり行きます。
   *Kanojo wa toshokan **ni bakari** ikimasu.*
   She always goes to the library.
6. After noun expressing length/quantity
   1週間ばかり留守にします。
   ***Isshūkan bakari** rusu ni shimasu.*
   I'll be away about a week.
   1か月で2キロばかり体重が増えました。

*Ikkagetsu de **ni kiro bakari** taijū ga fuemashita.*

I gained about two kilograms in one month.

→ See also *dake*

beki desu　べきです

PREDICATIVE PHRASE MEANING: should, ought to (do)

1. After dictionary form of verb
   一生けんめい働くべきです。
   *Isshōkenmei hatara**ku beki desu**.*
   You should work hard.
   そんなものを買うべきではない。
   *Sonna mono o ka**u beki dewa nai**.*
   You shouldn't buy such a thing.
   もっと早く来るべきでした。
   *Motto hayaku ku**ru beki deshita**.*
   I should have come much earlier.
   あなたはもっと勉強す(る)べきです。
   *Anata wa motto benkyō su**(ru) beki desu**.*
   You should study more.
   (*suru* + *beki* may be abbreviated to *subeki*)

2. Used as adjective
   それは注目すべき点だ。
   *Sore wa chūmoku **subeki ten da**.*
   That's the point you should pay attention to.
   (dictionary form of verb + *beki* directly precedes the noun and *da/desu* follows)

→ See also *nakereba naranai*

bun 分

NOUN INDICATING: a quantity, part, portion, degree

1. After dictionary form of verb
   食べる分はあります。
   *Taberu **bun** wa arimasu.*
   There is enough to eat.
2. After *ta*-form of verb
   すでに書いた分を見せてください。
   *Sudeni kaita **bun** o misete kudasai.*
   Please show me the part that you've already written.
   残った分は取っておきます。
   *Nokotta **bun** wa totte okimasu.*
   I'll keep the portion that is left.
3. After *nai*-form of verb
   要らない分は返しておいて下さい。
   *Iranai **bun** wa kaeshite oite kudasai.*
   Please return the portion you don't need.
4. After possessive particle *no*
   これは私の分です。
   *Kore wa watashi **no bun** desu.*
   This is my share.

cha ちゃ

INFORMAL EQUIVALENT of *te wa* or *tara* (usually used by women)
MEANING: if, when

It is used after the stem of *te*-form of verbs whose dictionary
form ends with *-u*, *-ku*, *-tsu*, or *-ru*. It becomes *ja* (the informal

version of *dewa*) after the stem of *te*-form of verbs whose dictionary form ends with *-bu*, *-gu*, *-mu*, or *-nu*.

1. After the stem of *te*-form of verb
   そこへ行っちゃいけません。
   *Soko e **itcha** ikemasen.*
   You must not go there.
   そんなことをされちゃ困ります。
   *Sonna koto o **sarecha** komarimasu.*
   I'll be distressed if you do that.
→ See also *ikenai*, *ja*, *naranai*, *tara*

chau ちゃう

INFORMAL EQUIVALENT of *te shimau* (usually used by women) meaning: be going to (do), finish (doing), (do something) completely

It is used after the stem of *te*-form of verbs whose dictionary form ends with *-u*, *-ku*, *-tsu*, or *-ru*. It becomes *jau* (the informal version of *de shimau*) after the stem of *te*-form of verbs whose dictionary form ends with *-bu*, *-gu*, *-mu*, or *-nu*. It is sometimes followed by *no* when forming a question. The past forms are *chatta/jatta* (plain) and *chaimashita/jaimashita* (polite).

1. After the stem of *te*-form of verb
   もう帰っちゃうんですか。
   *Mō **kaetchau** n desu ka.*
   Are you going to leave so soon?
   今日はどんどん飲んじゃいます。
   *Kyō wa dondon **nonjaimasu**.*

I'm going to drink like crazy today.
彼女に悪いことをしちゃいました。
*Kanojo ni warui koto o **shichaimashita**.*
I've done wrong to her.

→ See also *te shimau*

chittomo　ちっとも
ADVERB (used with a negative) MEANING: (not) at all, (not) a bit

1. Followed by negative verb
ちっともかまいません。
***Chittomo** kamaimasen.*
I don't mind at all.
(affirmative sentences use *sukoshi*)
すこし日本語が話せます。
***Sukoshi** nihongo ga hanasemasu.*
I can speak a little Japanese.

→ See also *amari, mattaku, sukoshi, zenzen*

chōdo　ちょうど
ADVERB MEANING: (have) just (done), exactly, precisely

1. Used with *ta*-form of verb, followed by *tokoro* (or *bakari*) + *da/desu*
ちょうど仕事を終えたところです。
***Chōdo** shigoto o oeta tokoro desu.*
I've just finished the work.

ちょうど今着いたばかりです。
Chōdo ima tsuita bakari desu.
I've just arrived.
2. Before number expression
ちょうど9時に来てください。
Chōdo ku ji ni kite kudasai.
Please come at nine sharp.

chū ni 中に

PHRASE (of time) MEANING: during, within

It often euphonically changes to *jū ni*.

1. After noun expressing period of time
夏休み中にアメリカに行くつもりです。
Natsu yasumi chū ni amerika ni iku tsumori desu.
I plan to go to America during the summer vacation.
今週中に休みをどこで過ごすか決めます。
Konshū chū ni yasumi o doko de sugosu ka kimemasu.
I'll decide within this week where to spend the vacation.
2、3日中に完成します。
Ni san nichi jū ni kansei shimasu.
I'll complete it within a few days.
→ See also *jū*

da だ
→ See *desu*

daga だが

CONJUNCTION (usually used in written language) MEANING: but, however

1. At the beginning of sentence
   戦争は終わった。だが多くの命が失われた。
   Sensō wa owatta. **Daga** *ōku no inochi ga ushinawareta.*
   The war is over. However, many people lost their lives.
2. After dictionary, *ta-*, or *nai*-form of verb/adjective + *no/n*
   この商品は安いのだが品質が良くない。
   Kono shōhin wa yasui **no daga** *hinshitsu ga yokunai.*
   These goods are cheap but the quality is not good.
   彼のうちを訪ねたのだが、会えなかった。
   Kare no uchi o tazuneta **no daga,** *aenakatta.*
   I dropped in at his house but I wasn't able to see him.
   高いんだが買わなければならない。
   Takai **n daga** *kawanakereba naranai.*
   It's expensive but I need to buy it.
   面白くなかったんだが最後まで見た。
   Omoshiroku nakatta **n daga** *saigo made mita.*
   Although it wasn't interesting, I watched it to the end.
3. After (adjectival) noun + *na* + *no/n*
   彼は誠実なのだが能力が足りない。
   Kare wa **seijitsu na no daga** *nōryoku ga tarinai.*
   He is sincere but lacks the ability.
→ See also *dakedo, ga (2), keredo(mo)*

dakara だから

CONJUNCTION MEANING: so, and so, that's why, therefore, because

1. At the beginning of sentence
   「事故があったそうですね。」「ええ、だから遅れました。」
   *"Jiko ga atta sō desu ne." "Ee, **dakara** okuremashita."*
   "I hear there was an accident." "Yes, that's why I was late."
2. After dictionary, *ta-*, or *nai*-form of verb/adjective + *no/n*
   あしたは早く起きるんだからもう寝なさい。
   *Ashita wa hayaku oki**ru n dakara** mō nenasai.*
   Go to bed now because you have to get up early tomorrow.
   お父さんはもう行ったんだからあなたも早く行きなさい。
   *Otōsan wa mō it**ta n dakara** anata mo hayaku ikinasai.*
   Your father has already gone so you should hurry and go too.
3. After (adjectival) noun + *na* + *no/n*
   あなたは学生なんだからもっと勉強しなくてはいけません。
   *Anata wa **gakusei na n dakara** motto benkyō shinakute wa ikemasen.*
   Because you are a student you have to study more.
→ See also *kara*

dake　だけ
PARTICLE MEANING: only, just, simply, as much as, as . . . as

1. After noun
   あなただけを愛しています。
   ***Anata dake** o ai shite imasu.*
   I love only you.
   それができるのは太郎だけです。
   *Sore ga dekiru no wa **tarō dake** desu.*

Taro is the only one who can do it.

2. After particle

あなたとだけ話したい。

*Anata **to dake** hanashitai.*

I want to talk just with you (alone).

その動物は沖縄にだけいます。

*Sono dōbutsu wa okinawa **ni dake** imasu.*

That animal exists only in Okinawa.

3. After dictionary form of verb/adjective, followed by *da/desu*

彼は眠っているだけです。

*Kare wa nemutte i**ru dake desu**.*

He is only sleeping.

これは高いだけです。あまりよくありません。

*Kore wa taka**i dake desu**. Amari yoku arimasen.*

This is just expensive. It's not so good.

4. After *ta*-form of verb/adjective, followed by *da/desu*

これを見に来ただけです。

*Kore o mi ni ki**ta dake desu**.*

I just came here to see this.

少し眠かっただけです。

*Sukoshi nemuka**tta dake desu**.*

I was just a little sleepy.

5. After *nai*-form of verb/adjective, followed by *da/desu*

彼とはあまり話をしないだけです。

*Kare to wa amari hanashi o shi**nai dake desu**.*

I simply don't talk with him so often.

行きたくないだけです。

*Ikitaku**nai dake desu**.*

I just don't want to go.

6. After adjectival noun + *na*

彼は有名なだけで大した政治家ではありません。

*Kare wa **yūmei-na dake** de taishita seijika dewa arimasen.*

He is merely famous, and not much of a politician.

7. In idiomatic expressions

(between *dekiru* and adverb)

あすまたできるだけ早くここに来てください。

*Asu mata **dekiru dake hayaku** koko ni kite kudasai.*

Please come here again tomorrow as soon as you can.

(after *suki-na* or *hoshii*)

好きなだけ食べてください。

***Suki-na dake** tabete kudasai.*

Please eat as much as you like.

8. Used instead of *hodo* in the pattern . . . *ba* . . . *hodo*

努力すればするだけうまくなります。

*Doryoku sureba suru **dake** umaku narimasu.*

The harder you try, the better you can do it.

9. Used in the pattern . . . *dake de naku* . . . *mo*

彼女は日本語だけでなくフランス語も話せます。

*Kanojo wa nihongo **dake de naku** furansugo **mo** hanasemasu.*

She can speak not only Japanese but also French.

→ See also *ba* . . . *hodo*, *kagiri*, *shika*

dakedo だけど

INFORMAL CONJUNCTION OR ADVERB MEANING: but, however, though, still, nevertheless

1. At the beginning of sentence

あの車がとてもほしい。だけど高すぎる。

*Ano kuruma ga totemo hoshii. **Dakedo** takasugiru.*

I want that car very much. However, it is too expensive for me.
だけどそんなことはしなければよかった。
***Dakedo** sonna koto wa shinakereba yokatta.*
I wish I hadn't done such a thing, though.
彼は親切です。だけどあまり好きではありません。
*Kare wa shinsetsu desu. **Dakedo** amari suki dewa arimasen.*
He is kind. Still, I don't like him very much.

2. After (adjectival) noun
今日は雨だけど出かけますか。
*Kyō wa **ame dakedo** dekakemasu ka.*
Will you go out though it is rainy today?

3. After dictionary form of verb/adjective + *no/n*
すもうを見たいんだけど、どこで切符を買ったらいいのか
わかりません。
*Sumō o mi**tai n dakedo** doko de kippu o kattara ii no ka
wakarimasen.*
I want to see sumo wrestling, but I don't know where I can buy
a ticket.

4. After *ta*-form of verb/adjective + *no/n*
ワープロを買ったんだけど使うのがむずかしいです。
*Wāpuro o kat**ta n dakedo** tsukau no ga muzukashii desu.*
I bought a word processor, but it is difficult to use.
高かったんだけどどうしても欲しかったのです。
*Takakat**ta n dakedo** dōshitemo hoshikatta no desu.*
It was expensive, but I really wanted it.

→ See also *daga, ga (2), keredo(mo)*

dare だれ
INTERROGATIVE PRONOUN MEANING: who

The subject indicator *wa* cannot be used after *dare*.

1. Used in subjective case with *ga*
   だれが勝つと思いますか。
   ***Dare ga** katsu to omoimasu ka.*
   Who do you think will win?
   だれがこれを壊したのか知っていますか。
   ***Dare ga** kore o kowashita no ka shitte imasu ka.*
   Do you know who broke this?

2. Used in objective case with *o/ni*
   だれをさがしているんですか。
   ***Dare o** sagashite iru n desu ka.*
   Who are you looking for?
   だれに会いたいのですか。
   ***Dare ni** aitai no desu ka.*
   Who do you want to see?

3. Used as complement that describes subject
   あそこに立っている人はだれですか。
   *Asoko ni tatte iru **hito** wa **dare** desu ka.*
   Who is the person standing over there?

4. Used in possessive case with *no*
   あれはだれの車ですか。
   *Are wa **dare no** kuruma desu ka.*
   Whose car is that?
   これはだれのかばんかわかりますか。
   *Kore wa **dare no** kaban ka wakarimasu ka.*
   Do you know whose bag this is?

5. Used with specific particle
   (*dare* + *ka*: someone, anyone)
   だれかがいるみたいです。

Dareka ga iru mitai desu.

Someone seems to be there.

(*dare + mo* [used with a negative]: no one, nobody)

だれも電話に出ません。

Daremo denwa ni demasen.

Nobody answers the phone.

(*dare + demo*: anybody, everybody)

だれでもこの機械を操作できます。

Daredemo kono kikai o sōsa dekimasu.

Anybody can operate this machine.

darō   だろう

→ See *deshō*

dasu   だす

VERB MEANING: abruptly begin (doing something), (do something) and take out, (do something) and go out

1. After conjunctive form of verb

   彼はたばこを吸いだした。

   *Kare wa tabako o **suidashita**.*

   He began to smoke.

   このカードでこの銀行からお金を引き出すことができます。

   *Kono kādo de kono ginkō kara o-kane o **hikidasu** koto ga dekimasu.*

   With this card you can withdraw money from this bank.

   私はよく授業を抜け出した。

*Watashi wa yoku jugyō o **nukedashita**.*

I would often skip out of classes.

→ See also *hajimeru*

datte だって

INFORMAL PARTICLE OR CONJUNCTION (usually used by women and children) MEANING: but, because, also, even

1. At the beginning of sentence
   (in answer to a question)
   「行きたくないの。」「だって疲れているんだもの。」
   *"Ikitakunai no?" "**Datte** tsukarete iru n da mono."*
   "You don't want to go?" "Because I'm tired."
   (in reply to an imperative)
   「もう寝る時間ですよ。」「だって眠くないんだもの。」
   *"Mō neru jikan desu yo." "**Datte** nemuku nai n da mono."*
   "It's time you went to bed." "But I'm not sleepy."

2. After noun
   金持ちだって不幸な時もある。
   ***Kanemochi datte** fukō-na toki mo aru.*
   Even rich people are unhappy sometimes.
   「あんなことはいやだ。」「私だっていやだ。」
   *"Anna koto wa iya da." "**Watashi datte** iya da."*
   "I hate such things." "I do, too."

3. Used with interrogative pronoun
   (*dare, nan,* and *doko* + *datte* mean everybody, everything, and everywhere respectively)
   だれだってそれには怒ります。
   ***Dare datte** sore ni wa okorimasu.*

Everybody gets angry at that.

彼はスポーツならなんだってできます。

*Kare wa supōtsu nara **nan datte** dekimasu.*

If it's sports, he can play everything.

→ See also *demo*

de で

PARTICLE MEANING: at, in, on, by, with, from, because of, for

Be careful not to confuse this with the conjunctive form *de* of the copula *da*.

1. After noun expressing place where an action is performed (takes the particle *o*)

   私は毎日学校で英語を勉強します。

   *Watashi wa mainichi **gakkō de** eigo o benkyō shimasu.*

   I study English at school every day.

   彼は部屋でテレビを見ています。

   *Kare wa **heya de** terebi o mite imasu.*

   He is watching television in his room.

2. After noun expressing place where an event is or where an action occurs

   (takes the particle *ga*)

   彼女の家でパーティがあります。

   *Kanojo no **ie de** pātii **ga** arimasu.*

   There will be a party at her house.

   屋根で何か音がする。

   ***Yane de** nanika oto **ga** suru.*

   I hear a sound on the roof.

3. After noun expressing range for comparison
   ポールはクラスで一番背が高い。
   *Pōru wa **kurasu de** ichiban se ga takai.*
   Paul is the tallest in the class.

4. After noun expressing method or means
   私は電車で仕事に行きます。
   *Watashi wa **densha de** shigoto ni ikimasu.*
   I go to work by train.
   そのニュースはきのうの新聞で読みました。
   *Sono nyūsu wa kinō no **shinbun de** yomimashita.*
   I read the news in yesterday's newspaper.
   名前はインクで書いてください。
   *Namae wa **inku de** kaite kudasai.*
   Please write your name in ink.

5. After noun expressing material or ingredients
   酒は米で作られる。
   *Sake wa **kome de** tsukurareru.*
   Sake is made from rice.

6. After noun expressing reason or cause
   佐藤さんは風で休んでいます。
   *Satō-san wa **kaze de** yasunde imasu.*
   Mr. Sato is absent with a cold.
   彼女のお父さんはがんで亡くなりました。
   *Kanojo no otōsan wa **gan de** nakunarimashita.*
   Her father died of cancer.
   あなたのおかげでうまくいきました。
   *Anata no **okage de** umaku ikimashita.*
   It went smoothly thanks to you.

7. After noun expressing how an action is performed
   新幹線は時速200キロ以上のスピードで走る。

*Shinkansen wa jisoku ni hyakkiro ijō no **supiido de** hashiru.*

The shinkansen runs at speeds of more than 200 kilometers per hour.

8. After noun expressing time taken to finish an action

1時間で帰ります。

***Ichi jikan de** kaerimasu.*

I'll be home in an hour.

9. After noun expressing point in time when something terminates

休みは明日で終わります。

*Yasumi wa **asu de** owarimasu.*

The vacation will be over tomorrow.

10. After noun expressing price

この時計は5千円で買いました。

*Kono tokei wa **gosen en de** kaimashita.*

I bought this watch for five thousand yen.

11. After noun expressing age

私は25才で結婚したい。

*Watashi wa **ni jū go sai de** kekkon shitai.*

I want to marry at the age of twenty five.

12. After noun expressing quantity

このトマトは4個で200円しました。

*Kono tomato wa **yon ko de** ni hyaku en shimashita.*

These tomatoes cost two hundred yen for four.

→ See also *desu, dewa (1), kara, ni*

de aru である

PREDICATIVE PHRASE used in written or formal language instead of *da/desu* to explicitly affirm the preceding statement

1. After (adjectival) noun
   金閣寺は14世紀に建てられた寺である。
   *Kinkakuji wa jū yon seiki ni taterareta **tera de aru**.*
   Kinkakuji is a temple built in the fourteenth century.
2. After dictionary form of verb/adjective + *no*
   こうすれば問題は解決されるのである。
   *Kō sureba mondai wa kaiketsu sare**ru no de aru**.*
   The problem will be solved in this way.
   結局彼のいうことが正しいのである。
   *Kekkyoku kare no iū koto ga tadashi**i no de aru**.*
   After all what he says is correct.
→ See also *desu, no desu*

dekiru できる
VERB MEANING: can perform something, can be done, be finished, be ready, be made, be born, become pregnant, be formed, be good (at), come into existence

1. After (object) noun + *ga*
   「車の運転ができますか。」「はい、できます。」
   *"Kuruma no **unten ga dekimasu** ka." "Hai, dekimasu."*
   "Can you drive a car?" "Yes, I can."
   マイクは日本語がよくできます。
   *Maiku wa **nihongo ga** yoku **dekimasu**.*
   Mike is very good at Japanese.
2. Used as intransitive verb
   仕事ができました。
   *Shigoto ga **dekimashita**.*
   The work is finished.

食事の用意ができました。

*Shokuji no yōi ga **dekimashita**.*

Preparation for dinner is finished. (Dinner is ready.)

みそは大豆からできます。

*Miso wa daizu kara **dekimasu**.*

Miso is made from soybeans.

彼女に子供ができた。

*Kanojo ni kodomo ga **dekita**.*

A child was born to her. (*or* She is going to have a baby.)

駅前に新しいビルができた。

*Ekimae ni atarashii biru ga **dekita**.*

A new building has been built in front of the station.

急用ができたので失礼します。

*Kyūyō ga **dekita** node shitsurei shimasu.*

Some urgent business has come up so I have to leave.

おもしろいクラブができました。

*Omoshiroi kurabu ga **dekimashita**.*

A unique club was set up.

→ See also *ga, koto ga dekiru*

demo でも

PARTICLE OR CONJUNCTION MEANING: but, or something, even, in spite of, any . . .

1. At the beginning of sentence

   でももう遅すぎるよ。

   ***Demo** mō ososugiru yo.*

   But it's too late now.

2. After interrogative word

だれでもそんなことは知っています。

Dare demo *sonna koto wa shitte imasu.*

Anybody knows such things. (Anybody knows that.)

食べ物は何でも食べます。

*Tabemono wa **nan demo** tabemasu.*

I eat any (kind of) food.

いつでもけっこうです。

Itsu demo *kekkō desu.*

Any time will be fine.

どこでも仕事に行きます。

Doko demo *shigoto ni ikimasu.*

I will go anywhere to work.

どうでもいいです。

Dō demo *ii desu.*

Any way is all right. (I don't care.)

3. After (adjectival) noun

コーヒーでも飲みたいな。

Kōhii demo *nomitai na.*

I'd like to drink coffee or something.

大人でもその漢字を知らない人がいます。

Otona demo *sono kanji o shiranai hito ga imasu.*

There are even some grown-ups who don't know that kanji.

彼は日曜日でも働きます。

*Kare wa **nichiyōbi demo** hatarakimasu.*

He works even on Sundays.

雨でも出発します。

Ame demo *shuppatsu shimasu.*

I'm going to leave even if it is rainy.

4. After specific particle

東京からでも富士山が見えます。

*Tōkyō **kara demo** fuji-san ga miemasu.*

Even from Tokyo Mt. Fuji can be seen.

→ See also *datte, ikura . . . temo/demo*

deshō　でしょう

AUXILIARY VERB MEANING: will (be), shall (be), would (be), probably

1. After noun
   あの人がホワイトさんでしょう。
   *Ano hito ga **howaito-san deshō**.*
   That man is probably Mr. White.
   東京はあす雨でしょう。
   *Tōkyō wa asu **ame deshō**.*
   It may be rainy in Tokyo tomorrow.
2. After dictionary form of verb/adjective
   ポールは5時までに帰るでしょう。
   *Pōru wa go ji made ni kae**ru deshō**.*
   Paul will be probably be back by five.
   あなたもいっしょに行くでしょう。(with rising intonation)
   *Anata mo isshoni i**ku deshō**.*
   You will go together, won't you?
   彼女はとてもきれいでしょう。(with rising intonation)
   *Kanojo wa totemo **kirei deshō**.*
   She is very beautiful, isn't she?
3. After *nai*-form of verb/adjective
   その仕事は土曜日までにできないでしょう。
   *Sono shigoto wa doyōbi made ni deki**nai deshō**.*
   The work will probably not be completed by Saturday.

→ See also *desu*

desu です

POLITE AUXILIARY VERB (similar to "be" in English) INDICATING: someone or something equals something else; someone or something is in some state or condition; someone or something has some quality; someone or something is in some place or position; something is at some time

1. After (adjectival) noun

   私の名前は佐藤健次です。

   *Watashi no namae wa **satō kenji desu**.*

   My name is Kenji Sato.

   きのうポールとマイクが欠席でした。

   *Kinō pōru to maiku ga **kesseki deshita.***

   Paul and Mike were absent yesterday.

   私はその決定にはとても満足です。

   *Watashi wa sono kettei ni wa totemo **manzoku desu**.*

   I am very much satisfied with the conclusion.

   兄は今京都です。

   *Ani wa ima **kyōto desu**.*

   My older brother is in Kyoto now.

   「コンサートは次の日曜日ですか。」「はい、そうです。」

   *"Konsāto wa tsugi no **nichiyōbi desu** ka." "Hai, sō desu."*

   "Is the concert next Sunday?" "Yes, it is."

   彼は日本人ではありません。

   *Kare wa **nihonjin dewa arimasen**.*

   He is not Japanese.

2. After dictionary form of adjective

   (*desu* at the end of the sentence makes it polite)

   彼のかいた絵はとてもすばらしいです。

   *Kare no kaita e wa totemo subarashii **desu**.*

The pictures he drew are very wonderful.

→ See also *arimasen, de aru, deshō, no desu*

dewa   では (1)

DOUBLE PARTICLE (made up of *de* and *wa*) MEANING: in, at, as for, judging from, by

Used in the same manner as *de*, the addition of *wa* serves to stress the preceding word.

1. After noun
東京では物価が高すぎます。
***Tōkyō dewa** bukka ga takasugimasu.*
In Tokyo prices are too high.
数学では彼はほかのクラスメートよりも優秀です。
***Sūgaku dewa** kare wa hoka no kurasumēto yori mo yūshū desu.*
In mathematics he is superior to all his classmates.
私の意見ではこちらの方がいいと思います。
*Watashi no **iken dewa** kochira no hō ga ii to omoimasu.*
In my opinion, I think this is better.
あの様子では彼は来そうもない。
*Ano **yōsu dewa** kare wa kisō mo nai.*
Judging from the looks of things, it doesn't seem he'll come.
私の時計では1時15分です。
*Watashi no **tokei dewa** ichi ji jū go fun desu.*
It is one fifteen by my watch.

→ See also *arimasen, de, ja*

dewa では (2)

CONJUNCTION MEANING: well, then, so, well then, if so

1. At the beginning of sentence
   ではこれで失礼します。
   Dewa *kore de shitsurei shimasu.*
   Well, I must be leaving now.
   ではなぜそうしたんですか。
   Dewa *naze sō shita n desu ka.*
   Then, why did you do it?
   ではもうあきらめます。
   Dewa *mō akiramemasu.*
   If so, I give up.

dō どう

INTERROGATIVE ADVERB MEANING: how, what, how about

1. Followed by verb + *no/n*
   (may be replaced with the phrase *dō yatte* or *dono yō ni shite*)
   それはどうするんですか。
   *Sore wa **dō suru n** desu ka.*
   How shall I do it?
   駅までどう行くんですか。
   *Eki made **dō iku n** desu ka.*
   How can I go to the station?
2. Followed by *desu*
   (may be replaced by the more polite word *ikaga*)
   今日は気分はどうですか。

*Kyō wa kibun wa **dō desu** ka.*
How are you feeling today?
コーヒーでも1杯どうですか。
*Kōhii demo ippai **dō desu** ka.*
How about a cup of coffee (or something)?
京都旅行はどうでしたか。
*Kyōto ryokō wa **dō deshita** ka.*
How did you like your trip to Kyoto?
それをやってみたらどうですか。
*Sore o yatte mitara **dō desu** ka.*
How would it be if you try it? (Why don't you try it?)
3. Used with the verb *omou*
この絵をどう思いますか。
*Kono e o **dō omoimasu** ka.*
What do you think of this picture?
→ See also *dōshite*

doko　どこ
INTERROGATIVE WORD MEANING: where, what

1. Followed by *desu*
「郵便局はどこですか。」「あの銀行の向こうです。」
*"Yūbinkyoku wa **doko desu** ka." "Ano ginkō no mukō desu."*
"Where is the post office?" "It's on the other side of that bank."
「田中さんは今どこですか。」「学校です。」
*"Tanaka-san wa ima **doko desu** ka." "Gakkō desu."*
"Where is Mr.Tanaka now?" " He is at school."
2. Followed by locational particle
彼女はどこに住んでいるんですか。

*Kanojo wa **doko ni** sunde iru n desu ka.*

Where is she living?

「休みにはどこへ行くんですか。」「どこにも行きません。」

*"Yasumi ni wa **doko e** iku n desu ka." "**Doko ni** mo ikimasen."*

"Where are you going for the vacation?" "I won't go anywhere."

どこで会うんですか。

***Doko de** au n desu ka.*

Where shall we meet?

彼女はどこから来ましたか。

*Kanojo wa **doko kara** kimashita ka.*

Where did she come from? (Where is she from?)

3. Followed by possessive particle *no*

どこのホテルに泊まるんですか。

***Doko no** hoteru ni tomaru n desu ka.*

At what hotel are you staying?

4. Followed by subject marker *ga*

それのどこが悪いんですか。

*Sore no **doko ga** warui n desu ka.*

What's wrong with it?

→ See also *dore, itsu, ka, nani*

dokoro de(wa) nai　どころで(は)ない

PHRASE MEANING: be out of the question, be more than . . . , this is
not an occasion for

1. After dictionary form of verb/adjective

旅行に行くどころではない。

*Ryokō ni **iku dokoro dewa nai**.*

Going on a trip is out of the question.

運がいいどころではありません。奇跡です。

*Un ga ii **dokoro dewa arimasen**. Kiseki desu.*

It is more than good luck. It is a miracle.

冗談を言っているどころでない。

*Jōdan o itte iru **dokoro de nai**.*

This is not an occasion for joking.

dokoro ka　どころか

PHRASE MEANING: far from, to say nothing of, not to speak of, much more, (not) . . . much less, not only . . . but . . . , not . . . on the contrary

1. After (adjectival) noun
   (the pattern . . . *dokoro ka* . . . *mo* emphasizes the second item in comparison with the first)

   彼は日本語どころか中国語も話せます。

   *Kare wa **nihongo dokoro ka** chūgokugo **mo** hanasemasu.*

   He can speak not only Japanese but Chinese as well.

   肉どころか魚も食べません。

   *Niku **dokoro ka** sakana **mo** tabemasen.*

   I don't even eat fish much less meat.

   ドイツ語どころか英語も私にはむずかしい。

   *Doitsugo **dokoro ka** eigo **mo** watashi ni wa muzukashii.*

   English is difficult for me, to say nothing of German.

   雨どころか雪になりそうです。

   *Ame **dokoro ka** yuki ni nari sō desu.*

   Rain—it looks more like snow.

2. After dictionary form of verb/adjective

彼は笑うどころか怒ってしまった。
*Kare wa warau **dokoro ka** okotte shimatta.*
Far from laughing, he got totally angry.
彼は賢いどころか天才だ。
*Kare wa kashikoi **dokoro ka** tensai da.*
He is not only clever but a genius.

3. After *nai*-form of verb
彼は手伝わないどころか文句を言っている。
*Kare wa tetsudawanai **dokoro ka** monku o itte iru.*
Not only does he not help, but he complains.

dōmo   どうも

INFORMAL WORD MEANING: hello, good-bye, thank you, sorry, very (much), somehow, just

1. Used in greetings
「やあ。」「やあ、どうも。」
*"Yā." "Yā, **dōmo**."*
"Hi." "Hi, how are you?" (Glad to see you.)
「これで失礼します。」「どうも。」
*"Kore de shitsurei shimasu." " **Dōmo**."*
"I'm leaving now." "Good-bye."

2. Used to express thanks
「お先にどうぞ。」「これは、どうも。」
*"O-saki ni dōzo." "Kore wa **dōmo**."*
"Please go ahead." (After you.) "Oh, thanks."

3. Used to express apology
「痛い。」「あ、どうも。大丈夫ですか。」
*"Itai." "A, **dōmo**. Daijōbu desu ka."*

"Ouch." "Oh, sorry. Are you all right?"
(*sumimasen* [I'm sorry] is dropped after *dōmo*)

4. Used as adverb
遅れてどうもすみません。
*Okurete **dōmo** sumimasen.*
I'm very sorry to be late.
ご親切どうもありがとうございます。
*Go-shinsetsu **dōmo** arigatō gozaimasu.*
Thank you very much for your kindness.

5. Used with negative
あなたの言うことがどうもわかりません。
*Anata no iū koto ga **dōmo** wakari**masen**.*
I just can't understand what you say.
どうもあの人は気に入らない。
***Dōmo** ano hito wa ki ni ira**nai**.*
Somehow I don't like that man.

→ See also *dōshitemo*

dono kurai   どのくらい

INTERROGATIVE PHRASE MEANING: how many, how much, how long, how far, how tall, how often

1. Before noun
どのくらい切手を集めましたか。
***Dono kurai** kitte o atsumemashita ka.*
How many stamps have you collected?

2. Used as adverb
ここから駅までどのくらいかかりますか。
*Koko kara eki made **dono kurai** kakarimasu ka.*

How long does it take from here to the station?

車はどのくらいかかりますか。

*Kuruma wa **dono kurai** kakarimasu ka.*

How much does a car cost?/How long does it take by car?

→ See also *kurai*

dore どれ

INTERROGATIVE PRONOUN MEANING: which

The polite form is *dochira*, which also means "who" or "where." *Dore* becomes *dono* before a noun it modifies. It becomes *doko* when expressing "where."

1. Used as subject

   このうちどれがいちばん安いですか。

   *Kono uchi **dore** ga ichiban yasui desu ka.*

   Which is the cheapest of them?

2. Used as object

   どれがいちばん好きですか。

   ***Dore** ga ichiban suki desu ka.*

   Which do you like best?

   この３つのうちどれを選びますか。

   *Kono mittsu no uchi **dore** o erabimasu ka.*

   Which do you choose of these three?

3. Before noun

   (changes to *dono*)

   どの本がおもしろいですか。

   ***Dono hon** ga omoshiroi desu ka.*

   Which book is interesting?

4. Used with specific particle
   (*dore + ka*: any)
   この内どれか頂戴できますか。
   *Kono uchi **dore ka** chōdai dekimasu ka.*
   Can you spare me any of these?
   (*dore + demo*: whichever, anything)
   どれでもいいから好きなのをお選び下さい。
   ***Dore demo** ii kara suki-na no o o-erabi kudasai.*
   Any one is fine, so please pick the one you like.
   (*dore + mo*: all, any)
   この本はどれも子供には難しすぎる。
   *Kono hon wa **dore mo** kodomo ni wa muzukashi-sugiru.*
   Any of these books is too difficult for a child.
→ See also *dōko*

dōshite　どうして
INTERROGATIVE ADVERB MEANING: why, in what way, how

1. Asking a reason
   どうして遅れたんですか。
   ***Dōshite** okureta n desu ka.*
   Why were you late?
2. Asking a method
   この字はどうして書くんですか。
   *Kono ji wa **dōshite** kaku n desu ka.*
   How do you write this character?
→ See also *dō, naze*

dōshitemo　どうしても

ADVERB MEANING: no matter what, (not) . . . by any means, at any cost, can't help (doing something), simply (not)

1. Used with affirmative
   どうしてもそれが必要です。
   Dōshitemo *sore ga hitsuyō **desu**.*
   I need it at any cost.
   どうしても彼女のことを考えてしまいます。
   Dōshitemo *kanojo no koto o kangaete shimai**masu**.*
   I can't help thinking of her.
2. Used with negative
   どうしてもそれを覚えられません。
   Dōshitemo *sore o oboerare**masen**.*
   I just can't memorize it .
   どうしても行きたくありません。
   Dōshitemo *ikitaku arima**sen**.*
   I simply don't want to go.
   どうしても明日までに終えなければなりません。
   Dōshitemo *ashita made ni oenakereba narima**sen**.*
   I must finish it by tomorrow no matter what.
→ See also *dōmo*

dōzo　どうぞ

ADVERB MEANING: please, certainly, sure, here it is

1. Used in imperative sentence

どうぞ座ってください。

Dōzo *suwatte kudasai.*

Please sit down.

こちらへどうぞ。

*Kochira e **dōzo**.*

This way, please.

2. Used in reply to a request

「電話を貸してくれませんか。」「はい、どうぞ。」

*"Denwa o kashite kuremasen ka." "Hai, **dōzo**."*

"Can I use your telephone?" "Yes, certainly."

「ちょっとペンを貸してくれませんか。」「どうぞ。」

*"Chotto pen o kashite kuremasen ka." "**Dōzo**."*

"Would you lend me your pen for a while?" "Sure." (Here it is.)

e へ

PARTICLE INDICATING: a destination or direction

1. After noun

ちょっとトイレへ行ってきます。

*Chotto **toire e** itte kimasu.*

I'm going to the rest room for a moment.

「京都へ行ったことがありますか。」「いえ、ありません。」

*"**Kyōto e** itta koto ga arimasu ka." "Ie, arimasen."*

"Have you been to Kyoto?" "No, I haven't."

角を右へ曲がるとバス停があります。

*Kado o **migi e** magaru to basutei ga arimasu.*

If you turn to the right at the corner, you'll find a bus stop.

→ See also *made, ni*

ga が (1)

PARTICLE INDICATING: the subject or object for specific verb or adjective

If the subject is contrasted with other things, or if only partial information about the subject is given, *wa* replaces *ga*.

1. After subject just introduced/recognized
   この人が鈴木さんです。彼は高校の先生です。
   *Kono **hito ga** suzuki-san desu. Kare wa kōkō no sensei desu.*
   This is Mr. Suzuki. He is a high school teacher.
   信号の向こうにガソリンスタンドがあります。
   *Shingō no mukō ni gasorin **sutando ga** arimasu.*
   There's a gas station on the other side of the traffic signal.
   とてもおいしいにおいがします。
   *Totemo oishii **nioi ga** shimasu.*
   It smells very delicious.
2. After stressed subject
   私がそれをします。
   ***Watashi ga** sore o shimasu.*
   I'll do it. (Let me do it./ I should do it.)
3. After interrogative
   何がそんなにおもしろいのですか。
   ***Nani ga** sonna ni omoshiroi no desu ka.*
   What is so funny?
4. After subject in a relative clause
   私が買ったカメラは日本製です。
   ***Watashi ga katta kamera** wa nihon sei desu.*
   The camera I bought is Japanese-made.
5. After subject in a subordinate clause

洋子が来たら教えてください。
Yoko ga kitara oshiete kudasai.
When Yoko comes, please tell me.
雨が降れば行くのをやめます。
Ame ga fureba iku no o yamemasu.
If it rains, I'll give up going.

6. After object of verb/adjective expressing possession, existence, ability, necessity, desire, emotion, or sensation
今お金がぜんぜんありません。
Ima o-kane ga zenzen arimasen.
I have no money now.
日本語ができますか。
Nihongo ga dekimasu ka.
Can you speak Japanese?
もっと自由時間がほしい。
Motto jiyū jikan ga hoshii.
I want much more free time.
本当のことが知りたい。
Hontō no koto ga shiritai.
I want to know the truth.
日本の食べ物の中ではすしがいちばん好きです。
Nihon no tabemono no naka dewa sushi ga ichiban suki desu.
Of Japanese foods I like sushi best.

→ See also *hoshii, no, wa*

ga が (2)
CONJUNCTION MEANING: but, and

1. Between two contrastive or opposing clauses

私はお酒は飲みますが、タバコは吸いません。
*Watashi wa **o-sake wa nomimasu ga tabako wa suimasen***.
I drink alcohol but don't smoke cigarettes.
がんばりましたが、だめでした。
Ganbarimashita ga dame deshita.
I tried hard but I failed.

2. To simply connect two clauses
田中と申しますが、社長にお会いできますか。
Tanaka to mōshimasu ga, shachō ni o-ai dekimasu ka.
My name is Tanaka. Would it be possible to see the boss?
その映画を見ましたが、とてもおもしろかったですよ。
Sono eiga o mimashita ga totemo omoshirokatta desu yo.
I saw that movie, and it was very interesting.

3. At the end of sentence
(states condition and leaves conclusion to the hearer)
今とても忙しいんですが...
*Ima totemo isogashii n desu **ga** . . .*
I'm very busy now . . . (so I can't help you).

→ See also *daga, dakedo, keredo(mo), nagara, no ni*

garu　がる

SUFFIX VERB (added to the stem of certain adjectives to give a more subjective feeling, or to *tai*-form of verb) MEANING: (someone) wants/feels (something)

Garu usually takes a 3rd person subject in the progressive form when the subject is specific.

1. After the stem of adjective expressing emotion

彼はもっといい車を欲しがっています。

Kare wa motto ii kuruma o hoshigatte imasu.

He wants a better car.

(the particle *ga* cannot be used after the direct object with *garu*)

子供はすぐおばけの話をこわがる。

Kodomo wa sugu obake no hanashi o kowagaru.

Children are easily scared by ghost stories.

2. After the stem of adjective expressing sensation

あのけが人はひどく痛がっています。

Ano kega nin wa hidoku itagatte imasu.

That injured person looks to be in terrible pain.

彼は外でとても寒がっています。

Kare wa soto de totemo samugatte imasu.

He is very sensitive to cold outside.

3. After conjunctive form of verb + *ta*

(*tai* + *garu* becomes *tagaru*)

彼女はヨーロッパに行きたがっています。

Kanojo wa yōroppa ni ikitagatte imasu.

She is eager to visit Europe.

ギターの人は歌を歌いたがる。

Gitā no hito wa uta o utaitagaru.

The guitarist wants to sing a song.

→ See also *tai, hoshii*

goro　ごろ

SUFFIX (of time) MEANING: about, around

1. After specified point in time

私とキャロラインは今朝は7時ごろ(に)起きました。
*Watashi to kyarorain wa kesa wa **shichi ji goro** (ni) oki-mashita.*
Caroline and I got up about seven o'clock this morning.

2. After *itsu/nan ji*
その橋はいつごろ出来上がりますか。
*Sono hashi wa **itsu goro** dekiagarimasu ka.*
About when will that bridge be completed?
何時ごろ(に)伺いましょうか。
Nan ji goro (ni) ukagaimashō ka.
At about what time shall I call on you?

gurai ぐらい
→ See *kurai*

hajimeru 始める
VERB MEANING: begin, start (doing)

1. After conjunctive form of verb
私の友達は去年日本語を勉強し始めました。
*Watashi no tomodachi wa kyonen nihongo o benkyō **shihajimemashita**.*
My friend began to study Japanese last year.
五月からピアノを習い始めます。
*Go gatsu kara piano o **naraihajimemasu**.*
I will start learning piano from May.
→ See also *dasu*

hazu desu はずです

PHRASE MEANING: be supposed/expected to (do), be sure to (do), ought to (do)

1. After dictionary form of verb/adjective
   彼はもう着くはずです。
   Kare wa mō tsuku hazu desu.
   He is supposed to arrive here soon.
   このカメラはもっと安いはずです。
   Kono kamera wa motto yasui hazu desu.
   This camera ought to be much cheaper.

2. After *ta*-form of verb/adjective
   そう言ったはずだ。
   Sō itta hazu da.
   I'm sure I told you that.

3. After (adjectival) noun + *na/no*
   ここは安全なはずです。
   Koko wa anzen-na hazu desu.
   This place ought to be safe.
   彼女は病気のはずです。
   Kanojo wa byōki no hazu desu.
   I'm sure she is sick.

3. After *nai*-form of verb/adjective
   彼女はそんなことをしないはずだ。
   Kanojo wa sonna koto o shinai hazu da.
   I don't expect that she is going to do such a thing.

→ See also *hazu ga nai*

hazu ga nai　はずがない

PHRASE MEANING: cannot (do), it is impossible that . . .

1. After dictionary form of verb/adjective
   そんなにお金が儲かるはずがない。
   Sonna ni o-kane ga mōkaru hazu ga nai.
   It is impossible that one would make so much money.
2. After *ta*-form of verb/adjective
   彼がミスをしたはずがない。
   Kare ga misu o shita hazu ga nai.
   He cannot have made a mistake.
3. After *nai*-form of verb/adjective
   彼女がまだ来ていないはずがない。
   Kanojo ga mada kite inai hazu ga nai.
   It is improbable that she has not arrived yet. (She should have already arrived.)
4. After adjectival noun + *na/no*
   彼の話がうそのはずがない。
   Kare no hanashi ga uso no hazu ga nai.
   His story cannot be false.

→ See also *hazu desu*

hō　ほう

NOUN INDICATING: one of two sides being compared with the other

It is always followed by the particle *ga*.

1. After the demonstrative adjectives *kono*, *sono*, *ano*
   この方が便利です。
   ***Kono hō** ga benri desu.*
   This is more useful.
2. After noun + *no*
   金曜日の方が忙しいです。
   ***Kinyōbi no hō** ga isogashii desu.*
   I am busier on Friday (than on other days of the week).
   パンよりごはんの方が好きです。
   *Pan yori **gohan no hō** ga suki desu.*
   I like rice better than bread.
   (*yori* often indicates the other side of a comparison)
3. After dictionary form of verb/adjective
   バスで行く方が便利でしょう。
   *Basu de i**ku hō** ga benri deshō.*
   It will be more convenient to go by bus.
   家で休む方がいい。
   *Ie de yasu**mu hō** ga ii.*
   I would rather take a rest at home.
   カメラは軽い方が便利ですよ。
   *Kamera wa karu**i hō** ga benri desu yo.*
   A lighter camera is handier.
4. After *nai*-form of verb
   そんな映画は見ない方がましです。
   *Sonna eiga wa mi**nai hō** ga mashi desu.*
   It is better for me not to see such a movie.
   (*mashi da/desu* is often used with *hō*)
5. After *ta*-form of verb
   歩いて行った方が速かったですね。
   *Aruite it**ta hō** ga hayakatta desu ne.*

It would have been faster to go on foot.

→ See also *hō ga ii, yori*

hodo ほど

PARTICLE MEANING: about, or so, (not) as . . . as . . . , to the extent of, enough to (do), the more . . . the more . . .

1. After noun expressing length/quantity
   京都駅はここから１キロほどです。
   *Kyōto eki wa koko kara **ichi kiro hodo** desu.*
   Kyoto Station is about one kilometer from here.
   10分ほどここで待ってください。
   ***Juppun hodo** koko de matte kudasai.*
   Please wait here ten minutes or so.
   そのコーヒーを１キロほどください。
   *Sono kōhii o **ichi kiro hodo** kudasai.*
   I'll take about one kilogram of that coffee.
2. After noun, followed by a negative
   英語は日本語ほどむずかしくありません。
   *Eigo wa **nihongo hodo** muzukashiku arimasen.*
   English is not as difficult as Japanese.
   時間ほど貴重なものはない。
   ***Jikan hodo** kichō-na mono wa **nai**.*
   There is nothing as precious as time.
3. After dictionary form of verb/adjective
   海外旅行ができるほどお金がたまりました。
   *Kaigai ryokō ga deki**ru hodo** o-kane ga tamarimashita.*
   I saved enough money to be able to travel abroad.
   この本は子供でも読めるほどやさしいです。

*Kono hon wa kodomo demo yome**ru hodo** yasashii desu.*
This book is so easy that even a child can read it.
彼とは話すほど好きになる。
*Kare to wa hana**su hodo** suki ni naru.*
The more I talk with him, the more I like him.

4. After *ta*-form of verb
   この中古の車は思ったほど高くはなかった。
   *Kono chūko no kuruma wa omo**tta hodo** takaku wa nakatta.*
   This used car was not as expensive as I had expected.

5. After *nai*-form of verb
   私はもう歩けないほど疲れました。
   *Watashi wa mō aruke**nai hodo** tsukaremashita.*
   I am so tired that I can't walk any more.

→ See also *ba . . . hodo, bakari, kurai*

hō ga ii　ほうがいい
PHRASE (expressing a suggestion or advice) MEANING: it would be better to (do), you had better (do)

When speaking to a person of higher status or in an indirect manner, it is better to add *to omoimasu* (I think) to the end of the phrase.

1. After dictionary form of verb
   (more direct than when following *ta*-form)
   彼女に謝る方がいい。
   *Kanojo ni ayama**ru hō ga ii**.*
   It is better to apologize to her.

2. After *ta*-form of verb

今日は傘を持って行ったほうがいい。
Kyō wa kasa o motte itta hō ga ii.
You had better take along an umbrella today.
もうやめたほうがいいと思います。
Mō yameta hō ga ii to omoimasu.
I think it would be better for you to give it up.

3. After *nai*-form of verb
そこへは行かないほうがいいですよ。
Soko e wa ikanai hō ga ii desu yo.
It really would be better for you not to go there.

→ See also *hō*

hoka ほか

NOUN whose meaning is determined by the particle which follows

Followed by *no*: another, (the) other(s), some other, else
Followed by *de*: somewhere/anywhere else
Followed by *ni*: some/any other, else
Preceded by *no* and followed by *ni/wa*: apart from, besides, in addition to, as well as, except (for), but

1. Followed by *no*, before noun it modifies
ほかの日がいいです。
Hoka no hi ga ii desu.
Some other day is better.
ほかの人に頼みます。
Hoka no hito ni tanomimasu.
I'll ask somebody else for it.

2. After noun + *no*, followed by *ni/wa*

彼女のほかに知り合いはいません。
Kanojo no hoka ni *shiriai wa imasen.*
I have no acquaintances besides her.
ビールのほかは何もいりません。
Biiru no hoka wa *nani mo irimasen.*
I don't need anything other than beer.

3. Used as noun, followed by *no*
ほかのを見せてください。
Hoka no *o misete kudasai.*
Please show me another.

4. Used as adverb, followed by *ni/de*
ほかでもっと安いのが手に入ります。
Hoka de *motto yasui no ga te ni hairimasu.*
You can get a cheaper one somewhere else.
ほかにだれが行くのですか。
Hoka ni *dare ga iku no desu ka.*
Who else is going?

→ See also *igai*

hoka nai ほかない

PHRASE MEANING: can do nothing but (do), cannot help (doing) something

1. After dictionary form of verb
あきらめるほかありません。
*Akirame**ru hoka arimasen**.*
I can do nothing but give up.

hoshii ほしい

ADJECTIVE MEANING: want, want (someone) to, would like (someone) to

The subject is usually the 1st person in declarative sentences, and the 2nd person in questions. However, when *hoshii* is followed by *garu*, the 3rd person subject must be used.

1. After object noun + *ga*
   私はとてもビデオカメラがほしいです。
   *Watashi wa totemo **bideo kamera ga hoshii** desu.*
   I want a video camera very much.
   何がほしいのですか。
   ***Nani ga hoshii** no desu ka.*
   What do you want?
2. After *te*-form of verb
   ちょっと手伝ってほしいのですが。
   *Chotto tetsuda**tte hoshii** no desu ga.*
   I want you to help me for a while.
   誕生日プレゼントにコンピューターを買ってほしいのです。
   *Tanjōbi purezento ni konpyūtā o ka**tte hoshii** no desu.*
   I want you to buy me a computer as a birthday present.
→ See also *ga (1), garu, morau*

hotondo ほとんど

ADVERB MEANING: almost, hardly, scarcely, little, few

1. In affirmative sentence
   仕事はほとんど終わりました。
   *Shigoto wa **hotondo** owarimashita.*
   The work is almost finished.
2. In negative sentence
   今週はほとんど日本語を勉強しませんでした。
   *Konshū wa **hotondo** nihongo o benkyō shimasen deshita.*
   I have hardly studied Japanese this week.
   ほとんどだれもそれを買いません。
   ***Hotondo** dare mo sore o kaimasen.*
   Hardly anybody buys it.
→ See also *metta ni, amari*

igai　以外

NOUN MEANING: except (for), but, besides, in addition to, apart from, (those) other than

It is often followed by the particle *ni* or *wa*.

1. After noun
   水曜日以外は毎日働いています。
   *Suiyōbi **igai** wa mainichi hataraite imasu.*
   I work every day except Wednesday.
   新聞以外はあまり何も読みません。
   *Shinbun **igai** wa amari nani mo yomimasen.*
   Other than the newspaper I read almost nothing.
   私はあなた以外に日本人の友人がいません。
   *Watashi wa **anata igai** ni nihonjin no yūjin ga imasen.*

I have no Japanese friends apart from you.

2. After dictionary form of verb
逃げる以外に方法がない。
Nigeru igai ni hōhō ga nai.
There is no other way except to run away.

3. After reported statement ending with *to iū koto*
私は彼が先生だということ以外は何も知りません。
Watashi wa kare ga sensei da to iū koto igai *wa nani mo shirimasen.*
I know nothing except that he is a teacher.

→ See also *hoka*

igo　以後

NOUN (used of time) MEANING: after, since, from (now) on

1. After noun expressing time
   (usually followed by a particle)
   午後7時以後に電話してください。
   *Gogo **shichi ji igo ni** denwa shite kudasai.*
   Please call me after 7 P.M.
   次の月曜日以後は大阪にいます。
   *Tsugi no **getsuyōbi igo wa** ōsaka ni imasu.*
   I'll be in Osaka from next Monday on.

2. Used as adverb
   以後気をつけてください。
   ***Igo** ki o tsukete kudasai.*
   Please be more careful from now on.

→ See also *ikō, irai, kara*

ijō 以上

NOUN MEANING: more than, over, mentioned above, (not) any longer, (no) more, once . . . , now that . . . , since, as long as

1. After noun expressing length/quantity/price
   そこまで行くのに1時間以上かかります。
   *Soko made iku no ni **ichi jikan ijō** kakarimasu.*
   It will take more than one hour to get there.
   このトンネルは2キロメートル以上あります。
   *Kono tonneru wa **ni kiromētoru ijō** arimasu.*
   This tunnel is more than two kilometers long.

2. Followed by *no* + noun
   以上の理由でこれは中止になりました。
   ***Ijō no riyū** de kore wa chūshi ni narimashita.*
   This was cancelled for the reasons mentioned above.
   18才以上の人しか入れません。
   *Jūhassai **ijō no hito** shika hairemasen.*
   Only people who are eighteen and over are allowed to enter.

3. After the demonstrative pronouns *kore*, *sore*, *are*
   これ以上ここで待てません。
   ***Kore ijō** koko de matemasen.*
   I can't wait here any longer.
   それ以上は無理です。
   ***Sore ijō** wa muri desu.*
   Any more than that is impossible.

4. At the end of a clause
   それをやると決めた以上努力しなければなりません。
   ***Sore o yaru to kimeta ijō** doryoku shinakereba narimasu.*
   Now that you've decided to do it, you must work hard.

(*kara niwa* can replace *ijō*)

ここまでやった以上完成しよう。

***Koko made yatta ijō** kansei shiyō.*

As long as we've come this far, let's complete it.

ichiban いちばん

ADVERB INDICATING: the superlative degree of an adjective/adverb

It is originally a noun meaning "the first," "number one," or "the first place."

1. Before adjective/(adjectival) noun/adverb

   どのカメラがいちばん安いですか。

   *Dono kamera ga **ichiban yasui** desu ka.*

   Which camera is the cheapest?

   「だれがいちばんじょうずに日本語を話しますか。」「マイクです。」

   *"Dare ga **ichiban jōzu** ni nihongo o hanashimasu ka." "Maiku desu."*

   "Who speaks Japanese the best?" "Mike does."

2. Used with predicate of emotion

   私はビールがいちばん好きです。

   *Watashi wa biiru ga **ichiban suki desu**.*

   I like beer best.

   私は今いちばんイギリスへ行きたい。

   *Watashi wa ima **ichiban** igirisu e ikitai.*

   I want to go to England most now.

→ See also *mottomo*

ikenai　いけない

ADJECTIVE MEANING: must not, have to, ought to, in case . . . , bad, wrong

1. After *te*-form of verb + *wa*
   ここでたばこを吸ってはいけません。
   Koko de tabako o sutte wa ikemasen.
   You must not smoke here.
   あまりお酒を飲んではいけないよ。
   Amari o-sake o nonde wa ikenai yo.
   You mustn't drink too much.
2. After the stem of *nai*-form of verb + *nakereba*
   もう行かなければいけません。
   Mō ikanakereba ikemasen.
   I have to go now.
   (*ikemasen* may be replaced by *narimasen*)
3. After dictionary form of verb + *to*, followed by *kara*
   雨が降るといけないから傘を持って行ったほうがいいです
   よ。
   Ame ga furu to ikenai kara kasa o motte itta hō ga ii desu yo.
   It's better to take an umbrella with you because it'll be bad if it
   rains. (You had better take an umbrella in case it rains.)
4. Used as adjective
   それのどこがいけないのですか。
   Sore no doko ga ikenai no desu ka.
   What's wrong with it?

→ See also *naranai*

ikō 以降

NOUN MEANING: from . . . on, after

1. After noun expressing point in time, followed by particle
   来週以降はとても忙しいです。
   Raishū ikō wa *totemo isogashii desu.*
   I'll be very busy from next week on.
   今晩9時以降に電話してください。
   *Konban **ku ji ikō ni** denwa shite kudasai.*
   Please call me after nine tonight.
→ See also *igo, irai, kara*

ikura . . . temo/demo いくら...ても／でも

PHRASE MEANING: no matter how (much/hard), at the . . . est, even . . .

1. Used with the stem of *te*-form of verb
   いくらがんばってもよくならない。
   Ikura ganbattemo *yoku naranai.*
   No matter how hard I try, it doesn't go well.
2. Used with *ku*-form of adjective
   いくら遅くても5時までに着きたい。
   *Ikura **osokutemo** go ji made ni tsukitai.*
   I want to arrive there by five at the latest.
3. Used with noun
   いくら天才でもその問題は解けない。

*Ikura tensai **demo** sono mondai wa tokenai.*
Even a genius cannot solve that problem.
→ See also *demo, temo*

inai 以内

NOUN MEANING: within, less than, not more than

1. After noun expressing length/quantity/price
   (followed by *ni*)
   10分以内に戻ります。
   *Juppun **inai ni** modorimasu.*
   I'll be back within ten minutes.
   (followed by *da/desu*)
   旅行の費用は5万円以内です。
   *Ryokō no hiyō wa **go man en inai desu**.*
   The expense for the trip will be less than fifty thousand yen.
   (followed by *no*)
   駅はここから歩いて20分以内の所です。
   *Eki wa koko kara aruite **ni juppun inai no** tokoro desu.*
   The station is within twenty minutes' walk from here.

irai 以来

CONJUNCTION MEANING: since

1. After noun expressing a past point in time
   先月以来雨が降っていません。
   *Sengetsu **irai** ame ga futte imasen.*
   It has not rained since last month.

2. After *te*-form of verb
   私は教師になって以来5年になります。
   Watashi wa kyōshi ni natte irai go nen ni narimasu.
   It is five years since I became a teacher.
→ See also *igo, ikō, kara*

iru　いる

VERB MEANING: be, there be, exist, stay, have, be . . . ing, have (done), be (done), have been . . . ing

1. Used for animate subject
   姉は今大阪にいます。
   Ane wa ima ōsaka ni imasu.
   My older sister is now staying (*or* living) in Osaka.
   この動物園には珍しい動物がいます。
   Kono dōbutsuen ni wa mezurashii dōbutsu ga imasu.
   There are unique animals in this zoo.
2. Used for animate object + *ga*
   私は兄弟が3人います。
   Watashi wa kyōdai ga san nin imasu.
   I have three brothers.
3. After *te*-form of verb
   私は今友人を待っています。
   Watashi wa ima yūjin o matte imasu.
   I am waiting for a friend of mine now.
   車の窓が開いていますよ。
   Kuruma no mado ga aite imasu yo.
   Your car window is open.
   私は英字新聞を読んでいます。

*Watashi wa eiji shinbun o yon**de imasu***.

I am reading an English language newspaper.

(*or* I read an English language newspaper. [habitual action])

その店はもう閉まっています。

*Sono mise wa mō shima**tte imasu***.

That store is closed already.

きのうからずっと雨が降っています。

*Kinō kara zutto ame ga fu**tte imasu***.

It has been raining since yesterday.

何をすべきか考えてます。

*Nani o subeki ka kangae**temasu***.

I am thinking what to do.

(informal spoken language often uses the abbreviated *ru/masu* instead of *iru/imasu* after *te*-form of verbs when expressing a continuing action or state)

あなたはとても疲れてるみたいだ。

*Anata wa totemo tsukare**teru** mitai da*.

You look very tired.

「この言葉を知っていますか。」「いいえ、知りません。」

*"Kono kotoba o shi**tte imasu** ka." "Iie, shirimasen."*

"Do you know this word?" "No, I don't know it."

(English verbs expressing a condition or state are usually translated into the progressive form in Japanese. However, the negative of *shitte iru* [*shitteru*] is the non-progressive form *shiranai*.)

→ See also *aru, oru, masu, temasu*

isshoni いっしょに

ADVERB MEANING: with (someone), together, at the same time

1. After noun + *to*
   「だれといっしょにそこへ行ったのですか。」「友達とです。」
   "***Dare to isshoni** soko e itta no desu ka.*" "*Tomodachi to desu.*"
   "Who did you go there with?" "With a friend."

2. Used as adverb
   今からいっしょに食事をしませんか。
   *Ima kara **isshoni** shokuji o shimasen ka.*
   Shall we have dinner together now?
   山本さんと山田さんがいっしょに着きました。
   *Yamamoto-san to yamada-san ga **isshoni** tsukimashita.*
   Mr. Yamamoto and Mr. Yamada arrived at the same time.

→ See also *to*

itadaku　いただく

RESPECTFUL VERB MEANING: be given, get, receive, eat, have (something) done

It is used to express respect to the giver.

1. As set phrase said before meals
   いただきます。
   ***Itadakimasu**.*
   (*Lit.*) I'll be given food.

2. After object noun + *o*
   学校の先生から手紙をいただきました。
   *Gakkō no sensei kara **tegami o itadakimashita**.*
   I got a letter from a teacher at my school.
   これをいただきたいのですが。

Kore o itadakitai no desu ga.
I'd like to have this.

3. After *te*-form of verb
そうしていただきます。
Sō shite itadakimasu.
I'll have you do so. (I hope you'll kindly do so.)
ちょっとこれを持っていただきたいのですが。
Chotto kore o motte itadakitai no desu ga.
I'd like you to hold this for a while.
この原稿を見ていただけますか。
Kono genkō o mite itadakemasu ka.
Would you look through this manuscript (for me)?
すみませんが、駅に行く道を教えていただけませんか。
Sumimasen ga, eki ni iku michi o oshiete itadakemasen ka.
Excuse me, but could you tell me the way to the station?

→ See also *morau*

itsu いつ

INTERROGATIVE WORD MEANING: when, what time

1. Used in a question
いつここへ来たんですか。
Itsu koko e kita n desu ka.
When did you come here?
いつできるのかたずねましたか。
Itsu dekiru no ka tazunemashita ka.
Did you ask when it will be finished?
(reported speech)

2. With specific particle in a question

彼女はいつから病気なのですか。

*Kanojo wa **itsu kara** byōki-na no desu ka.*

Since when has she been sick?

いつまで日本にいるんですか。

***Itsu made** nihon ni iru n desu ka.*

Until when (how long) are you in Japan?

3. Used in noun clause in a declarative sentence

いつ始まるのかわかりません。

***Itsu hajimaru no ka** wakarimasen.*

I don't know when it begins.

4. Followed by the subject marker *ga*

いつがよろしいですか。

***Itsu ga** yoroshii desu ka.*

When will be convenient for you?

ja　じゃ

INFORMAL PARTICLE that is a euphonic change of *dewa*

1. After (adjectival) noun

(used for making the negative form of *da/desu*)

これは私のかばんじゃありません。

*Kore wa watashi no **kaban ja arimasen**.*

This is not my bag.

(indicates a condition when followed by negative form of a potential verb)

この天気じゃ出かけられない。

*Kono **tenki ja** dekakerare**nai**.*

We can't go out in this weather.

このコンピューターじゃそれはできません。

*Kono **konpyūtā ja** sore wa dekimasen*.
It can't be done with this computer.

2. After the stem of *te*-form of verb whose dictionary form ends with *bu*, *gu*, *mu*, or *nu*, and followed by *ikenai*
ここで遊んじゃいけません。
*Koko de **asonja ikemasen***.
You must not play here.

→ See also *cha*, *dewa*, *ikenai*, *tewa*

jū 中

NOUN MEANING: throughout, within, all over

1. After noun expressing period of time
私は冬休み中スキーをしていました。
*Watashi wa **fuyu yasumi jū** sukii o shite imashita*.
I was skiing throughout the winter vacation.
1日中テレビを見ていました。
Ichi nichi jū terebi o mite imashita.
I was watching TV all day long.

2. After noun expressing period of time, followed by *ni*
今週中に仕上げてください。
Konshū jū ni shiagete kudasai.
Please complete it within this week.

3. After noun expressing place
日本中を旅行したいと思います。
Nihon jū o ryokō shitai to omoimasu.
I think I'd like to travel all over Japan.

→ See also *chū ni*

ka か

PARTICLE MEANING: (either) . . . or . . . , whether

It is also used to form questions, extend invitations, or make requests.

1. Between two or more nouns
   大学へはバスか地下鉄で行けます。
   *Daigaku e wa **basu ka chikatetsu** de ikemasu.*
   You can go to the university by either bus or subway.
2. After each of two or more verbs in dictionary form
   大学に行くか就職するか決めなければならない。
   *Daigaku ni **iku ka** shūshoku su**ru ka** kimenakereba naranai.*
   I have to decide either to go to university or get a job.
   遊園地に行くか映画を見に行くかしましょう。
   *Yūenchi ni **iku ka** eiga o mi ni **iku ka** shimashō.*
   Let's either go to an amusement park or go to see a movie.
3. After noun clause + *no*
   何が起ったのかわかりません。
   ***Nani ga okotta no ka** wakarimasen.*
   I don't know what happened.
   この字はどうやって書くのか教えてください。
   ***Kono ji wa dō yatte kaku no ka** oshiete kudasai.*
   Please teach me how to write this character.
   これが本物なのかどうかわかりません。
   ***Kore ga honmono na no ka** dōka wakarimasen.*
   I don't know whether or not this is the real thing.
   (if preceding clause has no question words, *dōka* [or not] may be put after *ka*)

4. At the end of question in indirect speech

   彼女にどこへ行くのかたずねましたが、答えませんでした。

   Kanojo ni doko e iku no ka *tazunemashita ga, kotaemasen deshita.*

   I asked her where she was going, but she didn't answer.

5. At the end of sentence

   「これはあなたのかばんですか。」「はい、そうです。」

   *"Kore wa anata no kaban desu **ka**." "Hai, sō desu."*

   "Is this your bag?" "Yes, it is. "

   「さしみは食べますか。」「はい、食べます。」

   *"Sashimi wa tabemasu **ka**." "Hai, tabemasu."*

   "Do you eat sashimi?" "Yes, I do."

   彼のことをどう思いますか。

   *Kare no koto o dō omoimasu **ka**.*

   What do you think of him?

6. After *masen*

   (to make an invitation)

   いっしょにコンサートに行きませんか。

   *Isshoni konsāto ni iki**masen ka**.*

   Would you like to go to the concert with me?

7. After *te*-form of verb + *kuremasen*

   (to make a request)

   自転車を貸してくれませんか。

   *Jitensha o kashi**te kuremasen ka**.*

   Would you please lend me your bicycle?

8. After interrogative word

   先生はだれかとどこかへ行きました。

   *Sensei wa **dare ka** to **doko ka** e ikimashita.*

   The teacher went somewhere with somebody.

何か飲むものが欲しいですね。
***Nani ka** nomu mono ga hoshii desu ne.*
I want something to drink, don't you?

→ See also *kureru, masen*

kagiri 限り

CONJUNCTION MEANING: as long as . . . , as far as . . . is concerned,
as . . . as possible, unless, not later than, just

1. After dictionary form of verb/adjective
   私の知る限り、彼はうそをついたことがない。
   *Watashi no shi**ru kagiri** kare wa uso o tsuita koto ga nai.*
   As far as I know he has never told a lie.
   ここにいる限り静かにしなければならない。
   *Koko ni i**ru kagiri** shizuka ni shinakereba naranai.*
   We must keep quiet as long as we stay here.
2. After *nai*-form of verb
   雨が降らない限り予定通り行われます。
   *Ame ga fura**nai kagiri** yotei dōri okonawaremasu.*
   It will be held as scheduled unless it rains.
3. After noun expressing time limit
   申し込みは明日限りです。
   *Mōshikomi wa **asu kagiri** desu.*
   Applications must be made no later than tomorrow.
4. After specific noun + *ni*
   今回に限り罰は与えません。
   ***Konkai ni kagiri** batsu wa ataemasen.*
   This time only I won't punish you.
5. After *dekiru*, followed by adverb

できる限り早く出かけたいと思います。
***Dekiru kagiri hayaku* dekaketai to omoimasu.**
I'd like to leave as soon as possible.

→ See also *dake*

kamoshirenai　かもしれない
ADJECTIVE MEANING: may, might, possibly

1. After dictionary form of verb/adjective
   あすは雪が降るかもしれない。
   *Asu wa yuki ga furu **kamoshirenai**.*
   It may snow tomorrow.
   彼の言うことが正しいのかもしれません。
   *Kare no iū koto ga tadashii **no kamoshiremasen**.*
   Possibly what he says is right.
2. After *ta*-form of verb/adjective
   その方が良かったのかもしれません。
   *Sono hō ga yoka**tta no kamoshiremasen**.*
   It might have been better.
   もう帰ったのかもしれない。
   *Mō kae**tta no kamoshirenai**.*
   She may have already gone.
3. After *nai*-form of verb
   彼はいっしょに行かないのかもしれない。
   *Kare wa isshoni ika**nai no kamoshirenai**.*
   He may not go together (with us).
4. After (adjectival) noun
   日本語はあなたには簡単かもしれません。

*Nihongo wa anata ni wa **kantan kamoshiremasen**.*
Japanese language might be easy for you.
→ See also *deshō*

kana かな

INFORMAL PARTICLE MEANING: I wonder if . . .

It can be replaced with *kashira* (used mostly by women).

1. At the end of sentence
   電車に間に合うかな。
   *Densha ni ma ni au **kana**.*
   I wonder if I will be in time for the train.
   彼女も来るかな。
   *Kanojo mo kuru **kana**.*
   I wonder if she will come, too.
   これでいいかな。
   *Kore de ii **kana**.*
   I wonder if this is all right.
2. After (adjectival) noun (+ *na no*)
   これはだれのかばん(なの)かな。
   *Kore wa dare no **kaban (na no) kana**.*
   I wonder whose bag this is.
   (*na no* after the adjectival noun is often dropped)
3. After conjunctive form of verb + *temo ii*
   窓を開けてもいいかな。
   *Mado o **aketemo ii kana**.*
   I wonder if it's okay to open the window?

kanarazushimo　必ずしも

ADVERB (used with a negative) MEANING: (not) always, (not) necessarily, (not) all

It can be shortened to *kanarazu*, or replaced by *itsumo*.

1. Used with negative
   お金は必ずしも必要ではない。
   *O-kane wa **kanarazushimo** hitsuyō dewa **nai**.*
   Money is not always necessary.
2. Used with dictionary form of verb/adjective + *to wa kagiranai*
   それが必ずしもうまく行くとは限らない。
   *Sore ga **kanarazushimo** umaku iku to wa kagiranai.*
   It will not necessarily go well.
   先生が必ずしも正しいとは限りません。
   *Sensei ga **kanarazushimo** tadashii to wa kagirimasen.*
   The teacher is not always right.

kara　から

PARTICLE MEANING: from, out of, at, through, since, after, because

When used to mean "because," it is the speaker's opinion that the statement expressed before *kara* is the reason or cause for the action expressed in the main clause. That is, the reason or cause may be subjective or emotional, unlike *node*.

1. After noun expressing point in time when something begins
   夏休みは7月20日からです。
   *Natsu yasumi wa **shichi gatsu hatsuka kara** desu.*

The summer vacation is from July twentieth.

学校は8時半から始まります。

*Gakkō wa **hachi ji han kara** hajimarimasu.*

School begins at eight thirty.

(*kara* may be replaced with *ni*)

あの店は午前10時から午後6時まで開いています。

*Ano mise wa gozen **jū ji kara** gogo roku ji made aite imasu.*

That store is open from 10 A.M. to 6 P.M.

きのうから風邪をひいています。

***Kinō kara** kaze o hiite imasu.*

I've had a cold since yesterday.

2. After noun expressing place

東京から京都まで新幹線で来ました。

***Tōkyō kara** kyōto made shinkansen de kimashita.*

I came from Tokyo to Kyoto by shinkansen.

彼女は怒って部屋から出て行った。

*Kanojo wa okotte **heya kara** dete itta.*

She got angry and went out of the room.

3. After noun expressing material/ingredients

日本酒は米から作られます。

*Nihonshu wa **kome kara** tsukuraremasu.*

Japanese *sake* is made from rice.

4. After *te*-form of verb

テレビを見てから勉強します。

*Terebi o mi**te kara** benkyō shimasu.*

I'll study after watching TV.

ここで休んでから帰ります。

*Koko de yasun**de kara** kaerimasu.*

I'll go home after taking a rest here.

日本に来てから6ヶ月になります。

*Nihon ni ki**te kara** rokkagetsu ni narimasu.*

It is six months since I came to Japan.

(here *kara* may be dropped)

5. After dictionary form of verb/adjective

雨が降るから傘を持って行った方がいい。

*Ame ga fu**ru kara** kasa o motte itta hō ga ii.*

It's better to take an umbrella with you because it's going to rain.

私がしますから休んでください。

*Watashi ga shima**su kara** yasunde kudasai.*

I'll do it, so please take a rest.

高いからそれは買いません。

*Taka**i kara** sore wa kaimasen.*

I don't buy it because it is expensive.

6. After *nai*-form of verb

だれにも言わないから教えて下さい。

*Dare ni mo iwa**nai kara** oshiete kudasai.*

I won't tell anybody so please tell me.

7. After (adjectival) noun + *da/desu*

あすは休みですからどこかへ遊びに行きましょう。

*Asu wa **yasumi desu kara** doko ka e asobi ni ikimashō.*

Let's go somewhere to have fun since tomorrow is a holiday.

8. After *ta*-form of verb/adjective

私が休んだのは風邪をひいたからです。

*Watashi ga yasunda no wa kaze o hii**ta kara** desu.*

It is because I caught cold that I was absent.

行きたくなかったから行きませんでした。

*Ikitaku naka**tta kara** ikimasen deshita.*

I didn't go because I didn't want to.

→ See also *dakara, de, ikō, igo, irai, ni, node, to*

kata　方

SUFFIX MEANING: how to (do), way/method of (doing)

1. After conjunctive form of verb
   かなの書き方を教えてください。
   *Kana no **kakikata** o oshiete kudasai.*
   Please teach me how to write *kana*.
   (the object of the verb *kaku* [*kana*] must be indicated by *no*,
   since the object of the main verb *oshieru* [*kakikata*] is already
   indicated by *o*)
   日本語の勉強の仕方がわかりません。
   *Nihongo no benkyō no **shikata** ga wakarimasen.*
   I don't know how to study Japanese.
   (*shikata*, the conjunctive form of *suru* + *kata*, is always preceded by noun + *no*)
   (the dictionary form of verb + *hōhō* also expresses "how to
   [do]"; object of the verb before *hōhō* must be indicated by *o*)
   コンピューターを操作する方法を教えてください。
   *Konpyūtā **o** sōsa suru **hōhō** o oshiete kudasai.*
   Please teach me how to operate the computer.

kawari ni　代わりに

PHRASE MEANING: instead of, for, as, in exchange for, in return (for),
to make up for

1. After noun + *no*
   彼が私の代わりにその会に出てくれました。
   *Kare ga **watashi no kawari ni** sono kai ni dete kuremashita.*
   He attended the meeting instead of me.

カメラはメモの代わりになる。

*Kamera wa **memo no kawari ni** naru.*

A camera will do for (taking) notes.

2. After dictionary form of verb

英語を教える代わりに日本語を教えてください。

*Eigo o oshie**ru kawari ni** nihongo o oshiete kudasai.*

Please teach me Japanese in exchange for teaching you English.

手伝う代わりにお金を貸してくれませんか。

*Tetsuda**u kawari ni** o-kane o kashite kuremasen ka.*

Will you lend me money in return for my helping you?

3. After *ta*-form of verb

彼はお金を無駄にした代わりに一生懸命働いている。

*Kare wa o-kane o muda ni shi**ta kawari ni** isshōkenmei hataraite iru.*

He is working hard to make up for having wasted money.

4. After *nai*-form of verb

何も食べない代わりにたくさんジュースを飲んだ。

*Nani mo tabe**nai kawari ni** takusan jūsu o nonda.*

I didn't eat anything but instead drank a lot of juice.

5. Used as adverb

代わりにこのペンダントをあげます。

Kawari ni *kono pendanto o agemasu.*

I will give you this pendant in return.

keredo(mo) けれど(も)

CONJUNCTION MEANING: though, although, but, however, and, I wish

The final *mo* is often dropped in more informal speech.

1. At the beginning of sentence
   私は彼に来るように何度も頼んだ。けれども来なかった。
   Watashi wa kare ni kuru yō ni nando mo tanonda. **Keredomo**
   konakatta.
   I repeatedly asked him to come. But he didn't.
2. At the end of sentence
   今ちょっと忙しいんですけれども。
   Ima chotto isogashii n desu **keredomo**.
   I'm a little too busy now (so I can't help you).
3. After dictionary form of verb/adjective
   太郎とはよく話すけれどもとてもいい人です。
   Taro to wa yoku hanasu **keredomo** *totemo ii hito desu.*
   I often talk with Taro, and I think he is a nice person.
4. After *tai*-form of verb
   旅行に行きたいけれどもひまがありません。
   Ryokō ni ikitai **keredomo** *hima ga arimasen.*
   Though I want to go on a trip, I have no time.
5. After *ta*-form of verb/adjective
   その店に行ったけれども閉まっていました。
   Sono mise ni itta **keredomo** *shimatte imashita.*
   I went to the store, but it was closed.
   そんなものは欲しくなかったけれども買ってしまいました。
   Sonna mono wa hoshiku nakatta **keredomo** *katte shimaimashita.*
   Though I didn't want such a thing, I bought it in spite of
   myself.
6. After *nai*-form of verb
   彼はあまり勉強しないけれども成績がいい。
   Kare wa amari benkyō shinai **keredomo** *seiseki ga ii.*

He doesn't study hard, but he gets good marks.

7. After (adjectival) noun + *da/desu*

   彼はまじめだけれども面白くありません。

   *Kare wa **majime da keredomo** omoshiroku arimasen.*

   He is earnest, but not interesting.

→ See also *daga, dakedo, ga (2), no ni*

kesshite 決して

ADVERB (used with a negative) MEANING: never, by no means, (not) at all, on no account

1. Used with negative

   あなたのことは決して忘れません。

   *Anata no koto wa **kesshite** wasuremasen.*

   I shall never forget you.

   この問題は決してむずかしくはありません。

   *Kono mondai wa **kesshite** muzukashiku wa arimasen.*

   This problem is by no means difficult.

   彼は決してそんなことをする人ではない。

   *Kare wa **kesshite** sonna koto o suru hito dewa **nai**.*

   He is the last person to do such a thing.

→ See also *mattaku, zenzen*

kore これ

DEMONSTRATIVE PRONOUN MEANING: this, these, it

It refers to an object or objects close to both the speaker and the hearer. The polite form is *kochira*, which also means "this person" or "this direction." *Kore* becomes *kono* before nouns it modifies. Moreover, it becomes *koko* when expressing "this place" or "here."

1. Followed by particle
   これがきのう買ったカメラです。
   Kore ga *kinō katta kamera desu.*
   This is the camera that I bought yesterday.
   これを見たことがありますか。
   Kore o *mita koto ga arimasu ka.*
   Have you ever seen this?
   これからがんばります。
   Kore kara *ganbarimasu.*
   I'll work hard from now on.
   こちらが山本さんです。
   Kochira ga *yamamoto-san desu.*
   This is Ms. Yamamoto.
   ここが私の家です。
   Koko ga *watashi no ie desu.*
   This is my house.
   「今日の新聞はどこですか。」「ここにあります。」
   "*Kyō no shinbun wa doko desu ka.*" "***Koko*** *ni arimasu.*"
   "Where is today's newspaper?" "Here it is."

2. Followed by *da/desu*
   神戸行きのプラットホームはここですか。
   Kōbe yuki no purattohōmu wa ***koko desu*** *ka.*
   Is this the platform for the train to Kobe?

3. Before noun
   この靴をください。
   Kono kutsu *o kudasai.*

Give me these shoes. (I'll take these shoes.)

→ See also *are*, *sore*

koso　こそ

PARTICLE stressing something that is worth mentioning

It essentially takes the place of the particle *ga* or *wa* after the subject.

1. After noun
   これこそ私のほしい本です。
   Kore koso *watashi no hoshii hon desu.*
   This is the very book that I want.
   私こそお礼を言わなければなりません。
   Watashi koso *o-rei o iwanakereba narimasen.*
   I (not you) should be expressing thanks.

koto　こと

NOUN AND NOMINALIZER MEANING: thing (in the abstract sense), . . . ing, to (do), (the fact) that

When used to nominalize the preceding clause, the nominalized phrase expresses a fact which is already accomplished or which the speaker supposes will be accomplished. *Koto* tends to be taken as an object by verbs of mental activity such as knowing, recognizing, understanding, hoping, learning, etc.

1. After noun + *no*

彼女のことはよく知っています。

***Kanojo no koto** wa yoku shitte imasu.*

I know things of her well. (I know her well.)

2. After dictionary form of verb/adjective

今日はすることがたくさんあります。

*Kyō wa su**ru koto** ga takusan arimasu.*

I have a lot of things to do today.

見ることは信じることです。

*Mi**ru koto** wa shinji**ru koto** desu.*

Seeing is believing.

よく休むことが必要です。

*Yoku yasu**mu koto** ga hitsuyō desu.*

It is necessary (for you) to get enough rest.

日本は物価が高いことはよく知られている。

*Nihon wa bukka ga taka**i koto** wa yoku shirarete iru.*

That prices are high in Japan is well known.

3. After *ta*-form of verb/adjective

私が言ったことを彼に伝えてください。

*Watashi ga i**tta koto** o kare ni tsutaete kudasai.*

Please tell him what I've said.

さち子さんがヨーロッパに行ったことを知っていますか。

*Sachiko-san ga yōroppa ni i**tta koto** o shitte imasu ka.*

Did you know that Sachiko has gone to Europe?

4. After declarative statement

(used as a command form in written notices)

敷地内に入らないこと。

*Shikichi nai ni hairanai **koto**.*

Don't enter the premises.

→ See also *koto ga aru, koto ga dekiru, koto ni naru, koto ni natte iru, koto ni shite iru, koto ni suru, mono, no, to, to iū*

koto ga aru   ことがある

PREDICATIVE PHRASE MEANING: there are occasions when, have (done), had an experience that

1. After dictionary form of verb
   あの人と話すことがありますか。
   *Ano hito to hanasu **koto ga arimasu** ka.*
   Do you have occasion to talk with that person?
2. After *ta*-form of verb
   「北海道へ行ったことがありますか。」「いいえ、ありません。」
   *"Hokkaidō e itta **koto ga arimasu** ka." "Iie, arimasen."*
   "Have you ever been to Hokkaido?" "No, I haven't."
   まだスキーをしたことがありません。
   *Mada sukii o shita **koto ga arimasen**.*
   I haven't ever skiied.
3. After *nai*-form of verb
   たまに食事をしないことがあります。
   *Tama ni shokuji o shinai **koto ga arimasu**.*
   There are occasions when I don't eat a meal.
→ See also *koto*

koto ga dekiru   ことができる

PREDICATIVE PHRASE MEANING: can (do), be able to (do)

1. After dictionary form of verb
   3時までに来ることができますか。
   *San ji made ni kuru **koto ga dekimasu** ka.*
   Are you able to come by three o'clock?

私はあまり漢字を書くことができません。
*Watashi wa amari kanji o ka**ku koto ga dekimasen***.
I cannot write many Chinese characters.
飛行機の予約を取ることができました。
*Hikōki no yoyaku o to**ru koto ga dekimashita***.
I was able to make a plane reservation.

2. After *nai*-form of verb
秘密を洩らさないことができますか。
*Himitsu o morasa**nai koto ga dekimasu** ka*.
Can you keep (from letting out) a secret?

→ See also *dekiru, koto*

koto ni naru　ことになる

PREDICATIVE PHRASE MEANING: it is decided/arranged that

1. After dictionary form of verb
今度東京に転勤することになりました。
*Kondo tōkyō ni tenkin su**ru koto ni narimashita***.
It is decided that I'll be transferred to the Tokyo office shortly.

koto ni natte iru　ことになっている

PREDICATIVE PHRASE MEANING: be scheduled to (do), be expected to (do)

1. After dictionary form of verb
彼は9時にここに着くことになっています。
*Kare wa ku ji ni koko ni tsu**ku koto ni natte imasu***.

He is due to arrive here at nine.

私たちは図書館で会うことになっています。

*Watashi tachi wa toshokan de a**u koto ni natte imasu***.

We are to meet at the library.

koto ni shite iru　ことにしている

PREDICATIVE PHRASE MEANING: make a practice of (doing), make it a rule to (do)

1. After dictionary form of verb
   寝る前に本を読むことにしています。
   *Neru mae ni hon o yo**mu koto ni shite imasu***.
   I make it a rule to read (a book) before going to bed.
2. After *nai*-form of verb
   夜ふかししないことにしています。
   *Yofukashi shi**nai koto ni shite imasu***.
   I make it a rule not to stay up late.

koto ni suru　ことにする

PREDICATIVE PHRASE MEANING: decide to (do), make up one's mind to (do)

1. After dictionary form of verb
   タバコをやめることにしました。
   *Tabako o yame**ru koto ni shimashita***.
   I've made up my mind to give up smoking.
2. After *nai*-form of verb

無駄遣いはしないことにしました。

*Muda zukai wa shi**nai koto ni** shimashita*.

I've decided not to waste money.

kudasai　ください

POLITE COMMAND FORM MEANING: please give . . . to me, please do something (for me)

It is usually used for expressing a request on the speaker's part.

1. After noun + *o*

   8時に電話をください。

   *Hachi ji ni **denwa o kudasai***.

   Please give me a call at eight.

   このジャケットとズボンをください。

   *Kono **jaketto to zubon o kudasai***.

   Please give me this jacket and these slacks. (I'll take this jacket and these slacks.)

2. After *te*-form of verb

   この漢字の書き方を教えてください。

   *Kono kanji no kakikata o oshie**te kudasai***.

   Please teach me how to write this kanji.

3. After *nai*-form of verb + *de*

   まだ行かないでください。

   *Mada ika**nai de kudasai***.

   Please don't leave yet.

→ See also *kureru,* Polite Language (II)

kurai　くらい

PARTICLE MEANING: about, approximately, as . . . as . . ., to the extent of . . ., only, at least, enough . . . to (do)

Gurai can be used in place of *kurai*.

1. After noun expressing quantity/length
   10冊くらい日本語の本を買いました。
   Jussatsu kurai *nihongo no hon o kaimashita.*
   I bought about ten Japanese language books.
   彼女はオーストラリアに3ヶ月くらいいました。
   *Kanojo wa ōsutoraria ni **san kagetsu kurai** imashita.*
   She was in Australia for about three months.
   毎日1時間くらいは勉強しなければならない。
   *Mainichi **ichi jikan kurai** wa benkyō shinakereba naranai.*
   One must study at least one hour every day.
   (*kurai* + *wa* means "at least")

2. After noun
   だれもあなたくらい上手にテニスができません。
   *Dare mo **anata kurai** jōzu ni tenisu ga dekimasen.*
   Nobody can play tennis as well as you.
   それができるのはあなたくらいです。
   *Sore ga dekiru no wa **anata kurai** desu.*
   You are the only one who can do it.

3. After demonstrative pronoun
   それくらい私でもわかります。
   Sore kurai *watashi demo wakarimasu.*
   Even I can understand that much.
   これくらいいい辞書は買ったほうがいい。
   Kore kurai *ii jisho wa katta hō ga ii.*

It's better to buy a dictionary as good as this one.

4. After *dono*

これはどのくらいしますか。

*Kore wa **dono kurai** shimasu ka.*

How much does this cost?

駅までどのくらいかかりますか。

*Eki made **dono kurai** kakarimasu ka.*

How long does it take to the station?

１週間にどのくらい喫茶店に行きますか。

*Isshūkan ni **dono kurai** kissaten ni ikimasu ka.*

How often do you go to a coffee shop in a week?

5. After dictionary form of verb

この本は子供が読めるくらいやさしいです。

*Kono hon wa kodomo ga yome**ru kurai** yasashii desu.*

This book is easy enough for a child to read.

6. After *nai*-form of potential verb

今日はとても我慢できないくらい寒いです。

*Kyō wa totemo gaman deki**nai kurai** samui desu.*

It is so cold today that I can't endure it. (It is colder than I can endure today.)

もう歩けないくらい疲れた。

*Mō aruke**nai kurai** tsukareta.*

I am tired to the extent that I can't walk any more. (I am too tired to walk any more.)

→ See also *dono kurai, hodo*

kureru　くれる

VERB MEANING: give (something), do (something) for, do a favor by doing (something), let (me) be satisfied with doing (something)

Kureru is used to express the "giving" of something to the speaker or to his/her family member. The first person is never the subject. *Kudasaru* may be substitued with persons of higher status or to whom the speaker wishes to show respect.

1. After object noun + *o*
   彼女は私の誕生日にすてきなプレゼントをくれました。
   *Kanojo wa watashi no tanjōbi ni suteki-na **purezento o kuremashita**.*
   She gave me a nice present for my birthday.
   (the recipient can be 2nd person with a past tense verb or in a simple question)
   彼は電話をくれましたか。
   *Kare wa **denwa o kuremashita** ka.*
   Did he give you a call?
2. After *te*-form of verb
   彼女がおいしい料理を作ってくれました。
   *Kanojo ga oishii ryōri o tsuku**tte kuremashita**.*
   She prepared a delicious dish for me.
   だれが手伝ってくれましたか。
   *Dare ga tetsuda**tte kuremashita** ka.*
   Who helped you?
   ペンを貸してくれませんか。
   *Pen o kashi**te kuremasen** ka.*
   Would you kindly lend me your pen?
   先生がていねいに日本語を教えてくださいます。
   *Sensei ga teinei ni nihongo o oshie**te kudasaimasu**.*
   The teacher teaches me Japanese respectfully.
   (*kudasaru* shows respect toward the teacher)
→ See also *ageru, kudasai, morau*

mada まだ

ADVERB MEANING: still, yet

1. In affirmative statement or question
   彼はまだ眠っています。
   *Kare wa **mada** nemutte **imasu**.*
   He is still sleeping.
   私の言ったことをまだ覚えていますか。
   *Watashi no itta koto o **mada** oboete **imasu** ka.*
   Do you still remember what I said?
   お父さんはまだお若いですか。
   *Otōsan wa **mada** o-wakai **desu** ka.*
   Is your father still young?
2. In negative sentence
   彼女はまだここに来ていません。
   *Kanojo wa **mada** koko ni kite imasen.*
   She has not arrived here yet.
   「もうできましたか。」「まだできません。」
   "Mō dekimashita ka." "Mada dekimasen."
   "Have you finished yet?" "No, not yet."
→ See also *mō*

made まで

PARTICLE MEANING: until, to, (from . . .) through, up to, as far as, before

1. After noun expressing temporal/spatial/quantitative limit
   火曜日から土曜日まで旅行に行きます。
   *Kayōbi kara **doyōbi made** ryokō ni ikimasu.*

I'll be traveling from Tuesday through Saturday.

事務所は来週の水曜日まで閉まっています。

*Jimusho wa raishū no **suiyōbi made** shimatte imasu.*

The office is closed through next Wednesday.

京都までの切符を2枚ください。

***Kyōto made** no kippu o ni mai kudasai.*

Give me two tickets for Kyoto, please.

東京まで新幹線で行きます。

***Tōkyō made** shinkansen de ikimasu.*

I'm going as far as Tokyo on the shinkansen.

25ページまで読んでください。

*Ni jū go **pēji made** yonde kudasai.*

Please read up to page twenty five.

この車は5人まで乗れます。

*Kono kuruma wa **go nin made** noremasu.*

This car can hold up to five persons.

2. After dictionary form of verb

雨がやむまで喫茶店で休みましょう。

*Ame ga ya**mu made** kissaten de yasumimashō.*

Let's take a rest in the coffee shop until it stops raining.

次の電車が来るまで15分ある。

*Tsugi no densha ga ku**ru made** jū go fun aru.*

There are fifteen minutes until the next train comes.

→ See also *kara, made ni*

made ni までに

PARTICLE MEANING: by (the time when . . .), before

1. After noun expressing time (limit)

今週の終わりまでにこの仕事を終えなければなりません。

*Konshū no **owari made ni** kono shigoto o oenakereba narimasen.*

I have to finish this work by the end of this week.

2. After dictionary form of verb

彼女が来るまでに用意しておきましょう。

*Kanojo ga ku**ru made ni** yōi shite okimashō.*

Let's be prepared by the time she comes.

→ See also *made*, *mae*

mae 前

NOUN (of space or time) MEANING: before, ago, previous, prior, last, former, in front of, forward

1. Used for telling time

今3時5分前です。

*Ima **san ji go fun mae** desu.*

It is five minutes to three o'clock.

2. After noun expressing length/duration of or point in time

私は半年前に日本に来ました。

*Watashi wa **hantoshi mae ni** nihon ni kimashita.*

I came to Japan half a year ago.

マイクはポールが来る5分前に帰りました。

*Maiku wa Pōru ga kuru **go fun mae ni** kaerimashita.*

Mike went home five minutes before Paul came.

1時前にここに戻ります。

*Ichi ji **mae ni** koko ni modorimasu.*

I'll be back here before one.

私は2ヶ月前からここで働いています。

*Watashi wa **ni kagetsu mae kara** koko de hataraite imasu.*
I've been working here since two months ago.

3. Used as adverb, followed by *ni*

前にどこかで会ったことがありませんか。
***Mae ni** dokoka de atta koto ga arimasen ka.*
Haven't we met somewhere before?

前に歩いてください。
***Mae ni** aruite kudasai.*
Walk in front, please.

4. After dictionary form of verb, followed by *ni*

いつも寝る前にココアを飲みます。
*Itsumo ne**ru mae ni** kokoa o nomimasu.*
I usually drink some cocoa before I go to bed.

私たちが着く前に電車が出た。
*Watashi tachi ga tsu**ku mae ni** densha ga deta.*
The train had left before we arrived.

5. After noun (positional) + *no*

湖の前にすてきなホテルがあります。
***Mizuumi no mae** ni suteki-na hoteru ga arimasu.*
There is a nice hotel in front of the lake.

彼女の前でその話はやめよう。
***Kanojo no mae** de sono hanashi wa yameyō.*
Let's stop talking about it in front of her.

6. Followed by *no* + noun

前の総理大臣はだれでしたか。
***Mae no** sōri daijin wa dare deshita ka.*
Who was the former Prime Minister?

鈴木さんの前の先生はだれでしたか。
*Suzuki-san no **mae no** sensei wa dare deshita ka.*
Who was the teacher prior to Mr. Suzuki?

前の土曜日に泳ぎに行って来ました。
***Mae no doyōbi** ni oyogi ni itte kimashita.*
I went swimming last Saturday.
そのことは前のページに書いてあります。
*Sono koto wa **mae no pēji** ni kaite arimasu.*
That matter is written about on the previous page.
トイレは前の車両にあります。
*Toire wa **mae no sharyō** ni arimasu.*
The restroom is in the front car (of the train).

→ See also *ato de, de, ni, no, uchi ni*

marude　まるで

CONJUNCTION OR ADVERB MEANING: entirely, (not) at all

When used together with *yō* or *mitai, marude* means "as if" or "as though."

1. Used with *yō*
   (*yō* usually follows a clause + *ka no*)
   彼はまるで何も知らないかのように話す。
   *Kare wa **marude** nani mo shiranai ka no **yō** ni hanasu.*
   He talks as if he knows nothing at all.
2. Used with *mitai*
   まるであなたがそれをしたみたいだ。
   ***Marude** anata ga sore o shita **mitai** da.*
   It sounds as though you had done it yourself.
3. Used as adverb
   ここに書いてあることはまるで話にならない。
   *Koko ni kaite aru koto wa **marude** hanashi ni naranai.*

What is written here is not at all worthy of discussion.
その文の意味がまるでわかりません。
*Sono bun no imi ga **marude** wakarimasen.*
I don't understand the meaning of the sentence at all.
→ See also *mattaku, mitai, yō, yō desu, zenzen*

masen ません
→ See *masu*

mashō ましょう
→ See *masu*

masu ます
AUXILIARY VERB expressing politeness

A verb that ends a sentence is usually followed by this auxiliary, while a verb that ends a relative or noun clause is not.

The *masu*-form usually expresses definite future actions or events, the speaker's intentions, present habitual actions, or potential actions. The progressive form with *masu* expresses continuing actions or states. *Masu* follows the conjunctive form of verbs.

Masu has the following forms:

Non-past negative form: *masen*
Past affirmative form: *mashita*
Past negative form: *masen deshita*
Volitional form: *mashō*

1. Expressing future action/event
   私は明日新幹線で京都に行きます。
   *Watashi wa ashita shinkansen de kyōto ni iki**masu**.*
   I will go to Kyoto by shinkansen tomorrow.
   彼女はいっしょに旅行には行きません。
   *Kanojo wa isshoni ryokō ni wa iki**masen**.*
   She is not going with me on the trip.
   閉会式は10時より行われます。
   *Heikaishiki wa jū ji yori okonaware**masu**.*
   The closing ceremony will be held from ten.

2. Expressing speaker's intention
   あとで電話します。
   *Ato de denwa shi**masu**.*
   I'll call you later.

3. Expressing habitual action
   私は毎朝ごはんとみそ汁を食べます。
   *Watashi wa mai asa gohan to miso shiru o tabe**masu**.*
   I eat rice and miso soup every morning.
   私はあまりタバコを吸いません。
   *Watashi wa amari tabako o sui**masen**.*
   I don't smoke much.

4. Expressing continuing action or state of being
   彼女は今あそこで新聞を読んでいます。
   *Kanojo wa ima asoko de shinbun o yon**de imasu**.*
   She is now reading a newspaper over there.
   私はとてもおなかがすいています。
   *Watashi wa totemo onaka ga sui**te imasu**.*
   I am very hungry.
   彼はもうその会社では働いていません。

*Kare wa mō sono kaisha dewa hatarai**te imasen***.

He is not working at that company any more.

5. Expressing present condition

このホテルは景色がよく見えます。

*Kono hoteru wa keshiki ga yoku mie**masu***.

We have a good view from this hotel.

6. Expressing past/perfect action

私はきのう図書館でマイクに会いました。

*Watashi wa kinō toshokan de maiku ni ai**mashita***.

I met Mike in the library yesterday.

もうその本は読みましたか。

*Mō sono hon wa yomi**mashita** ka*.

Have you read that book yet?

7. Expressing volition

いっしょにおいしい料理を食べましょう。

*Isshoni oishii ryōri o tabe**mashō***.

Let's eat some good food together.

8. Expressing suggestion

窓を閉めましょうか。

*Mado o shime**mashō** ka*.

Shall I shut the window?

9. Expressing invitation

お茶でもいっしょに飲みませんか。

*Ocha demo isshoni nomi**masen ka***.

Would you have tea (or something) with me?

→ See also *arimasen, temasu*, Polite Language (II), Verb Forms (II)

mattaku まったく

ADVERB MEANING: quite, completely, really, indeed, (not) at all, (not) in the least

1. In affirmative sentence
   まったく驚きました。
   Mattaku odoroki***mashita.***
   I was really surprised.
   まったくそのとおりです。
   Mattaku sono tōri ***desu***.
   You're quite right.
2. In negative sentence
   彼はまったく信用できません。
   Kare wa ***mattaku*** shin'yō dekima***sen***.
   He is not at all trustworthy.
   それが何かまったくわかりません。
   Sore ga nani ka ***mattaku*** wakarima***sen***.
   I don't have the faintest idea what it is.
→ See also *marude*, *zenzen*

metta ni めったに

ADVERB (used with a negative) MEANING: seldom, rarely, (not) very often

1. In negative sentence
   私はめったに飲みに行きません。

*Watashi wa **metta ni** nomi ni ikimasen*.
I rarely go out for a drink.
彼女とはめったに会いません。
*Kanojo to wa **metta ni** aimasen*.
I don't see her very often.
→ See also *amari*, *hotondo*

mitai みたい (1)
ADJECTIVE MEANING: would like to (do), feel like (doing), feel inclined to (do)

1. After *te*-form of verb
   いつか外国に行ってみたい。
   *Itsuka gaikoku ni itte **mitai***.
   I'd like to travel abroad some day.
   海でひと泳ぎしてみたい。
   *Umi de hito oyogi shite **mitai***.
   I feel like a swim in the sea.
→ See also *tai*

mitai みたい (2)
NOUN MEANING: like . . ., seem to, look like

In the same manner as adjectival nouns, *mitai* is followed by *da/desu* or *na/ni*.

1. After (adjectival) noun

あなたみたいに日本語が話せません。

Anata mitai *ni nihongo ga hanasemasen.*

I can't speak Japanese like you.

彼は先生みたいです。

*Kare wa **sensei mitai** desu.*

He looks like a teacher.

彼は芸術家みたいな格好をしている。

*Kare wa **geijutsuka mitai**-na kakkō o shite iru.*

He is dressed just like an artist.

2. After dictionary or *nai*-form of verb/adjective

彼女は疲れているみたいだ。

*Kanojo wa tsukarete **iru mitai** da.*

She seems to be tired.

彼女はすもうに興味がないみたいです。

*Kanojo wa sumō ni kyōmi ga na**i mitai** desu.*

It looks like she is not interested in sumo wrestling.

3. After *ta*-form of verb/adjective

彼は試験に合格したみたいです。

*Kare wa shiken ni gōkaku shit**a mitai** desu.*

He seems to have passed the exam.

パーティーは楽しかったみたいです。

*Pātii wa tanoshikatt**a mitai** desu.*

It seems that the party was fun.

→ See also *marude, rashii, sō desu (2), yō*

mo も

PARTICLE MEANING: too, also, (not) either, as many/much/long as, no less than, both . . . and . . ., as well as, neither . . .nor . . ., (not) even, even if, any. . .

Mata is sometimes added after *mo*. This simply means "too" or "also."

1. After noun
   私も相撲が好きです。
   ***Watashi mo** sumō ga suki desu.*
   I like sumo, too.
   「とてもおなかがすきました。」「私もです。」
   *"Totemo onaka ga sukimashita." **"Watashi mo** desu."*
   "I am very hungry." "So am I."
   「納豆は好きではありません。」「私もです。」
   *"Nattō wa suki dewa arimasen." **"Watashi mo** desu."*
   "I don't like fermented soybeans." "Neither do I."

2. After noun, with negative verb
   私も漢字は読めません。
   ***Watashi mo** kanji wa yomemasen.*
   I can't read kanji, either.
   私は簡単な漢字もわかりません。
   *Watashi wa kantan-na **kanji mo** wakarimasen.*
   I don't know even simple kanji.

3. After each of two nouns
   私はひらがなもカタカナも覚えました。
   *Watashi wa **hiragana mo katakana mo** oboemashita.*
   I learned both hiragana and katakana.

4. After noun expressing length/quantity/cost
   このジャケットは2万円もしました。
   *Kono jaketto wa **ni man en mo** shimashita.*
   This jacket cost as much as twenty thousand yen.
   きのうは3時間も日本語を勉強しました。

*Kinō wa **san jikan mo** nihongo o benkyō shimashita.*
I studied Japanese as long as three hours yesterday.

5. After interrogative word (+ particle)
だれもここに来ませんでした。
***Dare mo** koko ni kimasen deshita.*
Nobody came here.
あしたはどこにも行きません。
*Ashita wa **doko ni mo** ikimasen.*
I won't go anywhere tomorrow.

mō　もう
ADVERB MEANING: already, yet, have already begun to (do), (not) any more, soon, by now, another, more

1. Used with past form of verb
もう仕事を終えました。
***Mō** shigoto o oemashita.*
I have already finished the work.
「彼女はもう来ましたか。」「いいえ、まだです。」
*"Kanojo wa **mō** kimashita ka." "Iie, mada desu."*
"Has she come yet?" "No, not yet."
もうできたんですか。
***Mō** dekita n desu ka.*
Have you finished it already?

2. In negative sentence
もう待てません。
***Mō** matemasen.*
I can't wait any more.

冷蔵庫にはもう何も食べるものがありません。

*Reizōko ni wa **mō** nani mo taberu mono ga arima**sen**.*

There is nothing more to eat in the refrigerator.

3. Used with progressive form

マイクはもう到着しています。

*Maiku wa **mō** tōchaku shite **imasu**.*

Mike has already arrived.

4. Used with progressive form + *deshō*

(expressing assumptions about present actions)

山田さんはもう駅に着いているでしょう。

*Yamada-san wa **mō** eki ni tsui**te iru deshō**.*

Mr. Yamada has probably arrived at the station by now.

(*ta*-form of verb may replace the progressive form)

*Yamada-san wa **mō** eki ni tsui**ta deshō**.*

5. Expressing length of time, used with *ni naru*

日本に来てもう3年になります。

*Nihon ni kite **mō** san nen **ni narimasu**.*

It has already been three years since I came to Japan.

6. In future sentence

彼女はもう準備ができるでしょう。

*Kanojo wa **mō** junbi ga deki**ru deshō**.*

She will be ready soon.

もう夜中になります。

***Mō** yonaka ni nari**masu**.*

It will soon be midnight.

7. Before number + counter

父はもう2、3日で帰ります。

*Chichi wa **mō** ni san nichi de kaerimasu.*

My father will be back in another two or three days.

もう1度見に行きたいですね。

Mō ichido *mi ni ikitai desu ne.*
I want to go and see it again.
もう1杯コーヒーを飲みたいです。
Mō ippai *kōhii o nomitai desu.*
I'd like to have another cup of coffee.

→ See also *mada*

mono もの (物、者)

NOUN MEANING: thing/one which . . ., person, (one's) belongings, what . . ., would often, it is common that . . ., generally tend to (do), indeed

Unlike *koto*, the object expressed by *mono* must be a concrete inanimate object.

1. Used as noun
   物をもっと大切にしてください。
   Mono *o motto taisetsu ni shite kudasai.*
   Please handle the things more carefully.
   私は伊藤という者です。
   *Watashi wa itō to iū **mono** desu.*
   I am a person called Ito. (My name is Ito.)
   (using *mono* to refer to oneself is humble)

2. After pronoun/name + *no*
   「この傘はあなたのものですか。」「いいえ、ジョンのものです。」
   *"Kono kasa wa **anata no mono** desu ka." "Iie, **jon no mono** desu."*
   "Is this umbrella yours?" "No, it's John's."

(*mono* may be dropped after the possessive *no*)

3. After dictionary form of verb/adjective

   彼女が買う物はブランドものばかりだ。

   *Kanojo ga ka**u** **mono** wa burando mono bakari da.*

   The things she buys are all top-brand articles.

   私が今欲しい物はビデオカメラです。

   *Watashi ga ima hoshi**i** **mono** wa bideo kamera desu.*

   What I want now is a video camera.

4. After *ta*-form of verb/adjective

   あなたのテープレコーダーは私が買った物よりいいですね。

   *Anata no tēpu rekōdā wa watashi ga kat**ta** **mono** yori ii desu ne.*

   Your tape recorder is better than the one I bought, isn't it?

5. Followed by *da/desu*.

   休暇を１ヶ月取ってみたいものです。

   *Kyūka o ikkagetsu totte mitai **mono desu**.*

   I'd like to take a one-month vacation if possible.

   だれでも新しい物に興味を持つものです。

   *Dare demo atarashii mono ni kyōmi o motsu **mono desu**.*

   Anybody tends to take an interest in new things.

   楽しい時間のたつのは早いものです。

   *Tanoshii jikan no tatsu no wa hayai **mono desu**.*

   Pleasant time passes quickly indeed.

   私はよくうちでパーティーを開いたものです。

   *Watashi wa yoku uchi de pātii o hiraita **mono desu**.*

   I would often have parties at my house.

→ See also *koto, no*

morau もらう

VERB MEANING: get, be given, receive, have something (done), get (somebody) to (do something), get benefit (from somebody doing something)

The subject is usually the 1st person or his/her family members, but can also be the 2nd person in questions. The potential form, *moraeru*, is often used in questions. The respectful form, *itadaku*, or its potential form, *itadakeru*, is used instead of *morau* when receiving something from someone of higher status or to whom the speaker wishes to show respect.

1. After object noun + *o*
   アメリカにいる友人から手紙をもらいました。
   *Amerika ni iru yūjin kara **tegami o moraimashita**.*
   I got a letter from my friend in America.
   (*kara* may be replaced by *ni*)
   「このカタログをもらえますか。」「どうぞ。」
   *"Kono **katarogu o moraemasu ka**." "Dōzo."*
   "Could I get this catalog?" "Sure."

2. After *te*-form of verb
   友人からお金を貸してもらいました。
   *Yūjin kara o-kane o kashite **moraimashita**.*
   I was lent some money by a friend.
   先生に作文を見ていただきました。
   *Sensei ni sakubun o mite **itadakimashita**.*
   I had my composition looked through by the teacher.
   みんなに教室を掃除してもらいます。

*Minna ni kyōshitsu o sōji shite **moraimasu**.*

I will get you all to clean the classroom.

彼に手伝ってもらった。

*Kare ni tetsudatte **moratta**.*

I got benefit from his helping me. (He kindly helped me.)

その本を見せてもらえますか。

*Sono hon o misete **moraemasu** ka.*

Can I get you to show me the book?

(compare the above 1st person subject with the following 2nd person subject:)

*Sono hon o misete **kuremasu** ka.*

Will you show me the book?

(the subject "you" does the favor for object "me")

3. Used with *tai*-form

彼にそれをしてもらいたいと思います。

*Kare ni sore o shite **moraitai** to omoimasu.*

I think I want to get him to do that.

→ See also *ageru, itadaku, kureru*

moshi　もし

ADVERB MEANING: if, in case, when

It is used to stress the subjunctive when the action or state in the conditional clause is probable, improbable, unreal, or didn't happen. *Moshi + mo* is even more emphatic.

1. At the beginning of conditional clause

もし雨なら中止です。

Moshi ame nara chūshi desu.

In case of rain, it will be called off.
もしもっとお金があればそれを買うのに。
Moshi motto o-kane ga areba *sore o kau no ni.*
If I had more money, I would buy it.
もしあなたの助けがなかったらうまく行かなかっただろう。
Moshi anata no tasuke ga nakattara *umaku ikanakatta darō.*
If it had not been for your help, it probably would not have gone well.

→ See also *ba*, *nara*, *tara*

mottomo　もっとも
ADVERB forming the superlative of adjective or adverb

It may be replaced with its informal equivalent *ichiban* (*lit.* "number one").

1. Before adjective
   これは今まで読んだうちでもっともおもしろい本です。
   *Kore wa ima made yonda uchi de **mottomo omoshiroi** hon desu.*
   This is the most interesting book that I have ever read.
2. Before adverb
   だれがもっとも上手に日本語が話せますか。
   *Dare ga **mottomo jōzu ni** nihongo ga hanasemasu ka.*
   Who can speak Japanese the best?
3. Used with verb/adjective of emotion
   私はこの絵がもっとも好きです。
   *Watashi wa kono e ga **mottomo suki** desu.*

I like this painting best.

→ See also *ichiban*

na な

PARTICLE MEANING: never (do), don't (do), how I wish

It also has the following functions: seeking agreement to the preceding statement, making exclamatory sentences, or making rude affirmative commands. When used with *yokumo* it means "how dare . . ."

1. After dictionary form of verb
   そんなばかな事はするな。
   Sonna baka-na koto wa suru na.
   Don't do such stupid things.
   (the negative command with *na* is not polite; however, putting *yo* after *na* makes it more friendly)
   Sonna baka-na koto wa suru na yo.
2. After *ta*-form of verb, with *yokumo*
   よくもそんなことが言えたな。
   Yokumo sonna koto ga ieta na.
   How dare you say such a thing?
3. After the plain copula *da*
   (used only in informal speech)
   あれはジョージの車だな。
   Are wa jōji no kuruma da na.
   That's George's car, isn't it?
4. After conjunctive form of verb
   (rude affirmative command form)

早く来な。
*Hayaku **kina***.
Hurry up and get over here!

5. After conditional clause
   (the final *nā* is prolonged)
   もっとお金があればなあ。
   Motto o-kane ga areba nā.
   How I wish I had more money!

6. After dictionary form of verb/adjective
   (informal and uses a prolonged *nā*)
   これは高いなあ。
   *Kore wa taka**i nā***.
   How expensive this is!
   よく食べるなあ。
   *Yoku tabe**ru nā***.
   You eat a lot!

→ See also *kudasai, nasai*

nado など

PARTICLE MEANING: and so on, etc., and the like, or something like that, things such as . . ., the likes of, (not) . . . absolutely

Ya is usually used in place of *to* between nouns before *nado*.

1. After noun
   私はよくコンビニでパンやケーキなどを買います。
   *Watashi wa yoku konbini de **pan ya kēki nado** o kaimasu.*
   I often buy bread, cakes, and so on at the convenience store.
   私はよく景色などを描きます。

*Watashi wa yoku **keshiki nado** o egakimasu.*

I often paint scenery and the like.

ゴルフなどはしますか。

***Gorufu nado** wa shimasu ka.*

Do you play golf or anything like that?

2. Followed by *no* + noun

   すしやさしみなどのなま物は食べられますか。

   *Sushi ya sashimi **nado no namamono** wa taberaremasu ka.*

   Can you eat raw foods such as sushi, sashimi, and the like?

3. In negative sentence

   パチンコなどはしません。

   *Pachinko **nado** wa shima**sen**.*

   I don't play things like pachinko.

   私などには無理です。

   *Watashi **nado** ni wa **muri desu**.*

   It is impossible for the likes of me.

nagara　ながら

PARTICLE MEANING: while, as, although, in spite of

It is used to express the occurence of two simultaneous or contrastive actions, both having the same subject.

1. After conjunctive form of verb

   いつもラジオを聞きながら眠ります。

   *Itsumo rajio o **kikinagara** nemurimasu.*

   I usually fall asleep while listening to the radio.

   喫茶店でコーヒーを飲みながら話しましょう。

   *Kissaten de kōhii o **nominagara** hanashimashō.*

Let's talk over a cup of coffee in a coffee shop.

彼女は約束をしながらあまり守りません。

*Kanojo wa yakusoku o **shinagara** amari mamorimasen.*

Although she makes promises, she seldom keeps them.

2. After dictionary form of adjective

このコンピューターは小さいながらたくさん機能を持っている。

*Kono konpyūtā wa chiisai **nagara** takusan kinō o motte iru.*

Though it is small, this computer has many functions.

3. After adjectival noun

彼は病気ながらやってきました。

*Kare wa **byōki nagara** yatte kimashita.*

He came up in spite of illness.

→ See also *ga (2), keredo(mo), no ni*

nai ない

ADJECTIVE used as the negative of the verb *aru/da*, or for making the negative form of verb or adjective

It conjugates as an adjective.

Ta-form: *nakatta* (plain)/*nakatta desu* (polite)

Te-form: *naide* (after verb)/*nakute* (after adjective or after verb when expressing a cause for some emotion)

1. Used as negative of *aru*

ここに置いてあったかばんがない。

*Koko ni oite atta kaban ga **nai**.*

The bag I left sitting here is missing.

遊ぶ時間がなくて不満だ。

*Asobu jikan ga **nakute** fuman da.*

I am discontented because I have no time to play.

2. Used as negative of *da*

これは日本製の車ではない。

*Kore wa nihonsei no kuruma dewa **nai**.*

This is not a Japanese-made car.

(*dewa* must be used between [adjectival] noun and *nai*)

3. Used to make *nai*-form of verb

(added to the stem of verb)

今パスポートをもっていない。

*Ima pasupōto o motte **inai**.*

I don't have my passport now.

もう電車に間に合わない。

*Mō densha ni ma ni **awanai**.*

It's already too late to make the train.

4. Used in *te*-form

ここでタバコは吸わないでほしい。

*Koko de tabako wa **suwanaide** hoshii.*

I want you not to smoke here. (I don't want you to smoke here.)

努力しないで成功はしません。

*Doryoku **shinaide** seikō wa shimasen.*

You won't succeed without making efforts.

彼はお礼も言わないで帰ってしまった。

*Kare wa o-rei mo **iwanaide** kaette shimatta.*

He went home without expressing thanks.

彼女が来られなくて残念です。

*Kanojo ga **korarenakute** zannen desu.*

It is a pity that she cannot come.

5. After *ku*-form of adjective

このカメラは思ったほど高くはなかった。

*Kono kamera wa omotta hodo taka**ku** wa **nakatta**.*
This camera was not as expensive as I had expected.
(wa or *mo* used between *ku*-form and *nai* adds emphasis)
→ See also *aru, arimasen, desu, masu, zu ni,* Verb Forms (II)

nai uchi ni　ないうちに
PHRASE MEANING: before (an undesirable thing occurs)

Note that this phrase includes a negative form in Japanese, but becomes an affirmative expression in English translation.

1. After the stem of *nai*-form of verb
    暗くならないうちに帰りましょう。
    *Kuraku **naranai uchi ni** kaerimashō.*
    Let's go home before it gets dark.
    忘れないうちに彼女に電話しておこう。
    ***Wasurenai uchi ni** kanojo ni denwa shite okō.*
    I'll call her before I forget.
→ See also *mae ni, uchi ni*

nakereba ikenai　なければいけない
PREDICATIVE PHRASE (expressing obligation imposed by the speaker) MEANING: (you) must

Nakereba is the *ba*-form of the negative adjective *nai*. It may be replaced with *nakutewa, nai to,* or the informal *nakya*.

1. After the stem of *nai*-form of verb

もっと勉強しなければいけません。
*Motto benkyō **shinakereba ikemasen**.*
You must study harder.
「私も行かなければいけませんか。」「いえ、結構です。」
*"Watashi mo **ikanakereba ikemasen** ka." "Ie, kekkō desu."*
"Do I have to go, too?" "No, you don't need to."

2. After *ku*-form of adjective
もっと軽くなければいけません。
*Motto karu**ku nakereba ikemasen**.*
It needs to be lighter.

3. After (adjectival) noun + *de*
老人にしんせつでなければいけません。
*Rōjin ni **shinsetsu de nakereba ikemasen**.*
You must be kind to old people.

→ See also *nakereba naranai, nakutemo yoi*

nakereba naranai　なければならない
PREDICATIVE PHRASE (expressing obligation/necessity of the speaker) MEANING: have to

　Nakereba may be replaced with *nakutewa* or the informal *nakya*.

1. After the stem of *nai*-form of verb
9時までに会社に行かなければなりません。
*Ku ji made ni kaisha ni **ikanakereba narimasen**.*
I have to go to the company by nine o'clock.
もっと単語を覚えなければなりません。
*Motto tango o **oboenakereba narimasen**.*

I have to learn more words.

2. After *ku*-form of adjective

アパートは駅にもっと近くなければならない。

Apāto wa eki ni motto chikaku nakereba naranai.

The apartment house needs to be much closer to the station.

3. After (adjectival) noun + *de*

話は論理的でなければならない。

Hanashi wa ronriteki de nakereba naranai.

The speech needs to be logical.

→ See also *nakereba ikenai, nakutemo yoi, neba naranai*

nakutemo yoi　なくてもよい

PREDICATIVE PHRASE (expressing absence of obligation/necessity)

MEANING: need not, (not) have to

Yoi may be replaced by *ii*.

1. After the stem of *nai*-form of verb

そんなに急いでやらなくてもいいです。

Sonna ni isoide yaranakutemo ii desu.

You need not do it so hastily.

電話をしてくれればわざわざ来なくてもよかったですよ。

Denwa o shite kurereba wazawaza konakutemo yokatta desu yo.

If you had given me a call you need not have come all this way.

これは書かなくてもよいですか。

Kore wa kakanakutemo yoi desu ka.

Is it all right if I don't write this?

2. After *ku*-form of adjective

車は動けば新しくなくてもよいです。

Kuruma wa ugokeba atarashiku nakutemo yoi desu.

As long as the car moves it needn't be new. (The car needn't be new; it just has to run.)

3. After (adjectival) noun + *de*

返事は今日でなくてもいいです。

Henji wa kyō de nakutemo ii desu.

The answer does not need to be given today.

説明は完全でなくてもよい。

Setsumei wa kanzen de nakutemo yoi.

The explanation does not need to be perfect.

→ See also *nakereba ikenai, nakereba naranai, neba naranai, temo*

nan なん

INTERROGATIVE ADJECTIVE MEANING: what, how many, several, a few, many

Nan is a euphonically changed form of *nani* and is used to modify a noun.

1. Followed by counter

「今何時ですか。」「2時15分です。」

"Ima nan ji desu ka." "Ni ji jū go fun desu."

"What time is it now?" "It's two fifteen."

「終わるまで何分かかりますか。」「半時間です。」

"Owaru made nan pun kakarimasu ka." "Han jikan desu."

"How many minutes will it take to finish it?" "Half an hour. "

外国に何回行ったことがありますか。

*Gaikoku ni **nan kai** itta koto ga arimasu ka.*

How many times have you been abroad?

2. Followed by counter + *ka*

やっと何人か来ました。

*Yatto **nan nin ka** kimashita.*

Some people have finally come.

ジェーンには何日か前に会いました。

*Jēn ni wa **nan nichi ka** mae ni aimashita.*

I saw Jane a few days ago.

3. Followed by (number +) counter + *mo*

私は何十冊も本を買いました。

*Watashi wa **nan jussatsu mo** hon o kaimashita.*

I bought dozens of books.

外国語を覚えるのに何年もかかります。

*Gaikokugo o oboeru no ni **nan nen mo** kakarimasu.*

It takes many years to master a foreign language.

4. Followed by *no* + noun

何の音楽が好きですか。

Nan no ongaku *ga suki desu ka.*

What (kind of) music do you like?

→ See also *nani*

nani　何

INTERROGATIVE PRONOUN MEANING: what

1. Used as subject

この袋には何が入っていますか。

*Kono fukuro ni wa **nani** ga haitte imasu ka.*

What is in this bag?

2. Used as object
   デパートで何を買うんですか。
   *Depāto de **nani** o kau n desu ka.*
   What are you going to buy in the department store?
   いま何がいちばん欲しいですか。
   *Ima **nani** ga ichiban hoshii desu ka.*
   What do you want most now?
   何を話しているんですか。
   ***Nani** o hanashite iru n desu ka.*
   What are you talking about?

3. Used for describing subject
   将来何になりたいのですか。
   *Shōrai **nani** ni naritai no desu ka.*
   What do you want to be in the future?

→ See also *nan*

nara なら

PARTICLE MEANING: if, supposing . . ., on condition that . . ., as for

1. After (adjectival) noun in conditional clause
   明日雨ならば延期します。
   *Ashita **ame naraba** enki shimasu.*
   If it is rainy tomorrow, we will postpone it.
   (*nara* derives from the conditional form of the copula *da* and
   may be followed by the conditional particle *ba*)
   彼が病気ならば仕方がありません。
   *Kare ga **byōki naraba** shikata ga arimasen.*
   If he is ill, there is nothing we can do about it.
   遊園地ならディズニーランドがいい。

Yūenchi nara dizuniirando ga ii.

As for amusement parks, Disneyland is nice.

2. After *sore*

それならなぜやめないんですか。

Sore nara naze yamenai n desu ka.

If that's the case, why don't you stop?

3. After subject

私ならそんなものは買いません。

Watashi nara sonna mono wa kaimasen.

If it were me, I would not buy such a thing.

彼女なら喜んでしてくれるでしょう。

Kanojo nara yorokonde shite kureru deshō.

Certainly she'd be happy to do it for you.

4. After object

お金なら要りません。

O-kane nara irimasen.

If it's money (you're offering), I don't need it.

英語なら話せます。

Eigo nara hanasemasu.

If it's English (you need), I can speak it.

5. After particle

来週までならでき上がります。

*Raishū **made nara** dekiagarimasu.*

I will be able to complete it by next week (if you let me do it).

6. After dictionary form of verb/adjective + *no/n*

ちゃんと返してくれるのなら貸してあげましょう。

Chanto kaeshite kureru no nara kashite agemashō.

On condition that you return it to me without fail, I will lend it to you.

そんなに安いんなら買います。

*Sonna ni yasui **n nara** kaimasu.*
If it is so cheap, I'll buy it.

7. After *nai*-form of verb/adjective + *no/n*
あなたができないのなら私がしましょう。
*Anata ga deki**nai no nara** watashi ga shimashō.*
If you cannot do it, I will do it for you.

8. After *ta*-form of verb/adjective + *no/n*
欲しかったのなら言ってくれればよかったのに。
*Hoshika**tta no nara** itte kurereba yokatta no ni.*
If you wanted it, you should have told me.

→ See also *ba, tara, to, to sureba*

naru　なる

VERB MEANING: become, get, turn, come (grow) to, learn to

Naru is used with a word that describes the subject.

1. After (adjectival) noun + *ni*
兄は高校教師になりました。
*Ani wa kōkō **kyōshi ni narimashita**.*
My big brother became a high school teacher.
私はデザイナーになりたいです。
*Watashi wa **dezainā ni naritai** desu.*
I want to be a designer.
よく休みなさい、そうしないと病気になりますよ。
*Yoku yasumi nasai, sō shinai to **byōki ni narimasu** yo.*
Sleep well—if you don't you'll become sick.
実際に見れば相撲が好きになりますよ。

*Jissai ni mireba sumō ga **suki ni narimasu** yo.*

If you actually watch sumo, you'll grow to like it.

2. After *ku*-form of adjective

外はもう暗くなりました。

*Soto wa mō kura**ku narimashita**.*

It has already grown dark outside.

彼女はそれを見て青くなった。

*Kanojo wa sore o mite ao**ku natta**.*

She saw it and turned pale.

いつから彼女と会わなくなったのですか。

*Itsu kara kanojo to awana**ku natta** no desu ka.*

Since when did you stop meeting her?

3. After dictionary form of verb + *yō ni*

私は日本語がわかるようになりました。

*Watashi wa nihongo ga waka**ru yō ni narimashita**.*

I have come to understand the Japanese language.

最近よく酒を飲むようになった。

*Saikin yoku sake o no**mu yō ni natta**.*

I've come to drink a lot recently.

ギターが弾けるようになりました。

*Gitā ga hike**ru yō ni narimashita**.*

I came to be able to play the guitar. (I learned to play the guitar.)

→ See also *yō ni,* Polite Language (II)

nasai なさい

AUXILIARY VERB used for making a strong, emphatic, or rude command form

The standard negative command form is made by adding *na* to the dictionary form of the verb. It is safer to use *nasai* only toward children. Adding *yo* after *nasai* will soften the tone, however.

1. After conjunctive form of verb
   答を紙に書きなさい。
   *Kotae o kami ni **kakinasai**.*
   Write your answers on the paper.
   早くしなさい。
   *Hayaku **shinasai**.*
   Hurry up and do it.
→ See also *kudasai, na*

naze　なぜ
INTERROGATIVE ADVERB MEANING: why

1. In a question
   「なぜ休んだのですか。」「かぜをひいたからです。」
   "***Naze** yasunda no desu ka.*" "*Kaze o hiita kara desu.*"
   "Why were you absent?" "Because I caught a cold."
   なぜ彼は来たのですか。
   ***Naze** kare wa kita no desu ka.*
   Why did he come?
   彼になぜ約束を破ったのかたずねましたか。
   *Kare ni **naze** yakusoku o yabutta no ka tazunemashita ka.*
   Did you ask him why he broke his promise?
→ See also *dōshite, ka*

nazenaraba . . . kara なぜならば...から
CONJUNCTION MEANING: (why?) . . . because

Desu may be put after *kara* to end a sentence more politely, and the *ba* after *nazenara* may be dropped. The reason for the action is stated in the clause between *nazenaraba* and *kara*.

1. With sentence inserted in the middle
   彼は来ないでしょう。なぜならば行きたくないと言ってたからです。
   Kare wa konai desu. *Nazenaraba ikitaku nai to itteta kara desu.*
   He may not come. (The reason why is) because he said he didn't want to come.
→ See also *kara*

ne ね
COLLOQUIAL PARTICLE used for requesting agreement or confirmation from the hearer, or for softening the tone of a statement

It may function as an English tag question or may be used after any word in a sentence in order to call the listener's attention to it.

1. At the end of declarative sentence
   「今日は天気がとてもいいですね。」「そうですね。」
   "Kyō wa tenki ga totemo ii desu ne." "Sō desu ne."
   "The weather is very nice today, isn't it?" "Yes, it is."

本田さんも行きますね。

Honda-san mo ikimasu ne.

You're going too, Mr. Honda, aren't you?

2. After *nasai/kudasai*

ぜひパーティーに来てくださいね。

*Zehi pātii ni kite **kudasai ne**.*

By all means please come to our party, OK?

3. After any elements of sentence

だからね、もっとねがんばってほしいんですよ。

*Dakara **ne**, motto **ne** ganbatte hoshii n desu yo.*

That's why, you know, I want you to work/study harder.

→ See also *yo*

neba naranai　ねばならない

PREDICATIVE PHRASE (expressing obligation) MEANING: have to, must

1. After the stem of *nai*-form of verb

もう行かねばなりません。

Mō ikaneba narimasen.

I have to leave now.

若いうちはもっと仕事せねばなりません。

*Wakai uchi wa motto shigoto **seneba narimasen**.*

You must work harder while you are young.

(this uses the antiquated form *se*[*neba*] instead of the more common stem *shi*)

→ See also *nakereba naranai*

ni　に

PARTICLE MEANING: at, in, on, for, from, to, toward, per, in order to (do), and

It also indicates the object of specific verbs, the indirect object, the agent in passive voice, the person who is caused to do something, a result describing the subject or object, or regret. Moreover, it makes adjectival nouns into adverbs (used only in modifying verbs).

1. After noun expressing time
   「何時に電話をくれましたか。」「6時にしました。」
   *"**Nan ji ni** denwa o kuremashita ka." "**Roku ji ni** shimashita."*
   "(At) what time did you give me a call?" "I called at six."
   来週の日曜日に京都へ行きます。
   *Raishū no **nichiyōbi ni** kyōto e ikimasu.*
   I'll go to Kyoto (on) next Sunday
   夏休みに外国へ行こうかと考えています。
   *Natsu **yasumi ni** gaikoku e ikō ka to kangaete imasu.*
   I'm thinking of going abroad for summer vacation.
2. After noun expressing location/existence/state
   (usually used with *iru/aru* except when expressing ocurrence of an event)
   「彼女は今どこにいますか。」「あそこにいます。」
   *"Kanojo wa ima **doko ni** imasu ka." "**Asoko ni** imasu."*
   "Where is she now?" "She is over there."
   加藤さんは広島に住んでいます。
   *Katō-san wa **hiroshima ni** sunde imasu.*

Mr. Kato lives in Hiroshima.

郵便局は図書館の左側にあります。

*Yūbinkyoku wa toshokan no **hidari gawa ni** arimasu.*

The post office is to the left of the library.

3. After noun expressing direction/destination

彼らは今朝飛行機でバンコクに向かいました。

*Karera wa kesa hikōki de **bankoku ni** mukaimashita.*

They left for Bangkok by plane this morning.

私の別荘は海に面しています。

*Watashi no bessō wa **umi ni** menshite imasu.*

My cottage faces the sea.

壁に変な虫がいる。

***Kabe ni** hen-na mushi ga iru.*

A strange insect is on the wall.

荷物は棚に置いてください。

*Nimotsu wa **tana ni** oite kudasai.*

Please put your baggage on the shelf.

4. After noun expressing purpose

彼女はデパートへ買物に行きました。

*Kanojo wa depāto e **kaimono ni** ikimashita.*

She went to the department store to shop.

彼は香港へ旅行に行った。

*Kare wa honkon e **ryokō ni** itta.*

He has gone on a trip to Hong Kong.

あなたは遊びにお金を使いすぎます。

*Anata wa **asobi ni** o-kane o tsukaisugimasu.*

You spend too much money on play.

5. Between two nouns

私の好きな食べ物は魚に野菜です。

*Watashi no suki-na tabemono wa **sakana ni yasai** desu.*

My favorite foods are fish and vegetables.

6. After conjunctive form of verb
(usually used with *iku* or *kuru*)
「映画を見に行きませんか。」「いいですね。」
*"Eiga o **mi ni** ikimasen ka." "Ii desu ne."*
"Wouldn't you (like to) go and see a movie?" "That would be nice."
カメラを買いに来たんですが。
*Kamera o **kai ni** kita n desu ga.*
I came to buy a camera, but . . . (will you help me?)

7. After object of verb
さっき本屋でトムに会いました。
*Sakki hon'ya de **tomu ni** aimashita.*
I met Tom at a bookstore a while ago.
この質問に答えてください。
*Kono **shitsumon ni** kotaete kudasai.*
Please answer this question.
彼女にもう電話しましたか。
***Kanojo ni** mō denwa shimashita ka.*
Have you called her yet?
この作品は独創力に欠ける。
*Kono sakuhin wa **dokusōryoku ni** kakeru.*
This work lacks originality.

8. After indirect object expressing a recipient
私は彼にあの本をあげました。
*Watashi wa **kare ni** ano hon o agemashita.*
I gave him that book.
毎週フランクに日本語を教えています。
*Maishū **furanku ni** nihongo o oshiete imasu.*
I teach Frank Japanese every week.

9. After agent in passive sentence
   犬が車にはねられた。
   *Inu ga **kuruma ni** hanerareta.*
   A dog was hit by a car.

10. After noun expressing giver, followed by *morau*
    この絵はがきは神田さんにもらいました。
    *Kono ehagaki wa **kanda-san ni moraimashita**.*
    I got this picture postcard from Ms. Kanda.

11. After the agent in the pattern *te-morau*
    その仕事は彼に手伝ってもらった。
    *Sono shigoto wa **kare ni** tetsudatte **moratta**.*
    I got him to help me with the work.

12. After noun expressing person who is let/made to do something in a causative sentence
    私にそれを説明させて下さい。
    ***Watashi ni** sore o setsumei sasete kudasai.*
    Please let me explain it.

13. After (adjectival) noun describing the subject
    彼は働きすぎて病気になった。
    *Kare wa hatarakisugite **byōki ni** natta.*
    He overworked and became ill.
    私は建築家になりたいです。
    *Watashi wa **kenchikuka ni** naritai desu.*
    I want to be an architect.

14. After noun describing the object of verb
    この小麦粉はクッキーにします。
    *Kono komugiko wa **kukkii ni** shimasu.*
    I'll make this flour into cookies.
    このお金をドルに換えてください。
    *Kono o-kane o **doru ni** kaete kudasai.*

Please change this money into dollars.

15. After noun expressing opportunity/occasion
子供の誕生日にファミコンを買ってやった。
*Kodomo no **tanjōbi ni** famikon o katte yatta.*
I bought my child a computer video game for her birthday.

16. After noun expressing length/quantity
ミーティングは年に3回開かれる。
*Miitingu wa **nen ni** san kai hirakareru.*
The meeting is held three times per year.
3人に一人が試験に合格した。
***San nin ni** hitori ga shiken ni gōkaku shita.*
One person out of three passed the examination.

17. After noun expressing a field of interest/ability
私はクラシック音楽に興味があります。
*Watashi wa kurashikku **ongaku ni** kyōmi ga arimasu.*
I have an interest in classical music.

18. After noun expressing reason/cause for a mental state
彼の話には飽きてしまいました。
*Kare no **hanashi ni** wa akite shimaimashita.*
I completely tired of his talk.

19. After noun expressing criterion for comparison/judgment
外国に比べると日本人はよく働くと言われる。
***Gaikoku ni** kuraberu to nihonjin wa yoku hataraku to iwareru.*
It is said that the Japanese work hard compared with (people of) foreign countries.
この日本語の本は一年生にはむずかしすぎる。
*Kono nihongo no hon wa **ichinensei ni** wa muzukashi sugiru.*
This Japanese book is too difficult for first year students.

20. After *darō/deshō* to express regret

あきらめなければうまく行くでしょうに。
*Akiramenakereba umaku iku **deshō ni**.*
If you don't give up, it will go well.

21. Used as suffix to change adjectival noun into adverbial
    彼ならそれは楽にできます。
    *Kare nara sore wa **raku ni** dekimasu.*
    He can do it easily (I assure you).
    彼女は積極的に手伝ってくれます。
    *Kanojo wa **sekkyoku teki ni** tetsudatte kuremasu.*
    She will enthusiastically help us.

→ See also *de, e, tame, to, to ka,* Adjectival Nouns (II)

ni chigai nai　にちがいない
PREDICATIVE PHRASE (indicating definite deduction) MEANING: must, must have (done)

It conjugates as an adjective.

1. After dictionary form of verb/adjective
   彼女はこの辺に住んでいるにちがいない。
   *Kanojo wa kono hen ni sunde i**ru ni chigai nai**.*
   She surely must be living around here.
   鈴木さんはもう来ているにちがいありません。
   *Suzuki-san wa mō kite i**ru ni chigai arimasen**.*
   Mr. Suzuki must have already arrived.
   お母さんは悲しいにちがいありません。
   *Okāsan wa kanashi**i ni chigai arimasen**.*
   Your mother must be sad.
2. After *nai*-form of verb/adjective

彼女は二度と手伝ってくれないにちがいない。

*Kanojo wa ni do to tetsudatte kure**nai ni chigai nai**.*

It is certain that she will not help us again.

3. After *ta*-form of verb/adjective

彼はあきらめたにちがいありません。

*Kare wa akirame**ta ni chigai arimasen**.*

He must have given up.

あの車は高かったにちがいない。

*Ano kuruma wa takakat**ta ni chigai nai**.*

That car must have been expensive.

4. After (adjectival) noun

このかばんはトムのかばんにちがいない。

*Kono kaban wa tomu no **kaban ni chigai nai**.*

This bag must be Tom's.

ティムは病気にちがいありません。

*Timu wa **byōki ni chigai arimasen**.*

Tim is definitely sick.

ni kakete　にかけて

ADVERBIAL PHRASE MEANING: (extending) to/over, in the . . . district

1. After noun

夏から秋にかけて台風がよく来ます。

*Natsu kara **aki ni kakete** taifū ga yoku kimasu.*

Typhoons often come (in the period) from summer to autumn.

週末にかけて天気がよくなるでしょう。

***Shūmatsu ni kakete** tenki ga yoku naru deshō.*

The weather will probably be good over the weekend.

北陸から関西にかけて雨が降るでしょう。

*Hokuriku kara **kansai ni kakete** ame ga furu deshō.*
It will be rainy (in the area) from Hokuriku to Kansai.

ni kansuru　に関する
ADJECTIVAL PHRASE MEANING: about, concerning, regarding, pertaining to

It is used in this form before a noun it modifies, and becomes *ni kanshite* when modifying a verb.

1. Used as adjectival phrase
   彼女の離婚に関するいろいろな噂がある。
   *Kanojo no **rikon ni kansuru iroiro-na uwasa** ga aru.*
   There are various rumors concerning her divorce.
   宗教に関する本を探しています。
   ***Shukyō ni kansuru hon** o sagashite imasu.*
   I am looking for books on religion.
2. Used as adverbial phrase
   そのことに関して何か言うことがありますか。
   *Sono **koto ni kanshite** nanika **iū koto ga arimasu** ka.*
   Regarding that matter, do you have anything to say?
   この点に関して意見を述べてください。
   *Kono **ten ni kanshite iken o nobete** kudasai.*
   Please express your opinion on this point.

nikui　にくい
ADJECTIVE MEANING: hard/difficult (to do), can not (do) easily

1. After conjunctive form of verb
   箸は使いにくいですね。
   *Hashi wa **tsukainikui** desu ne.*
   Chopsticks are hard to use, aren't they?
   彼女とは話しにくいです。
   *Kanojo to wa **hanashinikui** desu.*
   She is difficult to talk with.
   (follows the subject it describes)
   覚えにくい漢字がたくさんあります。
   ***Oboenikui** kanji ga takusan arimasu.*
   There are a lot of Chinese characters that are difficult to learn.
   (precedes the object it modifies)
→ See also *yasui*

ni mo kakawarazu　にもかかわらず

ADVERBIAL PHRASE (generally used in formal language) MEANING: in spite of, although, for all . . ., after all . . ., in defiance of, nevertheless

1. After noun
   ひどい雨にもかかわらず彼らは外で野球をした。
   *Hidoi **ame ni mo kakawarazu** karera wa soto de yakyū o shita.*
   They played baseball outside in spite of heavy rain.
2. After dictionary form of verb/adjective
   疲れているにもかかわらず彼は手伝ってくれました。
   *Tsukarete **iru ni mo kakawarazu** kare wa tetsudatte kure-mashita.*
   Although he was tired, he helped me.

彼女はお金があるにもかかわらず質素に暮らしている。

Kanojo wa o-kane ga aru ni mo kakawarazu shisso ni kura-shite iru.

Although she has a lot of money, she lives simply.

とても安いにもかかわらず彼はそれを買わなかった。

Totemo yasui ni mo kakawarazu kare wa sore o kawanakatta.

Although it was very cheap, he didn't buy it.

3. After *nai*-form of verb/adjective

だれも行かないにもかかわらず彼は1人で行った。

Dare mo ikanai ni mo kakawarazu kare wa hitori de itta.

Nobody would go, so he went alone nevertheless.

4. After *ta*-form of verb/adjective

忠告したにもかかわらず彼はまた同じミスをした。

Chūkoku shita ni mo kakawarazu kare wa mata onaji misu o shita.

Although I advised him, he made the same mistake again.

天気がよかったにもかかわらず私は家にいました。

Tenki ga yokatta ni mo kakawarazu watashi wa ie ni imashita.

Though the weather was good, I stayed at home.

5. At the beginning of sentence

それはほとんど不可能です。にもかかわらずアレキサンダーはあきらめません。

Sore wa hotondo fukanō desu. Ni mo kakawarazu, arekisandā wa akiramemasen.

It is almost impossible. Nevertheless, Alexander doesn't give up.

→ See also *keredo(mo)*

ni oite　において

ADVERBIAL PHRASE (generally used in formal language) MEANING: in, at, on, as for

It is used in this form when modifying a verb and becomes *ni okeru* before a noun it modifies.

1. After noun expressing location
   7階の広間において歓迎会を行います。
   *Nana kai no **hiroma ni oite** kangeikai o okonaimasu.*
   We will give a reception in the hall on the seventh floor.
   日本における技術革新はめまぐるしかった。
   ***Nihon ni okeru** gijutsu kakushin wa memagurushikatta.*
   The technological revolution in Japan has happened very rapidly.
2. After noun expressing criterion/domain
   能力において彼は他の学生にまさります。
   ***Nōryoku ni oite** kare wa hoka no gakusei ni masarimasu.*
   As for ability, he surpasses the other students.
   その品物は品質において問題がある。
   *Sono shinamono wa **hinshitsu ni oite** mondai ga aru.*
   As for quality, there are problems with these goods.
→ See also *de, ni*

ni sotte　に沿って

ADVERBIAL PHRASE MEANING: along, parallel to, in accordance with

1. After noun
   通りに沿ってたくさん店があります。
   Tōri ni sotte *takusan mise ga arimasu.*
   There are a lot of stores along the street.
   この線路は国道に沿って走っている。
   *Kono senro wa **kokudō ni sotte** hashitte iru.*
   This railroad runs parallel to the national highway.
   彼は上司の方針に沿ってそれを実行した。
   *Kare wa jōshi no **hōshin ni sotte** sore o jikkō shita.*
   He carried it out in accordance with his boss's policy.
   (*ni shitagatte* may replace *ni sotte* here)

ni taishite に対して
ADVERBIAL PHRASE MEANING: toward, to (in connection with), against, in regard to, whereas, in contrast to

It becomes *ni taisuru* when used as an adjectival phrase.

1. After noun
   この問題に対して質問がありますか。
   *Kono **mondai ni taishite** shitsumon ga arimasu ka.*
   Do you have any questions in regard to this problem?
   生徒たちは先生に対してすなおな態度をとります。
   *Seito tachi wa **sensei ni taishite** sunao-na taido o torimasu.*
   The students take an obedient attitude toward the teachers.
   私は彼女に対して好意を持っています。
   *Watashi wa **kanojo ni taishite** kōi o motte imasu.*
   I feel affection toward her.

私は他人のプライバシーに対して関心を持たない。

*Watashi wa tanin no **puraibashii ni taishite** kanshin o motanai.*

I have no interest in other people's private matters.

彼は私に対して恨みを持っているようです。

*Kare wa **watashi ni taishite** urami o motte iru yō desu.*

He seems to have a grudge against me.

5人に対して1台コンピューターがあります。

***Go nin ni taishite** ichi dai konpyūtā ga arimasu.*

There is one computer to every five persons.

2. After dictionary or *ta*-form of verb/adjective + *no*

空が青いのに対して山は赤だった。

*Sora ga aoi **no ni taishite** yama wa aka datta.*

In contrast to the blue sky was the red mountain.

与党がそれに賛成したのに対して野党は反対した。

*Yotō ga sore ni sansei shita **no ni taishite** yatō wa hantai shita.*

The ruling party supported it, whereas the opposition parties were against it.

3. After (adjectival) noun + *na* + *no*

彼は弱い者には親切なのに対して強い者には冷たい。

*Kare wa yowai mono ni wa **shinsetsu-na no ni taishite** tsuyoi mono ni wa tsumetai.*

He is kind toward the weak, whereas he is cool toward the strong.

4. Used as adjectival phrase

これが質問に対する答です。

*Kore ga **shitsumon ni taisuru kotae** desu.*

This is the answer to the question.

→ See also *ni*, *ni kansuru*

ni totte　にとって
PHRASE MEANING: to, as far as . . . concerned, for

1. After personal pronoun/noun
それは私にとって問題ではありません。
*Sore wa **watashi ni totte** mondai dewa arimasen.*
As far as I'm concerned that is not a problem.
あなたにとって日本語を覚えることはむずかしいですか。
***Anata ni totte** nihongo o oboeru koto wa muzukashii desu ka.*
Is it difficult for you to learn Japanese?
それは彼女にとって不都合なのですか。
*Sore wa **kanojo ni totte** futsugō-na no desu ka.*
Is it inconvenient for her?

ni tsuite　について
ADVERBIAL PHRASE MEANING: about, concerning, in regard to, as to/ for, of

It becomes *ni tsuite no* when modifying a noun.

1. After noun
だれのことについて話しているんですか。
*Dare no **koto ni tsuite** hanashite iru n desu ka.*
Who are you talking about?
その件についてまったく賛成です。
*Sono **ken ni tsuite** mattaku sansei desu.*
I quite agree with you concerning that matter.
日本語教育についてたくさん問題がある。
*Nihongo **kyōiku ni tsuite** takusan mondai ga aru.*

There are many problems with Japanese language education.
日本の政治についてどう思いますか。
Nihon no seiji ni tsuite dō omoimasu ka.
What do you think of Japanese politics?
2. Used as adjectival phrase
演劇についての資料はありませんでした。
Engeki ni tsuite no shiryō wa arimasen deshita.
There was no data concerning theater.
→ See also *ni kansuru, ni taishite*

ni tsurete　につれて
CONJUNCTION MEANING: as (in consequence of some change)

1. After dictionary form of verb
彼は年をとるにつれて温厚になった。
Kare wa toshi o toru ni tsurete onkō ni natta.
As he grew older, he became gentler.
年がたつにつれて生活は楽になって来ました。
Toshi ga tatsu ni tsurete seikatsu wa raku ni natte kimashita.
As the years go by, my life has become (more and more) comfortable.

ni yoreba　によれば
ADVERBIAL PHRASE MEANING: according to, from

It can be replaced with *ni yoru to*.

1. After noun

テレビのニュースによれば阿蘇山で大きな噴火があったらしい。

*Terebi no **nyūsu ni yoreba** aso-zan de ōki-na funka ga atta rashii.*

According to the television news, it seems there was a big eruption at Mt. Aso.

聞くところによれば彼女は結婚するそうです。

***Kiku tokoro ni yoreba** kanojo wa kekkon suru sō desu.*

From what I've heard, she is going to get married.

天気予報によれば明日は雨です。

*Tenki **yohō ni yoreba** ashita wa ame desu.*

According to the weather forecast, it will be rainy tomorrow.

ni yotte　によって

ADVERBIAL PHRASE MEANING: by (an agent), because of, due to, by means of, according to

Note that it takes a passive verb. It can be replaced with the more formal *ni yori*, and becomes *ni yoru* (which does not take a passive verb) before a noun it modifies.

1. After noun

その小説は夏目漱石によって書かれた。

*Sono shōsetsu wa **natsume sōseki ni yotte** kakareta.*

The novel was written by Soseki Natsume.

職場での喫煙は規則によって禁止されています。

*Shokuba de no kitsuen wa **kisoku ni yotte** kinshi sarete imasu.*

Smoking at the office is prohibited by regulation.

試合は大雨によって中止された。

*Shiai wa **ōame ni yotte** chūshi sareta.*

The game was called off due to a heavy rain.

デモは武力によって鎮圧された。

*Demo wa **buryoku ni yotte** chin'atsu sareta.*

The demonstration was quelled by means of force.

2. Used in adjectival phrase

   彼による話は信じがたい。

   ***Kare ni yoru hanashi** wa shinjigatai.*

   Talk from him is hard to believe. (What he says is difficult to believe.)

→ See also *de, o tōshite, tame ni*

ni wa には

DOUBLE PARTICLE MEANING: for (in regard to), in order to

It is usually used before a predicate that expresses state, degree, quality, evaluation, etc.

1. After noun

   この服は子供には大きすぎます。

   *Kono fuku wa **kodomo ni wa** ōkisugimasu.*

   This dress is too big for my child.

2. After dictionary form of verb

   出かけるにはまだ早すぎます。

   *Dekake**ru ni wa** mada hayasugimasu.*

   It is still too early to go out.

   外国を旅行するにはたくさんお金がかかる。

   *Gaikoku o ryokō su**ru ni wa** takusan o-kane ga kakaru.*

   In order to travel abroad it takes a great deal of money.

このパソコンは持ち運ぶにはたいへん便利です。

*Kono pasokon wa mochihako**bu ni wa** taihen benri desu.*

This personal computer is very handy to carry.

→ See also *no ni, tame ni, wa*

no　の

PARTICLE MEANING: of, at, in, on, to, from, by, for, one's

It also makes adjectivals, indicates apposition, makes possessive adjectives or pronouns, nominalizes verbs and adjectives, and indicates the subject or object in a relative clause. Note that it comes only before nouns.

1. After (adjectival) noun
   東京は日本の首都です。
   *Tōkyō wa **nihon no** shuto desu.*
   Tokyo is the capital of Japan.
   これはフランクのかばんと傘です。
   *Kore wa **furanku no** kaban to kasa desu.*
   These are Frank's bag and umbrella.
   テレホンカードは売店の自動販売機で売っています。
   *Terehon kādo wa **baiten no** jidō hanbaiki de utte imasu.*
   Telephone cards are sold at a vending machine at the stand.
   午後の授業は休みます。
   ***Gogo no** jugyō wa yasumimasu.*
   I will miss my afternoon classes.
   日曜日の祭りは延期されました。
   ***Nichiyōbi no** matsuri wa enki saremashita.*
   The festival on Sunday was postponed.

芥川龍之介の小説を読んだことがありますか。

Akutagawa ryūnosuke no *shōsetsu o yonda koto ga arimasu ka.*

Have you ever read a novel by Ryunosuke Akutagawa?

事故で16歳の少年が死にました。

*Jiko de **jū roku sai no** shōnen ga shinimashita.*

A sixteen-year-old boy was killed in the accident.

こちらが友人の田中です。 (apposition)

*Kochira ga **yūjin no** tanaka desu.*

This is my friend Tanaka.

別の靴を見せてください。

Betsu no *kutsu o misete kudasai.*

Please show me another pair of shoes.

2. After specific noun expressing position/space/time
   (often a noun + *no* + noun + *no* pattern)

ポケットの中のさいふを盗まれました。

*Poketto no **naka no** saifu o nusumaremashita.*

I had the wallet in my pocket stolen.

机の上のかばんはだれのですか。

*Tsukue no **ue no** kaban wa dare no desu ka.*

Whose is the bag on the desk?

食事の後のデザートは何にしますか。

*Shokuji no **ato no** dezāto wa nani ni shimasu ka.*

What will you have for dessert after the meal?

3. After adverbial particle
   (*E*, *kara*, *de*, and *made* are adverbial particles used before verbs. When a phrase using one of them is used to modify a noun, *no* must be put before the noun to link it with the preceding phrase.)

広島までの往復切符を1枚ください。

Hiroshima made no ōfuku kippu *o ichi mai kudasai.*
Please give me a round-trip ticket to Hiroshima.
彼女へのプレゼントは何がいいですか。
Kanojo e no purezento *wa nani ga ii desu ka.*
What is a good present for her?

4. After adverbial phrase
   (Like adverbial particles, when an adverbial phrase is used to modify a noun, *no* must be used to link the phrase with the noun. However, when the phrase ends in *ni*, like *no tame ni*, the *ni* is replaced with *no*.)
   その件についてのあなたの意見は極端です。
   *Sono ken **ni tsuite no** anata no iken wa kyokutan desu.*
   Your opinion concerning that matter is extreme.
   彼らのための援助は全く不要です。
   *Karera **no tame no** enjo wa mattaku fuyō desu.*
   The aid for them is quite unnecessary.

5. After personal pronoun/name
   (makes it possessive)
   「これはあなたのかばんですか。」「いいえ、マイクのです。」
   *"Kore wa **anata no** kaban desu ka." "Iie, **maiku no** desu."*
   "Is this your bag?" "No, it is Mike's."

6. After interrogative pronoun
   (makes it an interrogative adjective)
   「これはだれのバイクですか。」「私のです。」
   *"Kore wa **dare no** baiku desu ka." "Watashi no desu."*
   "Whose motorbike is this?" "It's mine."
   「あれは何の木ですか。」「さくらの木です。」
   *"Are wa **nan no** ki desu ka." "Sakura no ki desu."*
   "What (kind of) trees are they?" "They are cherry trees."

どこの銀行に行けばいいですか。

***Doko no** ginkō ni ikeba ii desu ka.*

Which bank do I need to go to?

7. Used as indefinite pronoun

(after dictionary or *ta*-form of verb/adjective)

これがＣＤで、私が持っているのがレーザーディスクです。

*Kore ga shiidii de, watashi ga **motte iru no** ga rēzā disuku desu.*

This is a compact disc, and the one I have is a laser disc.

このカメラは高すぎます。もっと安いのはありませんか。

*Kono kamera wa takasugimasu. Motto yasu**i no** wa arimasen ka.*

This camera is too expensive. Do you have any cheaper ones?

この方が私が買ったのよりいい。

*Kono hō ga watashi ga ka**tta no** yori ii.*

This is better than the one I bought.

8. Used to make a nominal, or to change preceding clause into a noun clause

(after dictionary, *ta*-, or *nai*-form of verb/adjective)

漢字を覚えるのはとてもむずかしいです。

*Kanji o oboe**ru no** wa totemo muzukashii desu.*

Memorizing Chinese characters is very difficult.

タバコを吸うのをやめたいと思います。

*Tabako o s**ū no** o yametai to omoimasu.*

I'd like to stop smoking.

書類を持ってくるのを忘れました。

*Shorui o motte ku**ru no** o wasuremashita.*

I forgot to bring the papers.

蒸し暑いのはいやですね。

*Mushiatsui **no** wa iya desu ne.*

Humidity is unpleasant, isn't it?

彼が事故で亡くなったのは事実です。

*Kare ga jiko de nakunatta **no** wa jijitsu desu.*

It is true that he was killed in an accident.

彼にそれができないのはおかしい。

*Kare ni sore ga deki**nai no** wa okashii.*

It is strange that he can't do that.

9. After subject in a relative clause
   (may be replaced by *ga*)

   彼女の作った料理はとてもおいしいです。

   ***Kanojo no** tsukutta ryōri wa totemo oishii desu.*

   The food she cooks is very delicious.

10. After object in a relative clause

    コーヒーの欲しい人は言ってください。

    ***Kōhii no** hoshii hito wa itte kudasai.*

    Those who want coffee speak up, please.

11. At the end of sentence (with rising intonation)
    (usually used by women and children)

    いっしょに行きたくないの。

    *Isshoni ikitaku nai **no**.*

    Don't you want to go together?

→ See also *ga (1)*, *koto*, *mono*, *ni tsuite*, *no desu*, *tokoro*

node ので

PARTICLE MEANING: because (of), on account of, as, since

The statement preceding *node* should be objective, whereas

kara is used to indicate the speaker's subjective judgement or insistence.

1. After (adjectival) noun + *na*
   今日は雨なので映画を見よう。
   *Kyō wa **ame-na node** eiga o miyō.*
   I'll see a movie today since it is rainy.
   彼女は病気なので来られません。
   *Kanojo wa **byōki-na node** koraremasen.*
   She is unable to come because she is sick.

2. After dictionary form of verb/adjective
   用事があるのでもう失礼します。
   *Yōji ga a**ru node** mō shitsurei shimasu.*
   Since I have an engagement, I'll be leaving now.
   この本はおもしろいので勧めます。
   *Kono hon wa omoshiro**i node** susumemasu.*
   I recommend this book to you because it is interesting.
   (if *kara* replaced *node*, the reason would be "because *I think* the book is interesting")

3. After *nai*-form of verb/adjective
   彼女が行かないので私も行きません。
   *Kanojo ga ika**nai node** watashi mo ikimasen.*
   Since she's not going, I won't go either.
   そんなに長くないので読むには余り時間がかかりません。
   *Sonna ni nagaku**nai node** yomu ni wa amari jikan ga kakarimasen.*
   It's not very long, so it won't take too long to read.

4. After *ta*-form of verb/adjective
   雨が降っていたのでゴルフはやめました。

*Ame ga futte **ita node** gorufu wa yamemashita.*
We stopped playing golf because it was raining.
あのカメラは高かったので買いませんでした。
*Ano kamera wa takakat**ta node** kaimasen deshita.*
I didn't buy that camera because it was expensive.

→ See also *kara*

no desu のです

PREDICATIVE PHRASE which stresses the preceding statement or softens the tone of a suggestion, request, or demand

No desu is often abbreviated to *n desu* in colloquial speech.

1. After dictionary form of verb/adjective
   ちょっとたずねたいことがあるんですが。
   *Chotto tazunetai koto ga ar**u n desu** ga.*
   I have a small question that I want to ask you, but . . . (can you help me?)
   今とても忙しいんです。
   *Ima totemo isogashi**i n desu**.*
   I am very busy now (so I can't help you).

2. After *ta*-form of verb/adjective
   さっき彼女に電話したのですが、出ませんでした。
   *Sakki kanojo ni denwa shi**ta no desu** ga, demasen deshita.*
   I telephoned her a little while ago, but she didn't answer.
   (if preceded by a past-tense sentence, a contrary statement usually follows)
   あの自転車は安かったのですが、お金が足りませんでした。

*Ano jitensha wa yasukatta **no desu** ga, o-kane ga tarimasen deshita.*

That bicycle was cheap, but I didn't have enough money.

3. After *nai*-form of verb/adjective

次の休暇はどこにも行かないのですか。

*Tsugi no kyūka wa doko ni mo ika**nai no desu** ka.*

Won't you go anywhere during the next vacation?

4. After (adjectival) noun + *na/datta*

今日はとてもひまなんです。

*Kyō wa totemo **hima-na n desu**.*

I am very free today (and am wondering what to do).

きのうはひまだったんですが、うちにいました。

*Kinō wa **hima datta n desu** ga, uchi ni imashita.*

I was free yesterday, but I stayed at home.

5. Used in question

(A question using this phrase is usually asking for some explanation, while a question without it may indicate a request or invitation. When interrogative words are used in questions, *no desu ka* usually comes at the end of the question to clearly indicate that some information is being asked for.)

どうしてここへ来たんですか。

*Dōshite koko e kita **n desu** ka.*

Why (*or* how) did you come here?

テニスはするんですか。

*Tenisu wa suru **n desu** ka.*

Do you play tennis?

(compare with *Tenisu o shimsu ka*, meaning "Will you play tennis?")

お酒は飲まないんですか。

*O-sake wa nomanai **n desu** ka.*

Don't you drink sake?

(compare with *O-sake o nomimasen ka*, meaning "Won't you drink some sake?")

no ni のに

PARTICLE MEANING: although, though, in spite of, while, to (do), for (doing), in (doing), I wish . . . , you should . . .

When connecting two contrary statements, the statement after *no ni* usually implies unexpected surprise, dissatisfaction, disappointment, regret, etc. When indicating the purpose of an action, the main verb after *no ni* expresses the action that is performed in the process toward the end to which the action is directed. An adjective or adjectival predicate after *no ni* expresses a judgment on the purpose.

1. After dictionary form of verb/adjective

   雨が降っているのに出かけるんですか。

   *Ame ga futte **iru no ni** dekakeru n desu ka.*

   Are you going out even though it is raining?

   みんな休んでいるのに彼は一生懸命働いています。

   *Minna yasunde **iru no ni** kare wa isshōkenmei hataraite imasu.*

   Though the others are taking a rest, he is working hard.

   同じものがあの店では高いのにこの店では安い。

   *Onaji mono ga ano mise dewa takai **no ni** kono mise dewa yasui.*

   While the same item in that store is expensive, it's cheap in this store.

   彼女は病気でないのによく学校を休みます。

*Kanojo wa byōki de nai **no ni** yoku gakkō o yasumimasu.*
Though she is not sick, she often takes off from school.

渋滞のために空港に着くのに2時間もかかりました。
*Jūtai no tame ni kūkō ni tsuku **no ni** ni jikan mo kakarimashita.*
It took no less than two hours to reach the airport on account of the traffic jam.

この魚を料理するのに油が要ります。
*Kono sakana o ryōri suru **no ni** abura ga irimasu.*
Oil is needed to cook this fish.

あの店はいろいろな物を買うのにとても便利です。
*Ano mise wa iroiro-na mono o kau **no ni** totemo benri desu.*
That store is very convenient for buying various things.

彼の家は歩いて行くのに遠すぎます。
*Kare no ie wa aruite iku **no ni** tōsugimasu.*
His house is too far to walk to.

2. After *nai*-form of verb

彼はそのことを何も知らないのに偉そうにしている。
*Kare wa sono koto o nani mo shira**nai no ni** erasō ni shite iru.*
Though he doesn't know anything about that he acts like a know-it-all.

3. After *ta*-form of verb/adjective

あれほど注意したのに彼女はやめなかった。
*Are hodo chūi shi**ta no ni** kanojo wa yamenakatta.*
Even though I cautioned her to that extent, she would not stop.

天気が良かったのにどこにも行きませんでした。
*Tenki ga yoka**tta no ni** doko ni mo ikimasen deshita.*
Even though the weather was good, I didn't go anywhere.

電話してくれるように頼んだのに。
*Denwa shite kureru yō ni tanon**da no ni**.*
Even though I asked you to call me . . . (you didn't).

4. After (adjectival) noun + *na/datta*
   彼は元気なのによく仕事をさぼります。
   *Kare wa **genki-na no ni** yoku shigoto o saborimasu.*
   Though he is healthy, he often skips out of work.
   今日は雨なのにつりに行くんですか。
   *Kyō wa **ame-na no ni** tsuri ni iku n desu ka.*
   Are you going fishing today in spite of the rain?
   彼はまだ学生なのにたくさんお金を稼いでいます。
   *Kare wa mada **gakusei na no ni** takusan o-kane o kaseide imasu.*
   He is making a lot of money though he is still a student.
   あの人は金持ちだったのに今は貧乏です。
   *Ano hito wa **kanemochi datta no ni** ima wa binbō desu.*
   Even though that person was rich, he is poor now.

5. After *ba/tara*-form of verb/adjective + *ii/yokatta*
   あなたもいっしょに来ればいいのに。
   *Anata mo issho ni kure**ba ii no ni**.*
   I wish you would come with me . . . (but you won't).
   往復切符を買えば良かったのに。
   *Ōfuku kippu o kae**ba yokatta no ni**.*
   You should have bought a round-trip ticket.

→ See also *ga (2), keredo(mo), tame ni*

o を

PARTICLE EXPRESSING: the direct object of a verb, the starting point of an action, a point of separation (from), a place where something or somebody is passing (through/along/in/across/over)

1. After direct object of verb
   「何を買ったんですか。」「珍しい切手を買いました。」
   *"**Nani o** katta n desu ka." "Mezurashii **kitte o** kaimashita."*
   "What did you buy?" "I bought some unique stamps."
   私は毎週1回トムに日本語を教えています。
   *Watashi wa maishū ikkai tomu ni **nihongo o** oshiete imasu.*
   I teach Japanese to Tom once a week.
   彼女は私を田中君と呼びます。
   *Kanojo wa **watashi o** tanaka-kun to yobimasu.*
   She calls me Tanaka-*kun*.
   どこかで財布を取られました。
   *Dokoka de **saifu o** toraremashita.*
   I had my wallet stolen somewhere.
   みんなを驚かせよう。
   ***Minna o** odorokaseyō.*
   I'll surprise everybody.
   夏休みを旅行して過ごしました。
   *Natsu **yasumi o** ryokō shite sugoshimashita.*
   I spent my summer vacation traveling.

2. After noun expressing place
   今朝は8時に家を出ました。
   *Kesa wa hachi ji ni **ie o** demashita.*
   I left home at eight this morning.
   彼女はさっき部屋を出て行きました。
   *Kanojo wa sakki **heya o** dete ikimashita.*
   She went out of the room a short while ago.
   新幹線はもう京都を通過しました。
   *Shinkansen wa mō **kyōto o** tsūka shimashita.*

The shinkansen already passed through Kyoto.
この通りをまっすぐに行って下さい。
*Kono **tōri** o massugu ni itte kudasai.*
Please go straight along this street.
2つめの角を右に曲がって下さい。
*Futatsume no **kado** o migi ni magatte kudasai.*
Please turn right at the second corner.
→ See also *ga (1)*, *kara*, *ni*, *to*, *wa*

o motte　をもって
FORMAL ADVERBIAL MEANING: by (means of), with

1. After noun
結果は書面をもって通知いたします。
*Kekka wa **shomen** o motte tsūchi itashimasu.*
I'll inform you of the result by letter.
彼の能力をもってしても不可能でしょう。
*Kare no **nōryoku** o motte shitemo fukanō deshō.*
Even with his ability it will be impossible.
→ See also *de*, *ni yotte*

o tōshite　を通して
FORMAL ADVERBIAL PHRASE MEANING: through (some method)

1. After noun
私たちの調査を通していろいろなことがわかって来た。

*Watashi tachi no **chōsa o tōshite** iroiro-na koto ga wakatte kita.*

Through our investigation, various facts came to be known.

→ See also *ni yotte*

oki ni　おきに

PHRASE MEANING: at intervals of

1. After number + counter
私はうちで1日おきにお酒を飲みます。
*Watashi wa uchi de **ichi nichi oki ni** o-sake o nomimasu.*
I drink (alcohol) at home every other day.
この駅では普通電車は15分おきに出ます。
*Kono eki de wa futsū densha wa **jū go fun oki ni** demasu.*
Local trains leave every fifteen minutes from this station.
この用紙には1行おきに書いて下さい。
*Kono yōshi ni wa **ichi gyō oki ni** kaite kudasai.*
Please write on every other line of this paper.
あの道路には5メートルおきに木が植えてあります。
*Ano dōro ni wa **go mētoru oki ni** ki ga uete arimasu.*
Trees are planted along that road at intervals of five meters.

oru　おる

FORMAL VERB that can be substituted for *iru*

The polite form, *orimasu*, is used to show humbleness on the speaker's part, while the respectful form, *oraremasu*, is used to show respect to another.

1. Used for expressing existence
「山田さんはうちにおられますか。」「いいえ、今おりませんが。」
   *"Yamada-san wa uchi ni **oraremasu** ka." "Iie, ima **orimasen ga.**"*
   "Is Mr. Yamada at home?" "No, he is out now."
   (the question shows respect, and the response humbleness)
2. After *te*-form of verb
   社長は今出かけております。
   *Shachō wa ima dekake**te orimasu.***
   The boss is out now.
   (speaking to another about one's own boss)
   2時に入口で待っております。
   *Ni ji ni iriguchi de matte **orimasu.***
   I'll be waiting for you at two o'clock at the entrance.

rashii らしい
ADJECTIVE MEANING: I hear, seem to, be likely to, like. . .

The supposition expressed by *rashii* is based on what the speaker has heard.

1. After (adjectival) noun
   彼女は風邪らしいです。
   *Kanojo wa **kaze rashii** desu.*

I hear she has a cold.

彼女は先週病気だったらしいです。

*Kanojo wa senshū **byōki** datta **rashii** desu.*

I hear she was sick last week.

(the past-tense verb must be placed before *rashii*)

そんなことをするのは彼女らしい。

*Sonna koto o suru no wa **kanojo rashii**.*

It is like her to do such a thing.

この町には図書館らしい図書館はありません。

*Kono machi ni wa **toshokan rashii** toshokan wa arimasen.*

There is no library-like library in this town.

2. After dictionary form of verb/adjective

天気予報によると明日は晴れるらしい。

*Tenki yohō ni yoru to ashita wa hare**ru rashii**.*

According to the weather forecast, it is likely to be clear tomorrow.

3. After *nai*-form of verb/adjective

彼は肉は食べないらしい。

*Kare wa niku wa tabe**nai rashii**.*

It seems that he doesn't eat meat.

彼はあまりよくないらしい。

*Kare wa amari yoku**nai rashii**.*

It seems that he is not doing very well.

4. After *ta*-form of verb/adjective

彼は先月ヨーロッパを旅行したらしい。

*Kare wa sengetsu yōroppa o ryokō shi**ta rashii**.*

I hear he traveled in Europe last month.

彼が買ったバイクは高かったらしい。

*Kare ga katta baiku wa takakat**ta rashii**.*

I hear that that motorcycle he bought was expensive.

→ See also *mitai, sō desu, yō desu*

shika　しか

PARTICLE (used with a negative) MEANING: nothing/nobody/no-where but . . ., no more than . . ., no other . . . than . . ., only

Note that though a negative verb is used in Japanese, the English equivalent does not always require one.

1. After subject/object
   (used in place of the particle which indicates the subject/object)
   洋子しか約束の時間に来なかった。
   Yoko shika *yakusoku no jikan ni konakatta.*
   Nobody but Yoko came at the appointed time.
   マイクは野菜しか食べません。
   *Maiku wa **yasai shika** tabemasen.*
   Mike eats nothing but vegetables.

2. After number + counter
   東京には1回しか行ったことがありません。
   *Tōkyō ni wa **ikkai shika** itta koto ga arimasen.*
   I've only been to Tokyo once.
   私は三人しか日本の友人がいません。
   *Watashi wa **san nin shika** nihon no yūjin ga imasen.*
   I have no more than three Japanese friends.
   今2千円しかお金を持っていません。
   *Ima **ni sen en shika** o-kane o motte imasen.*
   I only have two thousand yen now.

3. After particle
今日は6時にしか会えません。
*Kyō wa roku ji **ni shika** aemasen.*
Today I can meet you at no other time except six.
ここからしか出られません。
*Koko **kara shika** deraremasen.*
You can go out only from here.
このタイプのラジオはあの店でしか売っていません。
*Kono taipu no rajio wa ano mise **de shika** utte imasen.*
Radios of this type are sold nowhere but at that store.

4. After dictionary form of verb
ここで待つしかありません。
*Koko de ma**tsu shika** arimasen.*
There is nothing to do but wait here.

sō desu   そうです (1)

PREDICATIVE PHRASE MEANING: (I) hear (that), it is said (that)

It is used with reported speech or hearsay.

1. After dictionary form of verb/adjective
明日は晴れるそうです。
*Asu wa hare**ru sō desu**.*
I hear it will be sunny tomorrow.
このビルが日本でいちばん高いそうです。
*Kono biru ga nihon de ichiban taka**i sō desu**.*
It is said that this building is the tallest in Japan.

2. After *nai*-form of verb
田中さんは今日は来ないそうです。

*Tanaka-san wa kyō wa ko**nai sō desu***.
I hear Mr. Tanaka won't come today.

3. After *ta*-form of verb/adjective
   彼女は泣いていたそうです。
   *Kanojo wa naite i**ta sō desu***.
   I hear she was crying.
   それはうまく行かなかったそうです。
   *Sore wa umaku ikanaka**tta sō desu***.
   They say it didn't go well.

4. After (adjectival) noun + *da/datta*
   彼女は先週熱だったそうです。
   *Kanojo wa senshū **netsu datta sō desu***.
   I hear she had a fever last week.

→ See also *rashii*

sō desu　そうです (2)
PREDICATE PHRASE MEANING: look(s), seem(s)

The supposition expressed is based on the speaker's observation.

1. After conjunctive form of verb
   雨が降りそうですね。
   *Ame ga **furisō desu** ne*.
   It looks like rain, doesn't it?
   私は試験にパスしそうもありません。
   *Watashi wa shiken ni pasu **shisō mo arimasen***.
   It doesn't look like I'll pass the exam.

2. After stem of adjective
   あの人はとても優しそうです。
   *Ano hito wa totemo **yasashisō** desu.*
   That person looks very gentle.
   彼はあなたに会えてとてもうれしそうでした。
   *Kare wa anata ni aete totemo **ureshisō** deshita.*
   He looked very glad to see you.
3. After adjectival noun
   退屈そうでしたね。
   ***Taikutsu sō* deshita** ne.
   You looked bored.
   このケースは丈夫そうではありません。
   *Kono kēsu wa **jōbu sō** dewa arimasen.*
   This case doesn't look durable.
4. After *yosa-* or *nasa-*
   (the irregular stems of *yoi* and *nai* respectively)
   車の調子はよさそうです。
   *Kuruma no chōshi wa **yosasō** desu.*
   The condition of the car seems good.
   彼女は元気がなさそうです。
   *Kanojo wa genki ga **nasasō** desu.*
   She seems to be lacking in spirit. (She does not seem well.)
   この料理はあまりおいしくなさそうです。
   *Kono ryōri wa amari oishiku **nasasō** desu.*
   This dish doesn't look very good.
5. In answer to a question
   (used as affirmative answer to a question ending in *desu ka*)
   「これはあなたのかばんですか。」「はい、そうです。」
   *"Kore wa anata no kaban **desu ka**." "Hai, **sō desu**."*

"Is this your bag?" "Yes, it is."

→ See also *mitai, rashii, sō desu (1), yō desu*

sō ni natta   そうになった

PREDICATIVE PHRASE MEANING: almost (did), nearly (did)

It may be replaced by the dictionary form of a verb, followed by *tokoro datta*.

1. After conjunctive form of verb
   ねぼうして飛行機に遅れそうになりました。
   *Nebō shite hikōki ni **okuresō ni narimashita**.*
   I overslept and nearly missed the airplane.
   電車を間違えそうになった。
   *Densha o **machigaesō ni natta**.*
   I almost took a wrong train.

→ See also *tokoro*

sore   それ

DEMONSTRATIVE NOUN MEANING: that, those, it

It refers to an object or objects near the hearer and not far from the speaker, or something just mentioned and thus already known to both the speaker and the hearer. The polite form, *sochira*, means "that person" or "that direction." It becomes *sono* before a noun it modifies and it becomes *soko* when expressing "that place" or "there." *Sono* may also express the English definite article "the."

1. Followed by particle
   「それは何ですか。」「携帯用テレビです。」
   "***Sore wa*** *nan desu ka.*" "*Keitaiyō terebi desu.*"
   "What's that?" "It's a portable television."
   それを貸して下さい。
   Sore o *kashite kudasai.*
   Please lend it to me.
   それでいいです。
   Sore de *ii desu.*
   That will do.
   そこへ電車で行けますか。
   Soko e *densha de ikemasu ka.*
   Can I get there by train?
   そこで何をしていたんですか。
   Soko de *nani o shite ita n desu ka.*
   What were you doing there?
   すぐそちらに行きます。
   Sugu ***sochira ni*** *ikimasu.*
   I'll be there soon.

2. Followed by noun it modifies
   そのかばんはだれのですか。
   Sono kaban *wa dare no desu ka.*
   Whose is that bag?
   その時ちょうどテレビを見ていました。
   Sono toki *chōdo terebi o mite imashita.*
   Just at that time I was watching television.

3. Followed by *da/desu*
   「捜しているのはこれですね。」「それです。」
   "*Sagashite iru no wa kore desu ne.*" "***Sore desu.***"

"This is what you're looking for, isn't it?" "That's it."
→ See also *are*, *kore*

sorehodo　それほど

ADVERB (used with a negative) MEANING: (not) so, (not) very, (not) so many, (not) so much

It can be replaced by *sonna ni*.

1. Followed by adjective/adjectival noun/adverb
   今日はそれほど暑くないですね。
   *Kyō wa **sorehodo atsuku nai** desu ne.*
   It isn't very hot today, is it?
   これはそれほど高い時計ではありません。
   *Kore wa **sorehodo takai** tokei dewa arimasen.*
   This is not so expensive a watch.
   日本語はそれほど上手に話せません。
   *Nihongo wa **sorehodo jōzu ni** hanasemasen.*
   I cannot speak Japanese that well.
2. Before (or after) object
   今それほどお金は持っていません。
   *Ima **sorehodo** o-kane wa motte imasen.*
   or *Ima **o-kane** wa **sorehodo** motte imasen.*
   I don't have so much money now.

sorekara　それから

CONJUNCTION MEANING: and, then, after that, since then

1. After noun + *to*
   あのカメラとフィルムとそれから電池を下さい。
   *Ano kamera to **fuirumu to sorekara** denchi o kudasai.*
   Please give me that camera, film, and batteries.

2. After *te*-form of verb
   (stresses the succession of two actions)
   きのう映画を見てそれから買物をしました。
   *Kinō eiga o mi**te sorekara** kaimono o shimashita.*
   Yesterday I saw a movie, and after that I did my shopping.
   この喫茶店で休んでそれから帰ろう。
   *Kono kissaten de yasun**de sorekara** kaerō.*
   Let's take a rest at this coffee shop and then go home.

3. After noun + *de*
   (stresses the contrast of two things)
   これが大仏殿でそれからあれが五重の塔です。
   *Kore ga **daibutsuden de sorekara** are ga go jū no tō desu.*
   This is the Hall of the Great Buddha and that is the Five-Storied Pagoda.

4. At the beginning of sentence
   きのう加藤と会いました。それからいっしょにテニスをしました。
   *Kinō katō to aimashita. **Sorekara** issho ni tenisu o shimashita.*
   I met with Mrs. Kato yesterday. And then we played tennis together.

5. Used with progressive form
   それからずっとそこで働いています。
   ***Sorekara** zutto soko de hatarai**te imasu**.*
   I've been working there since then.

→ See also *soshite*

sore ni それに

CONJUNCTION MEANING: moreover, what is more, and also, besides

1. After *te*-form of adjective
   (stresses the addition of another quality of one person/thing)
   彼女は優しくて、それにきれいです。
   *Kanojo wa yasashikute, **sore ni** kirei desu.*
   She is kind and, what is more, she is pretty.
2. After adjectival noun + *de*
   (stresses the addition of another quality of one person/thing)
   彼は誠実で、それに勤勉です。
   *Kare wa **seijitsu de, sore ni** kinben desu.*
   He is honest and, moreover, he is industrious.
3. After dictionary form of adjective + *shi*
   (stresses the addition of another state)
   今日は寒いし、それに疲れています。
   *Kyō wa samui shi, **sore ni** tsukarete imasu.*
   Today is cold and, moreover, I am tired.
4. After noun + *to*
   私はスイスとフランスとそれにスペインに旅行しました。
   *Watashi wa suisu to **furansu to sore ni** supein ni ryokō shima-shita.*
   I took a trip to Switzerland, France, and also Spain.
5. At the beginning of sentence
   これは高すぎる。それにデザインがあまり好きでない。
   *Kore wa takasugiru. **Sore ni** dezain ga amari suki de nai.*
   This is too expensive. Besides, I don't like the design very much.

→ See also *sorekara*

sorezore　それぞれ

ADVERB MEANING: each, respectively, one's own

1. After subject
私たちはそれぞれ好きなようにします。
***Watashi tachi wa sorezore** suki-na yō ni shimasu.*
Each of us will do as each of us likes.
田中先生と山田先生はそれぞれ数学と歴史を教えています。
***Tanaka sensei to yamada sensei wa sorezore** sūgaku to rekishi o oshiete imasu.*
Mr. Tanaka and Mr. Yamada teach math and history respectively.
2. After indirect object
先生は生徒にそれぞれ問題を1問ずつ与えた。
*Sensei wa **seito ni sorezore** mondai o ichi mon zutsu ataeta.*
The teacher gave each of the students one question.
3. Followed by *no*
(to modify a noun)
彼らはそれぞれの仕事を一生懸命している。
*Karera wa **sorezore no** shigoto o isshōkenmei shite iru.*
They work hard at their respective jobs.

soshite　そして

CONJUNCTION MEANING: and, and then, and after that

1. After *te*-form of verb
これから本屋に行って、そしてデパートに行きます。

Kore kara hon'ya ni itte, soshite depāto ni ikimasu.

I will go to the bookstore, and then I will go to the department store.

2. At the beginning of sentence

これからがんばって勉強します。そして大学に入ろうと思います。

Kore kara ganbatte benkyō shimasu. **Soshite** *daigaku ni hairō to omoimasu.*

I will study hard from now on. And I think I'll try to get into a university.

→ See also *sorekara*

sō iū　そういう

PHRASE MEANING: that kind of, that type of, such (a)

It may be replaced by *sonna*.

1. Followed by noun it modifies

そういう本は私には向いていません。

Sō iū hon wa watashi ni wa muite imasen.

That type of book is not suited to me.

2. Used in idiomatic expression

そういうわけで予約をキャンセルしました。

Sō iū wake de yoyaku o kyanseru shimashita.

Such being the case, I canceled the reservation.

そういう風に言われても困ります。

Sō iū fū ni iwaretemo komarimasu.

I am at a loss if you speak like that.

sugiru　すぎる

VERB MEANING: too much, too many, too. . . , excessively

1. After conjunctive form of verb
   (may be substituted with *sugi* [conjunctive form of *sugiru*] plus
   desu)
   夕べは飲み過ぎました。
   *Yūbe wa **nomisugimashita**.*
   I drank too much last night.
   たくさんりんごを買いすぎました。
   *Takusan ringo o **kaisugimashita**.*
   I bought too many apples.
   あなたは働きすぎです。
   *Anata wa **hatarakisugi desu**.*
   You are working too hard.
2. After the stem of adjective
   この服は私には大きすぎます。
   *Kono fuku wa watashi ni wa **ōkisugimasu**.*
   These clothes are too big for me.
   あの車は高すぎて買えません。
   *Ano kuruma wa **takasugite** kaemasen.*
   That car is so expensive that I can't buy it.
3. After adjectival noun
   あなたは消極的すぎます。
   *Anata wa **shōkyoku teki sugimasu**.*
   You are too passive.
   その手続きは複雑すぎて1人ではできません。
   *Sono tetsuzuki wa **fukuzatsu sugite** hitori dewa dekimasen.*
   The procedure is too complicated to do alone.

sukoshi すこし

ADVERB MEANING: a few, some, a little, a bit, a moment, (not) at all

1. In affirmative sentence
   私は本を少し買いました。
   *Watashi wa hon o **sukoshi** kaimashita.*
   I bought a few books.
   少し日本語が話せますね。
   ***Sukoshi** nihongo ga hanasemasu ne.*
   You can speak a little Japanese, can't you?
   少しここで待って下さい。
   ***Sukoshi** koko de matte kudasai.*
   Wait here a moment, please.
2. Followed by *mo* in negative sentence
   そんなことはすこしも気にしません。
   *Sonna koto wa **sukoshi mo** ki ni shimasen.*
   I don't care a bit about that.
→ See also *amari, mattaku, takusan, totemo, yoku, zenzen, zuibun*

suru する

IRREGULAR VERB MEANING: do, play, work as . . ., perform (an action), cost, wear (an accessory), have (a meal, feeling), make (a sound), make (something into something else), treat (in some manner), decide on (something), possess (a figure/smell/etc.)

1. After object + *o*
   あなたはふだんどこで買物をしますか。
   *Anata wa fudan doko de **kaimono o shimasu** ka.*
   Where do you usually do your shopping?

後藤さんは毎週日曜日にゴルフをします。

*Gotō-san wa maishū nichiyōbi ni **gorufu o shimasu***.

Mr. Goto plays golf every Sunday.

私は英語の教師をしています。

*Watashi wa eigo no **kyōshi o shite imasu***.

I work as a teacher of English.

いい時計をしていますね。

***Ii tokei o shite imasu** ne*.

You are wearing a very nice watch.

レストランで軽い食事をしませんか。

*Resutoran de karui **shokuji o shimasen** ka*.

Won't you have a light meal at the restaurant?

あの車は変った形をしていますね。

*Ano kuruma wa kawatta **katachi o shite imasu** ne*.

That car has a unique shape, doesn't it?

女の子はみんな黒い髪の毛をしています。

*Onna no ko wa minna kuroi **kaminoke o shite imasu***.

All the girls have black hair.

2. After object + *ga*

このお茶はとてもいいにおいがします。

*Kono o-cha wa totemo ii **nioi ga shimasu***.

This tea has a very good smell. (This tea smells very good.)

このナイロンのかばんは柔らかい感じがします。

*Kono nairon no kaban wa yawarakai **kanji ga shimasu***.

This nylon bag has a soft feeling. (This nylon bag feels soft.)

変な音がしませんでしたか。

*Hen-na **oto ga shimasen** deshita ka*.

Didn't you hear a strange noise?

3. After object + *o* + (adjectival) noun + *ni*

(expresses the idea of making something/someone into something else or some other state)

彼は彼女を幸せにするでしょう。

*Kare wa **kanojo o shiawase ni suru** deshō.*

He will make her happy.

あなたのお父さんはあなたを医者にするつもりですか。

*Anata no otōsan wa **anata o isha ni suru** tsumori desu ka.*

Does your father intend to make you a doctor?

私は彼女からもらったプレゼントを大切にしています。

*Watashi wa kanojo kara moratta **purezento o taisetsu ni shite imasu**.*

I treasure the present I received from her.

4. After object + *o* + *ku*-form of adjective

もっとスープを甘くした方がいいです。

*Motto **sūpu o amaku shita** hō ga ii desu.*

It's better to make the soup sweeter.

5. After object + *ni* + *ku*-form of adjective

彼女に優しくしてあげなさい。

***Kanojo ni** yasashiku shite agenasai.*

Please treat her kindly.

6. After noun + *ni*

あの白い車にします。

*Ano shiroi **kuruma ni shimasu**.*

I'll take that white car.

7. After dictionary or *nai*-form of verb + *koto ni*

(*koto ni* adds the meaning "decide" or "pretend" [to do])

転職することにしました。

*Tenshoku suru **koto ni shimashita**.*

I decided to change my occupation.

8. After *ta*-form of verb + *koto ni*

その事は聞かなかったことにします。

Sono koto wa kikanakatta koto ni shimasu.

I'll pretend that I didn't hear that.

9. After noun expressing action/state
(nouns mainly of Chinese origin and foreign loanwords can be made into verbs by adding *suru*)

町を案内します。

*Machi o **annai shimasu**.*

I'll show you around the town.

(*itasu* can replace *suru* when the speaker wants to be humbler)

*Machi o **annai itashimasu**.*

ここに名前と住所を記入して下さい。

*Koko ni namae to jūsho o **kinyū shite** kudasai.*

Please fill in your name and address here.

階段から転げて膝をけがしました。

*Kaidan kara korogete hiza o **kega shimashita**.*

I fell down the stairs and hurt my knee.

今晩電話して下さい。

*Konban **denwa shite** kudasai.*

Please call me this evening.

やっとエンジンがスタートしましたが、またストップしました。

*Yatto enjin ga **sutāto shimashita** ga, mata **sutoppu shimashita**.*

At last the engine started, but it stopped again.

(using *dekiru* instead of *suru* expresses potential)

車を運転できますか。

  *Kuruma o **unten dekimasu** ka.*

  Can you drive a car?

10. After noun expressing price

この時計は1万円しました。

*Kono tokei wa **ichi man en shimashita**.*

This watch cost ten thousand yen.

11. After noun expressing period of time (in *ba/tara*-form)
2・3日すれば梅雨が明けます。

***Ni san nichi sureba** tsuyu ga akemasu.*

The rainy season will be over in two or three days.
10分したら終わります。

***Juppun shitara** owarimasu.*

It will be over in ten minutes.

12. After imitative words
緊張してどきどきします。

*Kinchō shite **dokidoki shimasu**.*

I get nervous and my heart pounds.
それを聞いてがっかりしました。

*Sore o kiite **gakkari shimashita**.*

I was disappointed to hear that.

13. After volitional form of verb + *to*
(expresses the idea of "trying to" do something)
タバコをやめようとしたけれどだめでした。

*Tabako o yameyō **to shita** keredo dame deshita.*

I tried to give up smoking but I couldn't.

→   See also *dekiru, te miru, yō ni suru*

ta   た

AUXILIARY VERB EXPRESSING: past action or state, completion of action or movement, lasting state as the result of an action or movement, experience at some undefined time

The *ta*-form is made by adding *ta* to the stem of the *te*-form of a verb. *Ta* euphonically changes to *da* after a verb whose dictionary form ends with *-bu*, *-gu*, *-mu*, or *-nu*.

1. Used in verb

   きのう私は新幹線で京都に行って来た。

   *Kinō watashi wa shinkansen de kyōto ni itte **kita**.*

   I went to Kyoto by shinkansen yesterday.

   最近私はタバコをやめた。

   *Saikin watashi wa tabako o **yameta**.*

   I stopped smoking recently.

   ドアの鍵がこわれた。

   *Doa no kagi ga **kowareta**.*

   The lock on the door is broken.

   仕事はもう終わった。

   *Shigoto wa mō **owatta**.*

   The work is finished.

   この本は3回読んだ。

   *Kono hon wa san kai **yonda**.*

   I've read this book three times.

   きのう見た映画はとても怖かった。

   *Kinō **mita** eiga wa totemo kowakatta.*

   The movie that I saw yesterday was very scary.

   (used as an adjectival, the *ta*-form of the verb directly precedes the noun it modifies)

2. Used in adjective

   (*desu* after the *ta*-form makes it more polite)

   きのう買ったカメラはとても安かったです。

*Kinō katta kamera wa totemo **yasukatta** desu.*

The camera I bought yesterday was very cheap.

「テストはむずかしかったですか。」「あまりむずかしくな
かったです。」

*"Tesuto wa **muzukashikatta** desu ka." "Amari muzukashiku **nakatta** desu."*

"Was the test difficult?" "It was not very difficult."

→ See also Verb Forms (II)

tabi ni 度に

CONJUNCTION MEANING: every time, each time, whenever

1. After dictionary form of verb
   彼は会う度に仕事の不満を言う。
   *Kare wa **au tabi ni** shigoto no fuman o iū.*
   Every time he meets me, he complains about his job.
   あの店に入る度に新しいソフトを買ってしまいます。
   *Ano mise ni **hairu tabi** ni atarashii sofuto katte shimaimasu.*
   Each time I go into that store I buy new software (in spite of myself).

tai たい

AUXILIARY VERB MEANING: want to, would like to, feel like (doing), wish to, hope to

The subject of verb + *tai* must be the 1st person in declarative simple sentences, and the 2nd person in simple questions or conditional clauses. The 3rd person subject is used with verb + *tai* only in reported speech or in a clause before *rashii* or *sō da*. In 3rd person subject declarative sentences *ta garu/gatte iru* must be used instead of *tai*.

The object of verb + *tai* is usually indicated by *o*, but *ga* may also be used in short sentences expressing direct desires.

Tai conjugates like an *i*-adjective.

1. After conjunctive form of verb
   少し休みたいです。
   *Sukoshi **yasumitai** desu.*
   I'd like to rest for a while.
   ビールを(が)飲みたい。
   *Biiru o (ga) **nomitai**.*
   I feel like drinking beer.
   日曜日は働きたくありません。
   *Nichiyōbi wa **hatarakitaku arimasen**.*
   I don't want to work on Sundays.
   またいっしょにお話をしたいですね。
   *Mata isshoni o-hanashi o **shitai** desu ne.*
   I hope to talk with you again.
   いつか日本語をマスターしたい。
   *Itsuka nihongo o masutā **shitai**.*
   I hope to master Japanese some day.
   歌舞伎を見たくありませんか。
   *Kabuki o **mitaku arimasen** ka.*
   Wouldn't you like to see a kabuki performance?
   ポールはアメリカに帰りたいと言ってます。
   *Pōru wa amerika ni **kaeritai** to ittemasu.*
   Paul says that he wants to go back to America.
   洋子はスキーに行きたくなかったらしい。

*Yoko wa sukii ni **ikitaku nakatta** rashii.*

It seems that Yoko didn't want to go skiing.

→ See also *hoshii*, *garu*

tame ni　ために

PHRASE MEANING: for, for. . .'s sake, because of, on account of, owing to, as a result of, in order to, so as to, for the purpose of

1. After noun + *no*

それはあなたのためになるでしょう。

*Sore wa **anata no tame ni** naru deshō.*

It will be good for you.

何のためにそれをするんですか。

Nan no tame ni sore o suru n desu ka.

For what purpose do you do that? (Why do you do that?)

飛行機は台風のために欠航しています。

*Hikōki wa **taifū no tame ni** kekkō shite imasu.*

The air service is being canceled because of a typhoon.

戦争のためにたくさんの難民が出た。

Sensō no tame ni takusan nanmin ga deta.

There were many refugees as a result of the war.

父はガンのために死にました。

*Chichi wa **gan no tame ni** shinimashita.*

My father died of cancer.

(*de* may replace *tame ni* when expressing cause)

外国旅行のために貯金をしなければなりません。

Gaikoku ryokō no tame ni chokin o shinakereba narimasen.

I have to save money for travel abroad.

将来のためにもっと勉強したいと思います。

Shōrai no tame ni *motto benkyō shitai to omoimasu.*

For the sake of my future I think I'll study harder.

2. Between noun + *no* and the noun it modifies

(changes to *tame no*)

これは初心者のための授業です。

Kore wa ***shoshinsha no tame no jugyō*** *desu.*

This is a class for beginners.

3 After adjectival noun + *na*

(to express reason/cause)

彼は不まじめなために嫌われている。

Kare wa ***fumajime-na tame ni*** *kirawarete iru.*

He is disliked because he is insincere.

4. After dictionary form of verb

(to express purpose)

私はお金を貯めるために一生懸命働いています。

Watashi wa o-kane o ***tameru tame ni*** *isshōkenmei hataraite imasu.*

I am working hard in order to save money.

5. After *nai*-form of verb

(to express purpose)

電車に遅れないために早く用意しなさい。

Densha ni okurenai tame ni hayaku yōi shinasai.

Get ready quickly so as not to miss the train.

6. After *ta*-form of verb/adjective

(to express reason/cause)

彼が休んだために何もできません。

Kare ga yasunda tame ni nani mo dekimasen.

We can't do anything because he is absent.

彼は忙しかったために来られませんでした。

Kare wa isogashikatta tame ni koraremasen deshita.

He wasn't able to come because he was busy.

7. After (adjectival) noun + *datta*
   (to express reason/cause)
   彼女は不注意だったために事故を起こしたんです。
   *Kanojo wa **fuchūi datta tame ni** jiko o okoshita n desu.*
   She caused the accident because she was careless.

8. After the demonstrative adjectives *kono*, *sono*, *ano*
   私たちはそのために協力しているんです。
   *Watashi tachi wa **sono tame ni** kyōryoku shite iru n desu.*
   That is why we are cooperating.

→ See also *de, kara, ni, node, no ni, yō ni*

tara　たら

PARTICLE MEANING: if, when, after (doing), if only, if you're talking about/looking for. . ., why don't you (do)

The stem of the *te*-form of a verb plus *tara* makes the *tara*-form. *Tara* is euphonically changed into *dara* after a verb whose dictionary form ends with *-bu, -gu, -mu,* or *-nu. Moshi* is often put at the beginning of the sentence to stress the conditional meaning.

1. After the stem of *te*-form of verb
   大雨が降ったらドライブに行くのはやめます。
   *Ōame ga **futtara** doraibu ni iku no wa yamemasu.*
   If it rains heavily I'll give up going for a drive.
   駅に着いたら電話して下さい。
   *Eki ni **tsuitara** denwa shite kudasai.*
   When you arrive at the station, please call me.
   その本を読んだら私に貸して下さい。

*Sono hon o **yondara** watashi ni kashite kudasai.*

After you read that book, please lend it to me.

買物をしたら帰ります。

*Kaimono o **shitara** kaerimasu.*

After shopping I'll go home.

(past actions expressed after *tara* must be done by someone else)

駅に着いたら彼女は待っていました。

*Eki ni **tsuitara** kanojo wa matte imashita.*

When I arrived at the station, she was waiting.

2. At the end of sentence (with rising intonation)

ちゃんと調べてもらったら。

*Chanto shirabete **morattara**.*

What about having it properly checked out?

3. After (adjectival) noun + *dat(tara)*

(*da* + *tara* becomes *dattara*)

もし私があなただったらそんなことはしません。

*Moshi watashi ga **anata dattara** sonna koto wa shimasen.*

If I were you, I wouldn't do such a thing.

明日いい天気だったらテニスをしませんか。

*Ashita ii **tenki dattara** tenisu o shimasen ka.*

If the weather is good tomorrow, would you like to play tennis?

山田さんだったら今入院しています。

***Yamada-san dattara** ima nyūin shite imasu.*

If you're looking for Mr. Yamada, he is in the hospital now.

日本語がもっと簡単だったらなあ。

*Nihongo ga motto **kantan dattara** nā.*

If only Japanese were much simpler.

4. After the stem of *ta*-form of adjective

よろしかったらうちに遊びに来て下さい。

Yoroshikattara uchi ni asobi ni kite kudasai.
If it is all right, please come to my house to see me.

→ See also *ba*, *nara*, *to*, *to sureba*, Euphonic Changes (II)

tari　たり

PARTICLE EXPRESSING: (some kind of) action/state like . . ., actions performed in turn, sometimes . . . and . . .

The actions or states expressed are often in contrast to each other. *Tari* is euphonically changed into *dari* after a verb whose dictionary form ends with *-bu*, *-gu*, *-mu*, or *-nu*. *Suru* usually follows the last *tari*.

1. After the stem of *te*-form of verb
   私は趣味で絵を書いたり俳句を作ったりします。
   *Watashi wa shumi de e o **kaitari** haiku o **tsukuttari** shimasu.*
   I do things like painting and composing haiku as my hobbies.
   彼女はよく泣いたり笑ったりします。
   *Kanojo wa yoku **naitari warattari** shimasu.*
   She often cries and laughs in turn.
   今日は雨が降ったりやんだりします。
   *Kyō wa ame ga **futtari yandari** shimasu.*
   It will rain on and off today.
   彼は手伝ってくれたりくれなかったりする。
   *Kare wa tetsudatte **kuretari kurenakattari** suru.*
   He sometimes helps me and sometimes not.
   映画を見たり買物をしたりで楽しかった。
   *Eiga o **mitari** kaimono o **shitari** de tanoshikatta.*

I had a good time seeing a movie and going shopping.

2. After the stem of *ta*-form of adjective
   その劇は楽しかったり悲しかったりします。
   *Sono geki wa **tanoshikattari kanashikattari** shimasu.*
   The play is sometimes happy and sometimes sad.

3. After (adjectival) noun + *dat(tara)*
   (*da + tara* becomes *dattara*)
   彼は親切だったり薄情だったりする。
   *Kare wa **shinsetsu dattari hakujō dattari** suru.*
   He is sometimes kind and sometimes cold-hearted.

→ See also *to ka,* Euphonic Changes (II)

te て

PARTICLE EXPRESSING: actions in succession, an unemphatical reason or cause, the process of action, a condition, contrastive or parallel actions or qualities

The conjunctive form of a verb + *te* makes the *te*-form. It is euphonically changed into *de* when following a verb whose dictionary form ends with *-bu, -gu, -mu,* or *-nu,* or when following adjectival nouns.

1. After conjunctive form of verb
   買物をして帰ります。
   *Kaimono o **shite** kaerimasu.*
   I'll do my shopping and go home.
   試験が終わってほっとした。
   *Shiken ga **owatte** hotto shita.*

The examination is over and I am relieved.

私は毎日自転車に乗って駅まで行きます。

*Watashi wa mainichi jitensha ni **notte** eki made ikimasu.*

I ride a bicycle to go to the station every day.

外国と比べて日本は物価が高い。

*Gaikoku to **kurabete** nihon wa bukka ga takai.*

Compared with foreign countries, the cost of living in Japan is high.

彼は助けてもらってお礼も言わなかった。

*Kare wa **tasukete moratte** o-rei mo iwanakatta.*

He was helped, but didn't express his thanks.

2. After *ku*-form of adjective

寒くてたまりません。

*Samu**kute** tamarimasen.*

It is so cold that I can't stand it.

この電車は速くてあの電車は遅いです。

*Kono densha wa haya**kute** ano densha wa osoi desu.*

This train is fast and that one is slow.

彼女はとても優しくてきれいです。

*Kanojo wa totemo yasashi**kute** kirei desu.*

She is very kind and pretty.

→ See also *da, de,* Euphonic Changes (II)

te ageru　てあげる
→ See *ageru*

te aru　てある
→ See *aru*

te hoshii　てほしい
→ See *hoshii*

te iku　て行く
PREDICATIVE PHRASE MEANING: keep (doing) from now on, get/ become (some state describing the subject) from now on, (do something) on the way

　It becomes *de iku* after a verb whose dictionary form ends with *-bu*, *-gu*, *-mu*, or *-nu*.

1. After the stem of *te*-form of verb
　毎日単語を10個覚えて行きたいと思います。
　Mainichi tango o jukko oboete ikitai to omoimasu.
　I want to memorize ten words every day from now on.
　あそこでお茶を飲んで行きませんか。
　Asoko de o-cha o nonde ikimasen ka.
　Shall we have tea over there before we go?
2. After *ku*-form of adjective
　(the *te*-form of *naru* [*natte*] must always be used between the *ku*-form of adjective and *iku*)
　物価はどんどん高くなって行きます。
　Bukka wa dondon takaku natte ikimasu.
　Prices keep on rising rapidly.
→ See also *te kuru*

te iru　ている
→ See *iru*

teki 的

SUFFIX making specific nouns into adjectivals or adverbs

1. After noun, followed by *da/desu*
   (becomes the predicate)
   会の雰囲気は家庭的です。
   *Kai no fun'iki wa **katei teki desu**.*
   The atmosphere of the meeting is homey.
2. After noun, followed by *na*
   (modifies noun)
   それはとても現実的な計画です。
   *Sore wa totemo **genjitsu teki-na** keikaku desu.*
   That is a very realistic plan.
3. After noun, followed by *ni*
   (modifies verb or adjective)
   経済的に国が豊かでも一人一人は苦しい。
   ***Keizai teki ni** kuni ga yutaka demo hitori hitori wa kurushii.*
   Even though the country is economically rich, each individual
   is badly off.

te kuru て来る

PREDICATIVE PHRASE MEANING: come to (do), begin to (do), have
done (to some extent), have been (doing), get/become (some state
describing the subject), (do something and then) come back

It becomes *de kuru* after a verb whose dictionary form ends
with *-bu*, *-gu*, *-mu*, or *-nu*.

1. After the stem of *te*-form of verb

日本語の話し方が分って来ました。
Nihongo no hanashikata ga wakatte kimashita.
I have come to understand how to speak Japanese.
雨が降って来ました。
Ame ga futte kimashita.
It began to rain (and will continue to rain).
これまでたくさん漢字を覚えて来ました。
Kore made takusan kanji o oboete kimashita.
I have learned a lot of kanji so far.
今の仕事に慣れて来ましたか。
Ima no shigoto ni narete kimashita ka.
Have you become accustomed to your present job?
デパートに買物に行って来ます。
Depāto ni kaimono ni itte kimasu.
I'll go shopping at a department store (and then come back).

2. After *ku*-form of adjective
   (the *te*-form of *naru* [*natte*] is always used between the *ku*-form of adjective and *kuru*)
   このごろだいぶ暖かくなって来ましたね。
   Kono goro daibu atatakaku natte kimashita ne.
   It is getting much warmer recently, isn't it?

→ See also *te iku*

temasu てます

ABBREVIATED INFORMAL FORM of the progressive form *te imasu*

It is used only in informal speech. After a verb whose dictionary form ends with *-bu*, *-gu*, *-mu*, or *-nu* it euphonically changes to *demasu*.

1. After the stem of *te*-form of verb
   彼女は今図書館で本を読んでます。
   *Kanojo wa ima toshokan de hon o **yondemasu**.*
   She is reading a book in the library now.
   彼がどこで仕事をしてるのか知ってますか。
   *Kare ga doko de shigoto o **shiteru** no ka **shittemasu** ka.*
   Do you know where he is doing his work?
   「何をしてたんですか。」「電話をしてました。」
   *"Nani o **shiteta** n desu ka." "Denwa o **shitemashita**."*
   "What were you doing?" "I was talking on the phone."
   → See *iru, masu*

temo ても
PARTICLE MEANING: even if, though, whether . . . or . . ., no matter

It euphonically changes to *demo* after a verb whose dictionary form ends with *-bu, -gu, -mu,* or *-nu,* and after adjectival nouns.

1. After the stem of *te*-form of verb
   うまく行っても油断しないようにして下さい。
   *Umaku **ittemo** yudan shinai yō ni shite kudasai.*
   Even if it goes well, please try not to be inattentive.
   そのことについて聞いても彼女は答えませんでした。
   *Sono koto ni tsuite **kiitemo** kanojo wa kotaemasen deshita.*
   Though I asked her about that matter, she didn't answer.
   雨が降っても遊びに行きます。
   *Ame ga **futtemo** asobi ni ikimasu.*

Even if it rains, I'm going out to have fun.

2. After interrogative word

何をしてもおもしろくありません。

Nani o shitemo omoshiroku arimasen.

No matter what I do, it's not interesting.

いつ行っても彼は留守です。

Itsu ittemo kare wa rusu desu.

No matter when I go, he isn't home.

どんなに速く走ってもバスに間にあいません。

Donna ni hayaku hashittemo basu ni ma ni aimasen.

No matter how fast we may run, we won't be able to catch the bus.

いくら言っても子供は言うことを聞きません。

Ikura ittemo kodomo wa iū koto o kikimasen.

No matter how often I say it, the children don't listen (to what I say).

3. After *ku*-form of adjective

たとえ行きたくなくても行かなければなりません。

Tatoe ikitaku nakutemo ikanakereba narimasen.

Even if you don't want to go, you have to.

どんなに高くてもあれが欲しい。

Donna ni takakutemo are ga hoshii.

No matter how expensive that is, I want it.

4. After adjectival noun

いくらいやでもそれを実行しなければならない。

Ikura iya demo sore o jikkō shinakereba naranai.

No matter how much you dislike it, you have to carry it out.

→ See also *demo*, *keredo(mo)*, *mo*

temo ii てもいい

PREDICATIVE PHRASE MEANING: may, can, it is all right (even) if . . ., (not) have to (do), do without . . ., (not) feel like (doing)

It euphonically changes to *demo* after a verb whose dictionary form ends with *-bu*, *-gu*, *-mu*, or *-nu*, and after adjectival nouns.

The *mo* is sometimes dropped, and *ii* may be replaced by its synonym *yoi/yoroshii*. However, *yoroshii* is usually used in affirmative sentences when speaking to a younger person, and is followed by *desu ka* in questions when speaking to a person who is older or of higher status. *Ii* may also be replaced by *kamawanai/kamaimasen*.

1. After the stem of *te*-form of verb
   このコピー機は自由に使ってもいいです。
   *Kono kopii ki wa jiyū ni **tsukattemo ii** desu.*
   You can use this copy machine freely.
   (*kekkō desu* should replace *ii desu* when giving permisison to a superior)
   「入っていいですか。」「ええ、もちろん。」
   "***Haitte ii** desu ka.*" "*Ee, mochiron.*"
   "May I come in?" "Yes, of course."
   (note that *mo* has been dropped)
   「もう帰ってもよろしいですか。」「いえ、いけません。」
   "*Mō **kaettemo yoroshii** desu ka.*" "*Ie, ikemasen.*"
   "May I leave now?" "No, you may not."
   (speaking to a superior)
2. After *ku*-form of adjective
   (*kekkō* can replace *ii*)
   動けば古くてもいいです。

*Ugokeba furu**kutemo ii** desu.*
If it works, it is all right even if it is old.

マニュアルはなくてもいいです。

*Manyuaru wa na**kutemo ii** desu.*
It's all right even if there isn't a manual. (I can do without a manual.)

天気は良くなくてもいいです。

*Tenki wa yokuna**kutemo ii** desu.*
It's all right even if the weather is not good.

そんなに急がなくてもいいですよ。

*Sonna ni isoga**nakutemo ii** desu yo.*
You don't have to hurry so much.

私は泳がなくてもいいです。見てます。

*Watashi wa oyoga**nakutemo ii** desu. Mitemasu.*
I don't feel like swimming. I'll just watch.

3. After (adjectival) noun or interrogative word

不便でもいいです。

*Fuben **demo** ii desu.*
It's alright even if it's inconvenient.

簡単でもいいですから書いてください。

*Kantan **demo ii** desu kara, kaite kudasai.*
Even something simple will be fine, so please write (something).

何でもいいです。

*Nan **demo ii** desu.*
Anything is fine.

何時でもいいですか。

*Itsu **demo ii** desu ka.*
Will anytime be alright?

→ See also *ikenai, temo, yoroshii*

te miru　てみる

PREDICATIVE PHRASE MEANING: try, try (doing), do (something) and see (the result)

1.　After the stem of *te*-form of verb
　　この本を読んでみます。
　　Kono hon o yonde mimasu.
　　I'll try reading this book.
　　この果物を一口食べてみよう。
　　Kono kudamono o hito kuchi tabete miyō.
　　I'll try a bite of this fruit and see (how it tastes).
　　あの靴をはいてみますか。
　　Ano kutsu o haite mimasu ka.
　　Will you try those shoes on?
　　この冬は北海道へスキーに行ってみたい。
　　Kono fuyu wa hokkaidō e sukii ni itte mitai.
　　I'd like to go skiing in Hokkaido this winter.
→　See also *suru*

te oku　ておく

PREDICATIVE PHRASE MEANING: do (something) for the next occasion, leave/keep (something) in some state, let (somebody do something)

1.　After the stem of *te*-form of verb
　　よく考えておきます。
　　Yoku kangaete okimasu.
　　I will think it over.
　　暑いので窓を開けておきます。

*Atsui node mado o ake**te okimasu***.

It's hot so I'll open the window (and leave it open).

その事は秘密にしておきましょう。

*Sono koto wa himitsu ni shi**te okimashō***.

Let's keep that matter a secret.

長い間待たせておいてごめんなさい。

*Nagai aida matase**te oite** gomen nasai*.

I'm sorry to have kept you waiting for so long.

そのことは知らないことにしておきます。

*Sono koto wa shiranai koto ni shi**te okimasu***.

I'll keep pretending that I don't know about that.

te shimau てしまう

PREDICATIVE PHRASE MEANING: finish (something), do (something) in spite of oneself, do by mistake/absent-mindedly/carelessly, do (something) completely

1. After the stem of *te*-form of verb

   私はこの本を一週間で読んでしまった。

   *Watashi wa kono hon o isshūkan de **yonde shimatta***.

   I finished reading this book in a week.

   私は彼女の作った料理を食べてしまいました。

   *Watashi wa kanojo no tsukutta ryōri o **tabete shimaimashita***.

   I ate up all the food she prepared in spite of myself.

   彼は東京駅でちがう電車に乗ってしまった。

   *Kare wa tōkyō eki de chigau densha ni **notte shimatta***.

   He took the wrong train at Tokyo Station by mistake.

   トイレに傘を忘れてしまった。

   *Toire ni kasa o **wasurete shimatta***.

I absent-mindedly left my umbrella in a restroom.

あの人が好きになってしまいそうです。

*Ano hito ga suki ni **natte shimaisō** desu.*

I feel I will really grow to like that person. (I have a feeling I'm going to fall for that person.)

to と

PARTICLE MEANING: and, or, with (accompanied by), when(ever), once . . ., if, no matter

It also indicates a quotation, a statement in indirect speech, the object of a specific verb, a word that describes the object of a sentence, a criterion for comparison, or how an action is performed.

1. Between nouns

フィルムと乾電池を下さい。

***Fuirumu to kandenchi** o kudasai.*

I'll take film and dry batteries.

水曜日と日曜日が私の休みです。

***Suiyōbi to nichiyōbi** ga watashi no yasumi desu.*

Wednesday and Sunday are my holidays.

ジュースとアイスクリームのどちらにしますか。

***Jūsu to aisu kuriimu** no dochira ni shimasu ka.*

Which would you like, juice or ice cream?

2. After noun expressing person

私は前の日曜日に妻と映画を見てきました。

*Watashi wa mae no nichiyōbi ni **tsuma to** eiga o mite kimashita.*

I went and saw a movie with my wife last Sunday.

「今だれと話していたんですか。」「友人のマイクとです。」

*"Ima **dare to** hanashite ita n desu ka." "Yūjin no **maiku to** desu."*

"Who were you talking with just now?" "With my friend Mike."

彼女はだれと結婚するんですか。

*Kanojo wa **dare to** kekkon suru n desu ka.*

Who is she going to marry?

3. After dictionary form of verb/adjective

今朝起きると頭痛がしました。

*Kesa oki**ru to** zutsū ga shimashita.*

When I got up this morning, I had a headache.

彼はカラオケを歌い出すとなかなかやめない。

*Kare wa karaoke o utaida**su to** nakanaka yamenai.*

Once he starts singing to karaoke he doesn't readily stop.

出かけるとすぐに雨が降り出した。

*Dekake**ru to** sugu ni ame ga furidashita.*

As soon as I left home, it began to rain.

あの角を右に曲がるとバス停があります。

*Ano kado o migi ni maga**ru to** basu tei ga arimasu.*

If you turn to the right at that corner there's a bus stop.

私は本屋に行くとよく立ち読みをしていた。

*Watashi wa hon'ya ni i**ku to** yoku tachiyomi o shite ita.*

I would often browse through books when I went to bookstores.

(unlike *tara*, the action expressed after *to* may be of the subject's own volition)

4. After interrogative word + volitional form of verb

彼が何をしようと私には関係ありません。

*Kare ga **nani o shiyō to** watashi ni wa kankei arimasen.*

No matter what he may do, I have nothing to do with it.

5. After statement in reported speech or quotation
(the statement must end with dictionary, *nai-,* or *ta*-form of
verb/adjective, *da*, a particle, or command form of verb)

彼女はもうすぐ来ると思います。

***Kanojo wa mō sugu kuru to** omoimasu.*

I think (that) she will come soon.

彼は行きたくないと言っていました。

*Kare wa **ikitaku nai to** itte imashita.*

He said that he didn't want to go.

彼は来月日本に行くと書いてきました。

*Kare wa **raigetsu nihon ni iku to** kaite kimashita.*

He wrote that he is coming to Japan next month.

彼女はいつでも遊びに来て下さいと言っていましたよ。

*Kanojo wa **itsu demo asobi ni kite kudasai to** itte imashita yo.*

She said to please come and see her any time.

これは何だと思いますか。

***Kore wa nan da to** omoimasu ka.*

What do you think this is?

店は8時から17時までと書いてあります。

***Mise wa hachi ji kara jū shichi ji made to** kaite arimasu.*

It is written that the shop is open from eight to seventeen (five)
o'clock.

6. After (adjectival) noun/adjective that describes the object

私は犬をケンと呼んでいます。

*Watashi wa inu o **ken to** yonde imasu.*

I call my dog Ken.

みんなそれをいいと思っています。

*Minna sore o **ii to** omotte imasu.*
Everybody thinks that is good.
彼らは彼の行為を無罪と見なした。
*Karera wa kare no kōi o **muzai to** minashita.*
They regarded his behavior as innocent.

7. After word/clause that describes some other word
   ファミコンと呼ばれるテレビゲームがはやっています。
   ***Famikon to** yobareru terebi gēmu ga hayatte imasu.*
   A video game called Famicon is popular.
   私はその町で最高だとされるホテルに泊った。
   *Watashi wa **sono machi de saikō da to** sareru hoteru ni tomatta.*
   I stayed at a hotel reputed to be the best in town.

8. After noun/clause expressing criterion for comparison
   あなたの時計は私が買ったのと同じです。
   *Anata no tokei wa **watashi ga katta no to** onaji desu.*
   Your watch is the same as the one that I bought.
   この本は私が注文したのと違います。
   *Kono hon wa **watashi ga chūmon shita no to** chigaimasu.*
   This book is not the one I ordered.

9. After specific adverb/imitative word
   (*to* may be dropped)
   もっとゆっくり(と)話してくれませんか。
   *Motto **yukkuri (to)** hanashite kuremasen ka.*
   Will you speak more slowly?
   酔っ払いがふらふら(と)歩いていますよ。
   *Yopparai ga **furafura (to)** aruite imasu yo.*
   A drunk is staggering around.

→ See also *ba, koto, tara, temo, to ka*

to ka　とか

PARTICLE MEANING: some kind of (things/persons/actions/states) like . . ., mainly . . . and. . .

1. Between nouns

   私はロックとかジャズをよく聞きます。

   *Watashi wa **rokku to ka jazu** o yoku kikimasu.*

   I usually listen to (music like) rock and jazz.

   私はトムとかマイクとよく親しい話をします。

   *Watashi wa **tomu to ka maiku** to yoku shitashii hanashi o shimasu.*

   I usually have intimate talks mainly with people like Tom and Mike.

2. After dictionary form of each of two successive verbs, followed by *suru*

   一人の時はテレビを見るとかレコードを聞くとかします。

   *Hitori no toki wa terebi o mi**ru to ka** rekōdo o ki**ku to ka** shimasu.*

   I watch television or listen to records when I'm alone.

3. After quoted statement

   (indicates a quotation of uncertain content)

   彼女は仕事をやめるとか言っていました。

   *Kanojo wa shigoto o yameru **to ka** itte imashita.*

   She said something like she would quit her job.

4. Followed by *iū*

   山本さんとかいう女の人から電話ですよ。

   *Yamamoto-san **to ka iū** onna no hito kara denwa desu yo.*

   There's a telephone call for you from a woman named something like Ms. Yamamoto.

→ See also *ni, tari, to, to iū, ya*

toki ni　時に

CONJUNCTION MEANING: (at the time) when . . ., as . . ., while, whenever, in case of

Toki literally means "time" and *ni* "at." *Ni* is sometimes omitted, replaced by *wa*, or followed by *wa*.

1. After dictionary form of verb/adjective

外国に行く時にはトラベラーズチェックを持っていきます。

*Gaikoku ni **iku toki ni** wa toraberāzu chekku o motte ikimasu.*

When I go abroad, I take traveler's checks.

家を出る時に雪が降って来ました。

*Ie o de**ru toki ni** yuki ga futte kimashita.*

It began to snow as I was leaving home.

私は読書をする時は音楽を聞きます。

*Watashi wa dokusho o su**ru toki wa** ongaku o kikimasu.*

I listen to music while reading books.

出かける時には戸締まりをしなさい。

*Dekake**ru toki ni** wa tojimari o shinasai.*

When you go out, make sure to lock the doors.

今度そこへ行く時にはカメラを持って行きましょう。

*Kondo soko e **iku toki ni** wa kamera o motte ikimashō.*

Let's take a camera with us the next time we go there.

暑い時はビールがうまい。

*Atsu**i toki wa** biiru ga umai.*

When it is hot, beer is tasty.

彼は私が悲しい時にはいつも励ましてくれます。

*Kare wa watashi ga kanashi**i toki ni** wa itsumo hagemashite kuremasu.*

He always cheers me up when I am sad.

2. After *ta*-form of verb/adjective

私が来た時には彼女はまだ来ていませんでした。

*Watashi ga ki**ta toki ni** wa kanojo wa mada kite imasen deshita.*

When I came, she had not yet arrived.

困った時はいつでもお手伝いします。

*Koma**tta toki wa** itsu demo o-tetsudai shimasu.*

I'll help you whenever you're in a bind.

食事をした時には「ごちそうさま」と言います。

*Shokuji o shi**ta toki ni** wa "gochisō-sama" to iimasu.*

After having a meal we say, "*gochisō-sama.*"

3. After noun + *no*

私は大学生の時に哲学を専攻していました。

*Watashi wa **daigakusei no toki ni** tetsugaku o senkō shite imashita.*

When I was a university student, I was specializing in philosophy.

火事の時にはこの赤いボタンを押して下さい。

***Kaji no toki ni** wa kono akai botan o oshite kudasai.*

Push this red button in case of fire.

(*bāi* may replace *toki* when expressing "in case of")

緊急の時には電話を下さい。

***Kinkyū no toki ni** wa denwa o kudasai.*

Please call me up in case of emergency.

4. After adjectival noun + *na*

これは必要な時に自由に使って下さい。

*Kore wa **hitsuyō-na toki ni** jiyū ni tsukatte kudasai.*

Please use this freely whenever you need it.

5. After (adjectival) noun + *datta*
   私が学生だった時には授業料は安かった。
   *Watashi ga **gakusei datta toki ni** wa jugyōryō wa yasukatta.*
   When I was a student, the tuition was cheap.
→ See also *ato de, mae ni, tara, to, tsuide ni, uchi ni*

tokoro　ところ

NOUN MEANING: a place, a point in time

Followed by a particle or *da/desu/datta/deshita* it expresses: where somebody is, a place which is . . ., be about to (do), be going to (do), on the verge of, in the middle of (some action or state), have just (done), have been (doing), just as, or nearly (did something).

1. After noun expressing person + *no*
   私のところに来て下さい。
   ***Watashi no tokoro** ni kite kudasai.*
   Please come to the place where I am. (Please come to me.)
   東京に行った時は兄のところに泊ります。
   *Tōkyō ni itta toki wa **ani no tokoro** ni tomarimasu.*
   When I visit Tokyo, I'll stay at my older brother's.
2. After word expressing length of time/distance + *no*
   大学は駅から歩いて15分のところにあります。
   *Daigaku wa eki kara aruite **jū go fun no tokoro** ni arimasu.*
   The university is at a place which is fifteen minutes from the station on foot. (The university is a fifteen-minute walk from the station.)

郵便局はここから約５百メートルのところです。

*Yūbinkyoku wa koko kara yaku **go hyaku mētoru no tokoro** desu.*

The post office is about five hundred meters from here.

3. After dictionary form of verb

ちょうど仕事を終わるところです。

*Chōdo shigoto o owa**ru tokoro** desu.*

I am just about to finish work.

「どこへ行くんですか。」「温泉に泊りに行くところです。」

*"Doko e iku n desu ka." "Onsen ni tomari ni i**ku tokoro** desu."*

"Where are you going?" "I'm about to go stay at a hot spring."

電話した時彼女は家を出るところでした。

*Denwa shita toki kanojo wa ie o de**ru tokoro** deshita.*

She was about to leave home when I called her.

新幹線に乗り遅れるところでした。

*Shinkansen ni noriokure**ru tokoro** deshita.*

We were on the verge of missing the shinkansen.

今そのことについて彼女と話しているところです。

*Ima sono koto ni tsuite kanojo to hanashite i**ru tokoro** desu.*

I am in the middle of talking to her about that now.

4. After *ta*-form of verb

ちょうど食事の準備ができたところです。

*Chōdo shokuji no junbi ga deki**ta tokoro** desu.*

Dinner preparations have just been completed.

さきほど着いたところです。

*Saki hodo tsui**ta tokoro** desu.*

I arrived just now.

銀行を出たところで彼女に会いました。

*Ginkō o de**ta tokoro** de kanojo ni aimashita.*

I met her just as I went out of the bank.
寝ようとしていたところへ電話がかかってきました。
*Neyō to shite **ita tokoro** e denwa ga kakatte kimashita.*
The telephone rang just as I was going to bed.

5. After dictionary form of adjective
お忙しいところ、どうもすいません。
*O-isogashii **tokoro**, dōmo suimasen.*
I'm sorry to trouble you when you are busy.

tokoro ga ところが

CONJUNCTION MEANING: but, however, and

1. After *ta*-form of verb
買物をしに来たところが店が閉まっていました。
*Kaimono o shi ni k**ita tokoro ga** mise ga shimatte imashita.*
I came to do my shopping, but the store was closed.
やってみたところがうまく行きました。
*Yatte m**ita tokoro ga** umaku ikimashita.*
I tried it, and it worked well.

2. At the beginning of sentence
彼にお金を貸してあげた。ところがまだ返してくれない。
*Kare ni o-kane o kashite ageta. **Tokoro ga** mada kaeshite kurenai.*
I lent him some money. But he has not returned it to me yet.
東京はいい町です。ところが暑すぎます。
*Tōkyō wa ii machi desu. **Tokoro ga** atsusugimasu.*
Tokyo's a good town. But it's too hot.

→ See also *daga, dakedo, ga (2), keredo(mo)*

to shitemo としても

CONJUNCTION MEANING: even though/if, no matter . . .

Tatoe may also be put at the beginning of the clause for emphasis. The *to* may be replaced by *ni*.

1. After dictionary form of verb/adjective
   お金を持っているとしてもそんな高い物を買ってはいけない。
   *O-kane o motte **iru to shitemo** sonna takai mono o kattewa ikenai.*
   Even though you have the money, you should not buy such an expensive thing.
   たとえ日本語がむずかしいとしてもあきらめずに勉強して下さい。
   *Tatoe nihongo ga muzukash**ii to shitemo** akiramezu ni benkyō shite kudasai.*
   Even if Japanese is difficult, continue studying and don't give up.

2. After *nai*-form of verb
   たとえ要らないとしても支払わなければなりません。
   *Tatoe ira**nai to shitemo** shiharawanakereba ikemasen.*
   Even if you don't need it, you must pay for it.

3. After *ta*-form of verb/adjective
   たとえ何が起こったとしてもあきらめません。
   *Tatoe nani ga okot**ta to shitemo** akiramemasen.*
   No matter what happens, I won't give up.
   彼がそれを知らなかったとしてもその過ちは許されない。
   *Kare ga sore o shiranakat**ta to shitemo** sono ayamachi wa yurusarenai.*

Even though he didn't know about it, that is an unforgivable mistake.

4. After (adjectival) noun + *da/datta*
それが当然だとしても納得できません。
*Sore ga **tōzen da to shitemo** nattoku dekimasen.*
Even if it is natural, I just can't understand it.
たとえそれが本当だったとしても彼女を軽蔑しません。
*Tatoe sore ga **hontō datta to shitemo** kanojo o keibetsu shimasen.*
Even if it were true, I wouldn't despise her.

→ See also *temo*

to sureba とすれば

CONJUNCTION MEANING: if . . . (ever), assuming that . . ., if that is the case

Sureba (the *ba*-form of *suru*) may be replaced with *shitara* or *suru to*.

1. After dictionary form of verb/adjective
車を買うとすれば小さいのがいい。
*Kuruma o ka**u to sureba** chiisai no ga ii.*
If I ever buy a car, a small one would be better.
彼がかしこいとすれば何か面白い計画しているにちがいない。
*Kare ga kashiko**i to sureba** nanika omoshiroi keikaku shite iru ni chigai nai.*
Assuming that he is clever, he is no doubt making some interesting plan.

2. After *nai*-form of verb
彼ができないとすればだれにしてもらおう。
*Kare ga deki**nai to sureba** dare ni shite moraō.*
Assuming that he can't, who shall we have do it?

3. After *ta*-form of verb/adjective
彼がうそをついたとすれば彼女にもたずねるべきだ。
*Kare ga uso o tsui**ta to sureba** kanojo ni mo tazuneru beki da.*
Assuming that he told a lie, you should ask her about it, too.

4. After (adjectival) noun + *da*
彼が先生だとすれば何を教えているのだろう。
*Kare ga **sensei da to sureba** nani o oshiete iru no darō.*
Assuming that he is a teacher, I wonder what he is teaching.
これがだめだとすればどんなものが良いのだろう。
*Kore ga **dame da to sureba** donna mono ga yoi no darō.*
Assuming that this is no good, what kind of things will be good?

5. At the beginning of sentence
彼はかぜをひいたと言っています。とすれば、あなたに頼まなければなりません。
*Kare wa kaze o hiita to itte imasu. **To sureba**, anata ni tanoma-nakereba narimasen.*
He says that he has a cold. If that is the case, I have to ask a favor of you.

→ See also *ba*, *nara*, *tara*, *to*

totemo とても
ADVERB MEANING: very, terribly, (not). . .at all, (not). . .possibly

1. Before adjective/adjectival noun

今日はとても暑いですね。
*Kyō wa **totemo atsui** desu ne.*
Today is very hot, isn't it?
そこはとても危険なので入ってはいけません。
*Soko wa **totemo kiken-na** node haittewa ikemasen.*
That place is very dangerous so you must not go in.

2. Used with negative potential verb
この寒さにはとても我慢できません。
*Kono samusa ni wa **totemo** gaman **dekimasen**.*
I can't possibly put up with this cold.

3. Used in statement expressing improbability
(takes a negative verb)
とても間に合う見込みはありません
***Totemo** mani au mikomi wa **arimasen**.*
There is no hope at all that we'll make it in time.

→ See also *amari, mattaku*

to iū   という

PHRASE MEANING: of, called, saying that, the fact that

1. After noun in apposition to the following word
私は神戸という都市に住んでいます。
*Watashi wa **kōbe to iū toshi** ni sunde imasu.*
I live in a city called Kobe. (I live in the city of Kobe.)
佐藤という人が会いに来ています。
***Satō to iū hito** ga ai ni kite imasu.*
A Mr. Sato is here to see you.

2. After statement in apposition to the following word
彼女は彼が無事だという知らせを聞いて喜んだ。

*Kanojo wa **kare ga buji da to iū shirase** o kiite yorokonda.*
She was happy to hear the news that he was all right.

3. After statement, followed by *no/koto*
(nominalizes the preceding statement)

彼が結婚したというのは本当です。

***Kare ga kekkon shita to iū no** wa hontō desu.*
It is true that he got married.

彼女が入院しているということを知っていますか。

***Kanojo ga nyūin shite iru to iū koto** o shitte imasu ka.*
Do you know that she is in the hospital?

→ See also *koto, no, to*

tsuide ni　ついでに

PHRASE MEANING: on the way, while . . ., incidentally

This phrase implies that some opportunity is taken advantage of in order to do something else.

1. After dictionary form of verb
銀行へ行くついでにこの手紙をポストに入れて下さい。

*Ginkō e i**ku tsuide ni** kono tegami o posuto ni irete kudasai.*
Please mail this letter on your way to the bank.

コーヒーを飲むついでにケーキも食べましょう。

*Kōhii o no**mu tsuide ni** kēki mo tabemashō.*
While we're drinking coffee, let's have some cake, too.

2. After *ta*-form of verb
彼に会ったついでにそれを頼みました。

*Kare ni at**ta tsuide ni** sore o tanomimashita.*
I asked him to do it since I met him.

映画を見に行ったついでに買物をして来ました。
*Eiga o mi ni itta **tsuide ni** kaimono o shite kimashita.*
While I went (out) to see a movie I did my shopping.

3. After noun + *no*
旅行のついでに昔の友人に会って来ました。
***Ryokō no tsuide ni** mukashi no yūjin ni atte kimashita.*
I met my old friend while traveling.

4. At the beginning of sentence
ついでにひとつ大事なことを言っておきます。
***Tsuide ni** hitotsu daiji-na koto o itte okimasu.*
While I am at it, let me tell you one important thing.

→ See also *toki ni*

tsumori desu　つもりです

PHRASE MEANING: be going to, intend to, plan to, mean to, expect (somebody) to, think/fancy that

Tsumori is a noun expressing intention, expectation, or fancy. It can also be used with *de*.

1. After dictionary form of verb
日本ではどんな仕事を探すつもりですか。
*Nihon de wa donna shigoto o saga**su tsumori desu** ka.*
What kind of job do you intend to look for in Japan?
一生懸命働いてお金をたくさん貯めるつもりです。
*Isshōkenmei hataraite o-kane o takusan tame**ru tsumori desu**.*
I plan to work hard and save a lot of money.
この写真は彼女にあげるつもりでした。
*Kono shashin wa kanojo ni age**ru tsumori deshita**.*

I intended to give this photograph to her.

傷つけるつもりはありませんでした。

Kizutsukeru tsumori wa arimasen deshita.

I didn't mean to hurt you.

少年は日本に住むつもりで日本語を勉強した。

Shōnen wa nihon ni sumu tsumori de nihongo o benkyō shita.

The boy studied Japanese with the intention of living in Japan.

2. After *nai*-form of verb

私は今年の夏はどこにも行かないつもりです。

*Watashi wa kotoshi no natsu wa doko ni mo ika**nai tsumori desu***.

I have no intention of going anywhere this summer.

3. After dictionary form of adjective

彼女は自分ではかわいいつもりでいる。

*Kanojo wa jibun de wa kawai**i tsumori de** iru.*

She fancies herself to be cute.

4. After *ta*-form of verb/adjective

ちゃんと書いたつもりですが。

*Chanto kai**ta tsumori desu** ga.*

I thought that I wrote it properly, but . . . (didn't I?)

それで十分良かったつもりですが。

*Sore de jūbun yoka**tta tsumori des**u ga.*

I thought it was good enough, but . . . (wasn't it?)

5. After noun + *no*

彼は芸術家のつもりでいます。

*Kare wa **geijutsuka no tsumori de** imasu.*

He fancies himself an artist.

何のつもりでそんなことをしたのですか。

***Nan no tsumori de** sonna koto o shita no desu ka.*

With what intention did you do such a thing?

6. After adjectival noun + *na/datta*

彼らは勤勉なつもりでいる。

*Karera wa **kinben-na tsumori de** iru.*

They fancy themselves diligent.

彼はそうするのが賢明だったつもりでいます。

*Kare wa sō suru no ga **kenmei datta tsumori de** imasu.*

He thinks it was wise of him to do so.

→ See also *toki ni*

tte って

INFORMAL PARTICLE (used mostly but not exclusively by women) that emotionally emphasizes the subject or object noun, a quoted statement, or a concessive clause

1. After subject/object
   (used in place of *wa* to emphasize the subject/object)

   マイクってとてもおもしろい人ですね。

   ***Maiku-tte** totemo omoshiroi hito desu ne.*

   Mike is a very interesting man, isn't he?

   あの事故って彼が起こしたんですよ。

   *Ano **jiko-tte** kare ga okoshita n desu yo.*

   That accident—he caused it, you know.

2. After dictionary form of verb
   (makes verb into noun equivalent)

   漢字を覚えるってむずかしいですね。

   *Kanji o **oboeru-tte** muzukashii desu ne.*

   Memorizing kanji is difficult, isn't it?

3. After *ta*-form of verb
   (expresses concessive clauses)
   今頃気付いたってもう遅いよ。
   *Ima goro **kizuita-tte** mō osoi yo.*
   Noticing now is really too late.

4. After quoted statement
   (a verb after *-tte* is often omitted when it is obvious)
   「彼女は行かないって言ってますよ。」「行かないって？」
   "*Kanojo wa **ikanai-tte** ittemasu yo.*" "***Ikanai-tte**?*"
   "She says she won't go." "She won't go? (Really?)"
   絶対に良くなるって。
   Zettai ni yoku naru-tte.
   No doubt it will get better.

→ See also *no, koto, to, wa*

uchi de/kara　うちで／から

PHRASE MEANING: among, between, of

Uchi can be replaced with *naka*.

1. After noun + *no*
   彼らのうちでだれが日本語を話せますか。
   ***Karera no uchi de** dare ga nihongo o hanasemasu ka.*
   Which of them can speak Japanese?
   3冊のうちから好きな本を1冊選んで下さい。
   ***San satsu no uchi kara** suki-na hon o issatsu erande kudasai.*
   Please choose your favorite book among the three.

→ See also *aida ni*

uchi ni　うちに

CONJUNCTION OR PHRASE MEANING: within, during, in (some state), out of, while, before (with a negative)

When it follows a verb, the main clause will state something that should be done in a hurry.

1. After noun + *no*

数か月のうちに日本語が話せるようになるでしょう。

Sūkagetsu no uchi ni nihongo ga hanaseru yō ni naru deshō.

You'll be able to speak Japanese within a few months.

朝のうちに出発の準備をしておきます。

Asa no uchi ni shuppatsu no junbi o shite okimasu.

I'll finish my preparations for the departure during the morning.

国会は混乱のうちに閉会した。

*Kokkai wa **konran no uchi ni** heikai shita.*

The National Diet closed in the midst of confusion.

彼は1年のうち3ヶ月は仕事で家にいません。

*Kare wa **ichi nen no uchi** san kagetsu wa shigoto de ie ni imasen.*

He is away from home on business three months a year.

(*ni* is dropped when a definite number is stated)

15人のうち10人が女性でした。

Jū go nin no uchi jū nin ga josei deshita.

Ten out of fifteen persons were female.

2. After dictionary form of verb/adjective

何でもできるうちにやっておくのがいいと思います。

*Nan demo deki**ru uchi ni** yatte oku no ga ii to omoimasu.*

I think it is good to get whatever possible done while you can.

時間があるうちにその仕事を片付けてしまいたい。

*Jikan ga a**ru uchi ni** sono shigoto o katazukete shimaitai.*

I want to get through with that task while there is time.

明るいうちに家へ帰ってきなさい。

*Akar**ui uchi ni** ie e kaette kinasai.*

Come back home while it is still light.

鉄は熱いうちに打て。

*Tetsu wa ats**ui uchi ni** ute.*

Strike while the iron is hot.

3. After *nai*-form of verb

雨が降らないうちにバスに乗りましょう。

*Ame ga fura**nai uchi ni** basu ni norimashō.*

Let's get on a bus before it rains.

忘れないうちにメモしておいた方がいい。

*Wasure**nai uchi ni** memo shite oita hō ga ii.*

It is better to jot it down before you forget.

さめないうちにスープをどうぞ。

*Same**nai uchi ni** sūpu o dōzo.*

Please have your soup before it gets cold.

4. After adjectival noun + *na*

まだここが安全なうちに去った方がいい。

*Mada koko ga **anzen-na uchi ni** satta hō ga ii.*

You had better leave here while it is safe.

→ See also *aida ni, mae, nai, uchi ni*

wa　は

PARTICLE INDICATING: the subject or object of verb as the topic of a sentence, something that is contrasted with some other thing, something that is singled out for special attention

Wa cannot be used in a relative clause, and is rarely used in other subordinate clauses (conditional/concessive clauses) when it has already been used to introduce a word as the topic of the whole sentence or the main clause.

Interrogative words such as *nani* or *dare* may not be followed by *wa* because they cannot be a topic themselves. Note that the particle *wa* is expressed by は, not by わ.

1. After subject
   (The predicate after *wa* only describes one attribute of the subject; therefore, the existence of the subject needs to be already known to the hearer. *Ga,* on the other hand, tells complete information about a subject at the time of speaking. The subject in a subordinate clause must be indicated by *ga.*)

   彼女は大学生です。英語を勉強しています。

   Kanojo wa *daigakusei desu. Eigo o benkyō shite imasu.*

   She is a college student. She is studying English.

   あの人がポールです。彼はアメリカから来ました。

   Ano hito ga pōru desu. ***Kare wa*** *amerika kara kimashita.*

   That man is Paul. He came from America.

   彼が買った車はドイツ製です。とてもいい車です。

   Kare ga katta kuruma wa *doitsu-sei desu. Totemo ii kuruma desu.*

   The car that he bought is German-made. It's a very nice one.

   日本語をマスターするのはむずかしいです。でも楽しいです。

Nihongo o masutā suru no wa muzukashii desu. Demo tanoshii desu.

It is difficult to master Japanese. But it's fun.

2. After object

(When the object of a verb is indicated by *wa*, the subject of the verb must be indicated by *ga* and placed after the object + *wa*, except when it is expressed in contrast with another subject.)

この本はマリがきのう貸してくれたんですが、もう読みました。

*Kono **hon wa** mari ga kinō kashite kureta n desu ga, mō yomimashita.*

Mari lent this book to me yesterday, and I've already read it.

英語は日本人が覚えるにはむずかしすぎるかもしれません。

Eigo wa nihonjin ga oboeru ni wa muzukashisugiru kamo shiremasen.

It may be too difficult for Japanese to learn English.

3. After topic of sentence

スポーツは何が好きですか。

Supōtsu wa nani ga suki desu ka.

Talking about sports, what do you like? (What sports do you like?)

ミチコさんは髪がきれいですね。

Michiko-san wa kami ga kirei desu ne.

As for Michiko, her hair is beautiful, isn't it? (Michiko has beautiful hair, doesn't she?)

4. After each of two contrasted words

今日は仕事を休みますが、明日は必ず働きます。

Kyō wa shigoto o yasumimasu ga, asu wa kanarazu hatarakimasu.

Today I'll take off from my job, but tomorrow I'll be sure to work.

彼は行くそうですが、私はわかりません。

Kare wa *iku sō desu ga,* ***watashi wa*** *wakarimasen.*

He says that he will go, but I don't know (whether I will go or not).

(the contrasted word is sometimes not stated)

彼はタバコは吸いません。

Kare wa ***tabako wa*** *suimasen.*

He doesn't smoke (but he may drink).

私は毎日3時間は勉強します。

Watashi wa mainichi ***san jikan wa*** *benkyō shimasu.*

I study at least three hours every day (and sometimes longer).

5. After noun + *de*, adjectival noun + *de/ni*, or *ku*-form of adjective

    (a word to be contrastively negated is first introduced with *wa*)

    これは私のかばんではありません。

    Kore wa ***watashi no kaban de wa*** *arimasen.*

    This is not my bag.

    彼女は病気ではありません。

    Kanojo wa ***byōki de wa*** *arimasen.*

    She is not sick.

    それは簡単にはできません。

    Sore wa ***kantan ni wa*** *dekimasen.*

    You can't do it easily.

    この時計は安くはありません。

    Kono tokei wa ***yasuku wa*** *arimasen.*

    This watch is not cheap.

6. After particle

    (the word preceding the particle is usually contrasted with

some other word that is not stated)

ここでは静かにして下さい。

*Koko **de wa** shizuka ni shite kudasai.*

Please keep quiet here. (You can talk somewhere else.)

あの服よりはこのほうがいい。

*Ano fuku **yori wa** kono hō ga ii.*

This dress is better than that one. (But possibly there is a better one.)

10時まではテレビを見てもよろしい。

*Jū ji **made wa** terebi o mitemo yoroshii.*

You may watch television until ten o'clock (but no later).

これからはがんばります。

*Kore **kara wa** ganbarimasu.*

From now on I'll do my best (since I've been lazy).

東京では物価が高すぎますね。

*Tōkyō **de wa** bukka ga takasugimasu ne.*

In Tokyo prices are too high, aren't they?

→ See also *dewa (1), ga (1)*

wake　わけ

NOUN MEANING: the reason why/for

It can be replaced with its synonym *riyū*.

1. After dictionary or *nai-* form of verb/adjective

   日本語を学ぶわけは興味があるからです。

   *Nihongo o mana**bu wake** wa kyōmi ga aru kara desu.*

   The reason why I learn Japanese is that I am interested in it.
2. Used in idiomatic expression (may not be replaced by *riyū*)

(followed by *ni wa ikanai*, meaning "should not")

あなたがしないなら私もするわけには行きません。

*Anata ga shinai nara watashi mo suru **wake ni wa ikimasen***.

If you don't do it, I shouldn't either.

(followed by *de wa nai*, meaning "it doesn't necessarily mean that")

あなたが悪いわけではない。

*Anata ga warui **wake dewa nai***.

It doesn't mean that you are wrong.

すべてあなたに賛成するわけではありません。

*Subete anata ni sansei suru **wake dewa arimasen***.

It doesn't mean that I quite agree with you.

(followed by *da/desu*, meaning "it's natural that," "that's why")

それでみんな集っているわけですね。

*Sore de minna atsumatte iru **wake desu** ne*.

That's why they are all gathering, isn't it?

3. After *nai*-form of verb

彼女を手伝わないわけには行きません。

*Kanojo o tetsudawa**nai wake ni wa ikimasen***.

I should not keep from helping her. (I have to help her.)

4. After *ta*-form of verb/adjective

仕事をやめたわけは言いたくありません。

*Shigoto o yame**ta wake** wa iitaku arimasen*.

I don't want to tell you why I quit my job.

子供がおとなしかったわけが分りました。

*Kodomo ga otonashika**tta wake** ga wakarimashita*.

I understand why the child was quiet.

必ずしもあなたの新しい提案に同意したわけではありません。

232 • GRAMMATICAL FUNCTION WORDS

*Kanarazushimo anata no atarashii teian ni dōi shita **wake** dewa arimasen.*

I don't necessarily agree to your new proposal.

それで遅れたわけですね。

*Sore de okureta **wake** desu ne.*

That's why you were late, isn't it?

5. After adjectival noun + *na*

彼がずっと健康なわけは早寝早起きをしているからだ。

*Kare ga zutto **kenkō-na wake** wa hayane hayaoki o shite iru kara da.*

The reason why he remains healthy is that he always goes to bed early and gets up early.

別にそれが嫌いなわけではありません。

*Betsu ni sore ga **kirai-na wake** dewa arimasen.*

It doesn't mean that I particularly hate it.

それではたいへんなわけだ。

*Sore dewa **taihen-na wake** da.*

If that is the case, it will of course be difficult.

6. After (adjectival) noun + *datta*

私たちはずっと無関心だったわけではありません。

*Watashi tachi wa zutto **mukanshin datta wake** dewa arimasen.*

We were not necessarily indifferent throughout.

そういう事情で消極的だったわけですね。

*Sō iū jijō de **shōkyoku teki datta wake** desu ne.*

You have a good reason to have been passive under the circumstances.

wo を

→ See *o*

wo motte　をもって
→ See *o motte*

wo tōshite　を通して
→ See *o tōshite*

ya　や
PARTICLE MEANING: and . . . (and the like), or, as soon as

1. Between nouns
   老人や子供を大切にすべきです。
   ***Rōjin ya kodomo** o taisetsu ni subeki desu.*
   You should care for old people and children.
   私はジャズやロックは聞きません。
   *Watashi wa **jazu ya rokku** wa kikimasen.*
   I don't listen to jazz or rock.
2. After dictionary form of verb
   地震が起こるや私はあわてて飛び出した。
   *Jishin ga oko**ru ya** watashi wa awatete tobidashita.*
   As soon as the earthquake occurred, I jumped out in a hurry.
→ See also *mo, nado, ni, tari, to, to ka*

yasui　やすい
ADJECTIVE MEANING: (be) easy to (do), (be) liable to (do), (be) apt to
(do)

1. After conjunctive form of verb

私は風邪にかかりやすい。

*Watashi wa kaze ni **kakariyasui**.*

I am prone to catching colds.

彼は飲むと怒りやすくなる。

*Kare wa nomu to **okoriyasuku naru**.*

He is apt to get angry when he drinks.

このカメラは扱いやすい。

*Kono kamera wa **atsukaiyasui**.*

This camera is easy to handle.

彼は親しくなりやすい人です。

*Kare wa shitashiku **nariyasui** hito desu.*

He is a man who is easy to make friends with.

→ See also *nikui*

yō 用

SUFFIX MEANING: suitable for, for (. . . use)

1. After noun

この本は初心者用です。

*Kono hon wa **shoshinsha yō** desu.*

This book is suitable for beginners.

(*no* may be used between *yō* and the noun it modifies)

家庭用 (の) 洗剤はありますか。

***Katei yō** (no) senzai wa arimasu ka.*

Do you have detergent for home use?

登山用 (の) 靴を買いましたか。

***Tozan yō** (no) kutsu o kaimashita ka.*

Did you buy shoes for mountain climbing?

yō desu　ようです

PREDICATIVE PHRASE MEANING: seem to, look like, be likely to, such as, like, as, such . . . as, to the effect

It is used to express a supposition the speaker makes based on observation. Its adjectival form is *yō-na* and its adverbial form is *yō ni*.

1. After dictionary form of verb/adjective
   彼は外国へ旅行に行くようです。
   *Kare wa gaikoku e ryokō ni **iku yō desu**.*
   He looks like he will travel abroad (because he is carrying his suitcase).
   その試験はやさしいようです。
   *Sono shiken wa yasashi**i yō desu**.*
   The examination seems easy (since many people passed it).
   彼女は仕事を辞めるようなことを言っていました。
   *Kanojo wa shigoto o yame**ru yō-na** koto o itte imashita.*
   She said that she might quit her job. (I heard so).
   もっと役に立つような道具を買いなさい。
   *Motto yaku ni ta**tsu yō-na** dōgu o kainasai.*
   You should buy more useful tools.
   その計画はあなたが思うようにはうまく行かないでしょう。
   *Sono keikaku wa anata ga omo**u yō ni** wa umaku ikanai deshō.*
   That plan will probably not work as well as you expect.
2. After *nai*-form of verb/adjective
   彼女は何も知らないようです。
   *Kanojo wa nani mo shira**nai yō desu**.*

She seems to know nothing about it.

彼女はあまり行きたくないようです。

*Kanojo wa amari ikitaku**nai yō desu**.*

It seems that she doesn't really want to go.

3. After *ta*-form of verb/adjective

彼女は入学試験に合格したようです。

*Kanojo wa nyūgaku shiken ni gōkaku shi**ta yō desu**.*

It seems that she passed the entrance examination.

彼の今日の仕事は厳しかったようです。

*Kare no kyō no shigoto wa kibishika**tta yō desu**.*

His work today seems to have been hard.

先に述べたように契約期間は1年です。

*Saki ni nobe**ta yō ni** keiyaku kikan wa ichi nen desu.*

As mentioned before, the term of the contract is one year.

4. After adjectival noun + *na*

彼は無事なようです。

*Kare wa **buji-na yō desu**.*

He seems to be all right (because I heard no bad news).

好きなようにして結構です。

***Suki-na yō ni** shite kekkō desu.*

You can do as you like.

5. After noun + *no*

彼は留守のようでした。

*Kare wa **rusu no yō deshita**.*

He seemed to be out (because there was no answer).

日本人ははちのように働くとよく言われる。

*Nihonjin wa **hachi no yō ni** hataraku to yoku iwareru.*

It is often said that the Japanese work like bees.

若い人は東京や大阪のような大都市に住みたがる。

*Wakai hito wa tōkyō ya **osaka no yō-na** dai toshi ni sumi-tagaru.*

Young people want to live in big cities like Tokyo and Osaka.

あなたのように日本語をうまく話してみたい。

***Anata no yō ni** nihongo o umaku hanashite mitai.*

I'd like to speak Japanese well like you.

いつものように家を出ましたが遅刻してしまいました。

***Itsumo no yō ni** ie o demashita ga chikoku shite shimai-mashita.*

I left home as usual but I was late.

6. Used with *marude*

   (precedes the noun and emphasizes the metaphor)

   あの犬はまるで熊のようだ。

   *Ano inu wa **marude kuma no yō da**.*

   That dog looks just like a bear.

   彼はまるで女のような人だ。

   *Kare wa **marude onna no yō-na** hito da.*

   He is exactly like a woman.

   彼女はまるで魚のように速く泳げます。

   *Kanojo wa **marude sakana no yō ni** hayaku oyogemasu.*

   She can swim as fast as a fish.

7. After the demonstrative nouns *kono, sono, ano*

   このようにお願いできますか。

   ***Kono yō ni** o-negai dekimasu ka.*

   Can you do me a favor like this?

   そのようなことを聞きました。

   ***Sono yō-na** koto o kikimashita.*

   I heard something to that effect.

   あのような美しい着物を見たことがありません。

Ano yō-na *utsukushii kimono o mita koto ga arimasen.*
I've never seen such a beautiful kimono.
→ See also *deshō, marude, mitai, rashii, sō desu*

yō ni　ように
ADVERBIAL PHRASE MEANING: so as to, in order to, so that . . . (can)

This *yō ni* differs from the adverbial form of *yō desu* mentioned above. The word or words before *yō ni* express a wish.

1. After dictionary form of verb
   私にも分るようにゆっくり日本語を話して下さい。
   *Watashi ni mo waka**ru yō ni** yukkuri nihongo o hanashite kudasai.*
   Please speak Japanese more slowly so that I can understand you too.
2. After *nai*-form of verb
   飛行機に遅れないように早く出発しましょう。
   *Hikōki ni okure**nai yō ni** hayaku shuppatsu shimashō.*
   Let's start early so as not to be late for the plane.
→ See also *naru, no ni, tame ni*

yō ni suru　ようにする
PREDICATIVE PHRASE MEANING: make sure that, take care that, try to (do), make it a rule to (do)

The progressive form *yō ni shite iru* expresses an habitual action.

1. After dictionary form of verb
   あす9時までにここに来るようにして下さい。
   *Asu ku ji made ni koko ni ku**ru yō ni shite** kudasai.*
   Please make sure that you come here by nine tomorrow.
   この頃は早寝早起きをするようにしています。
   *Kono goro wa hayane hayaoki o su**ru yō ni shite** imasu.*
   Recently I am going to bed and getting up early.
   毎日漢字をみっつ覚えるようにします。
   *Mainichi kanji o mittsu oboe**ru yō ni shimasu**.*
   I'll make it a rule to learn three kanji every day.

2. After *nai*-form of verb
   バスに遅れないようにして下さい。
   *Basu ni okure**nai yō ni shite** kudasai.*
   Please make sure that you don't miss the bus.

→ See also *suru*

yō ni iū　ように言う

PREDICATIVE PHRASE MEANING: tell (somebody) to (do something)

1. After dictionary form of verb
   きのう彼女に今日の3時にここへ来るように言いました。
   *Kinō kanojo ni kyō no san ji ni koko e ku**ru yō ni iimashita**.*
   Yesterday I told her to come here at three o'clock today.

2. After *nai*-form of verb
   彼にあまり飲まないように言いなさい。
   *Kare ni amari noma**nai yō ni iinasai**.*
   Tell him not to drink too much.
   (replacing *tanomu* with *iu* changes the meaning to "ask [some-
   body] to [do something]")

彼に手伝ってくれるように頼みましたか。

Kare ni tetsudatte kureru yō ni tanomimashita ka.

Did you ask him to help you?

→ See also *yō ni*

yori   より

PARTICLE MEANING: than, (not) . . . but, from, since, (out) of

In Japanese *yori*, *hodo*, and *hō* are used to express the comparative degree of adjectives and adverbs. The emphatic particle *mo* is often used after *yori*.

1. After noun
   日本語は英語よりもずいぶんむずかしいですね。

   *Nihongo wa **eigo yori** mo zuibun muzukashii desu ne.*

   Japanese is much more difficult than English, isn't it?

   あの特急の方がこの電車より早く着きます。

   *Ano tokkyū no hō ga kono **densha yori** hayaku tsukimasu.*

   That special express will arrive earlier than this train.

   今日はいつもより遅くなります。

   *Kyō wa **itsumo yori** osoku narimasu.*

   It will be later than usual today.

   香港行きの飛行機は3番ゲートより出発します。

   *Honkon yuki no hikōki wa san ban **gēto yori** shuppatsu shimasu.*

   The plane for Hong Kong departs from Gate 3.

   (when meaning "from," *yori* may be replaced by *kara*)

   開会式は10時より始まります。

Kaikaishiki wa jū ji yori hajimarimasu.

The opening ceremony will be held from ten.

2. After dictionary form of verb/adjective

家でテレビを見るより外へ出かける方がいい。

Ie de terebi o miru yori soto e dekakeru hō ga ii.

I like going out better than watching television at home.

こうするよりほかに方法がない。

Kō suru yori hoka ni hōhō ga nai.

There is nothing else to do but this.

同じものなら高いより安い方がいいに決まっています。

Onaji mono nara takai yori yasui hō ga ii ni kimatte imasu.

If they are the same, naturally the cheap one is better than the expensive one.

わずかなお金でもないよりはましです。

Wazuka-na o-kane demo nai yori wa mashi desu.

Even a small sum of money is better than none.

3. After *ta*-form of verb

その仕事は思ったよりやさしかったです。

Sono shigoto wa omotta yori yasashikatta desu.

That work was easier than I had expected.

4. After *nai*-form of verb

この本は読まないより読んだ方がいい。

Kono hon wa yomanai yori yonda hō ga ii.

It is better to read this book than not.

→ See also *hō, hō ga ii, hodo, kara, ni*

yoroshii　よろしい

ADJECTIVE MEANING: all right, okay

When used toward a person of higher status or to whom one wishes to show respect, it should be followed by *desu*.

1. After noun + *de*
   それでよろしいです。
   Sore de yoroshii *desu.*
   That will do.
   駅へ行くのにこの道でよろしいですか。
   *Eki e iku no ni kono **michi de yoroshii** desu ka.*
   Is this the right street to the station?
2. After interrogative word + *demo*
   いつでもよろしいですよ。
   Itsu demo yoroshii *desu yo.*
   Any time will be all right.
   どちらでもよろしいです。
   Dochira demo yoroshii *desu.*
   Either will do.
3. After *te*-form of verb (+ *mo*)
   電話を使ってもよろしい。
   *Denwa o tsuka**ttemo yoroshii**.*
   You may use the telephone.
   もう帰ってよろしいですか。
   *Mō kae**tte yoroshii** desu ka.*
   Is it all right if I go home now?
   ここでタバコを吸って (も) よろしいですか。
   *Koko de tabako o su**tte(mo) yoroshii** desu ka.*
   Is it all right if I smoke here?
   バス停までついて行って (も) よろしいですよ。

Basutei made tsuite itte(mo) yoroshii desu yo.
I'd be glad to accompany you to the bus stop.

4. After *ta*-form of verb + *hō ga*
やめた方がよろしいですよ。
Yameta hō ga yoroshii desu yo.
It would be better to stop it.

5. In conditional *ba*-form
よろしければ映画を見に行きませんか。
Yoroshikereba eiga o mi ni ikimasen ka.
If you feel like it, would you like to go to a movie?

→ See also *hō ga ii, temo ii*

zaru o enai　ざるを得ない

PREDICATIVE PHRASE MEANING: cannot help (doing), cannot help but (do), be obliged to (do), have no choice but to (do)

1. After the stem of *nai*-form of verb
私は旅行する計画をあきらめざるを得ません。
*Watashi wa ryokō suru keikaku o **akiramezaru o emasen**.*
I am obliged to give up the plan to take a trip.
あれには笑わざるを得ませんでした。
*Are ni wa **warawazaru o emasen** deshita.*
I could not help laughing at that.
彼らに協力せざるを得ない。
*Karera ni kyōryoku **sezaru o enai**.*
I have no choice but to cooperate with them.
(note the irregular stem of *suru* is *se*)

zenzen 全然

ADVERB MEANING: (not) at all, (not) in the least, (not) a bit, (not) anything, entirely, completely

1. Used with negative
   (total negation)
   日本語は全然書けません。
   *Nihongo wa **zenzen** kakemasen.*
   I cannot write in Japanese at all.
   そのことについては全然知りません。
   *Sono koto ni tsuite wa **zenzen** shirimasen.*
   I know nothing at all about it.
   彼女の言ったことは全然気にしていません。
   *Kanojo no itta koto wa **zenzen** ki ni shite imasen.*
   I don't care a bit about what she said.
2. Used with affirmative
   あなたの言うことは彼の言うことと全然違います。
   *Anata no iū koto wa kare no iū koto to **zenzen** chigaimasu.*
   What you say is entirely different from what he says.
→ See also *marude, mattaku*

zu ni ずに

PHRASE MEANING: without (doing), not (do something) but (do another thing)

It is equivalent to *nai de*.

1. After the stem of *nai*-form of verb
   あきらめずにがんばって下さい。

***Akiramezu ni** ganbatte kudasai.*

Do your best and don't give up.

チケットを見せずに会場に入ることはできません。

*Chiketto o **misezu ni** kaijō ni hairu koto wa dekimasen.*

You cannot enter the hall without showing the ticket.

彼は勉強もせずに遊んでいた。

*Kare wa benkyō mo **sezu ni** asonde ita.*

He was playing and didn't study.

(note the irregular stem of *suru* is *se*)

2. Followed by the verb *sumu*

    (meaning "can manage without [doing]," "not have to [do]")

    銀行からお金を借りずにすみそうです。

    *Ginkō kara o-kane o **karizu ni** sumisō desu.*

    I looks like we'll manage without borrowing money from the bank.

    わざわざ東京まで行かずにすみました。

    *Wazawaza tōkyō made **ikazu ni sumimashita**.*

    I didn't have to make a special trip to Tokyo.

→ See also *nai*

PART TWO

Grammatical Explanations

ADJECTIVAL NOUNS (also known as *na*-adjectives)
Words in this category can function as adjectives, adverbs, or less often, as ordinary nouns in the subject or object of a sentence.

Adjectival Noun Forms

Most adjectival nouns are followed by -*na* before a noun they modify, though some are followed by *no* (refer to List of Common Adjectival Nouns below). When used as adverbs, or as complements that describe the subject or object, they are followed by *ni*.

NOUN FORM	ADJECTIVE FORM	ADVERB FORM
shinsetsu (kindness)	*shinsetsu-na* (kind)	*shinsetsu ni* (kindly)
kirei (beauty)	*kirei-na* (beautiful)	*kirei ni* (beautifully)
byōdō (equality)	*byōdō no* (equal)	*byōdō ni* (equally)
jiyū (freedom)	*jiyū-na* (free)	*jiyū ni* (freely)
muda (waste)	*muda-na* (wasteful)	*muda ni* (wastefully)

1. NOUN FORM
   *Watashi wa motto **jiyū** ga hoshii.*
   I want more freedom.
   *Amari no **muda** wa sakenakereba naranai.*
   We have to avoid too much waste.
2. ADJECTIVE FORM
   *Kare wa **shinsetsu-na** hito desu ne.*
   He is a kind person, isn't he?
   *Dare demo koko dewa **byōdō no** kenri ga aru.*
   Everybody has equal rights here.
3. ADVERB FORM
   *Kare wa watashi tachi ni **shinsetsu ni** shite kuremashita.*
   He treated us kindly.
   *Kono shashin wa **kirei ni** torete imasu.*
   This photograph is taken beautifully.
4. AS COMPLEMENT
   *Kanojo wa totemo **kirei ni** narimashita.*

She became very beautiful.
*Te o **kirei ni** shite okinasai.*
Keep your hands clean.

Used in a Predicate

1. LIST OF VERBS/VERBAL PHRASES WHICH FOLLOW
   ADJECTIVAL NOUN
   When used in a predicate, the adjectival noun is followed by a
   verb or verbal phrase at the end of the sentence. The chart
   below lists these.

da/desu	Plain/polite aff. non-past
datta/deshita	Plain/polite aff. past
darō/deshō	Plain/polite aff. presumptive present
datta darō/deshō	Plain/polite aff. presumptive past
*ni naru darō/deshō	Plain/polite aff. presumptive future
dewa nai/arimasen	Plain/polite neg. non-past
dewa nakatta (*desu*)	Plain (polite) neg. past
dewa arimasen deshita	Polite neg. past
dewa nai darō/deshō	Plain/polite neg. presumptive present
dewa nakatta darō	Plain neg. presumptive past
dewa nakatta deshō	Polite neg. presumptive past

   (**ni naru* means "to become")

• When used at the end of a relative or other type of subordinate
  clause, *-na* or *-no* must be put at the end of the clause.
  *Kanojo wa **byōki-na** node koraremasen.*
  She cannot come because she is sick.
  *Sore wa wareware ni totte taihen **shinkoku-na** mondai desu.*
  It is a problem that is very serious to us.

List of Common Adjectival Nouns
aimai-na 曖昧(な) ambiguous, vague
akiraka-na 明らか(な) obvious, clear

anzen-na 安全(な) safe, secure
baka-na ばか(な) foolish, silly, stupid
benri-na 便利(な) convenient, useful
byōki no 病気(の) sick, diseased
chikaku no 近く(の) near, close
chūko no 中古(の) secondhand, used
daiji-na 大事(な) important, valuable
daijōbu-na 大丈夫(な) all right, safe
dame-na だめ(な) no good, impossible
detarame-na でたらめ(な) inaccurate, random
dokutoku no 独特(の) peculiar, unique
dōyō no 同様(の) the same, similar
fuben-na 不便(な) inconvenient
fukanō-na 不可能(な) impossible
fukuzatsu-na 複雑(な) complicated, complex
fushigi-na 不思議(な) strange, mysterious
futsū no 普通(の) usual, common, normal, ordinary
genki-na 元気(な) energetic, lively, healthy
gōka-na 豪華(な) deluxe, gorgeous
heibon-na 平凡(な) commonplace, ordinary
hen-na 変(な) odd, queer, strange
heta-na 下手(な) unskillful, awkward, clumsy
hima-na 暇(な) not busy, not engaged, free
hitsuyō-na 必要(な) necessary, indispensable
hontō no 本当(の) true, real, actual
ijō-na 異常(な) unusual, abnormal
iroiro-na いろいろ(な) various
jiyū-na 自由(な) free, liberal
jōbu-na 丈夫(な) durable, firm, tough
jōzu-na 上手(な) expert
jūbun-na 十分(な) enough, sufficient
jūyō-na 重要(な) important
kawaisō-na かわいそう(な) poor, pitiful
kanzen-na 完全(な) perfect, complete

kantan-na 簡単(な) simple, easy, brief
kiken-na 危険(な) dangerous, risky
kirei-na きれい(な) pretty, beautiful
majime-na まじめ(な) eanest, serious, honest
manzoku-na 満足(な) satisfactory, sufficient
mare-na まれ(な) rare, unusual
meiwaku-na 迷惑(な) troublesome, annoying
migoto-na 見事(な) splendid, excellent, skillful
muda-na 無駄(な) useless, wasteful, fruitless
muri-na 無理(な) impossible
nama no 生(の) raw, uncooked
nami no 並み(の) ordinary, common, average
nise no にせ(の) false, fake, counterfeit
o-kiniiri no お気に入り(の) favorite, pet
raku-na 楽(な) easy, comfortable
rippa-na 立派(な) splendid, great, superb
saigo no 最後(の) final, ultimate
saisho no 最初(の) first, original
seijitsu-na 誠実(な) sincere, honest
seikaku-na 正確(な) exact, accurate, precise
shinchō-na 慎重(な) careful
shinsetsu-na 親切(な) kind, kindly
shitsurei-na 失礼(な) impolite, rude
shizuka-na 静か(な) quiet, calm
suki-na 好き(な) favorite
sunao-na すなお(な) obedient, yielding
suteki-na すてき(な) nice, splendid
taihen-na 大変(な) terrible, serious, difficult
taikutsu-na 退屈(な) boring, tedious
taisetsu-na 大切(な) important, precious
tanjun-na 単純(な) simple, simple-minded
tashika-na 確か(な) definite, certain, sure
tegaru-na 手軽(な) handy, simple, light
teinei-na 丁寧(な) polite, courteous

tekitō-na 適当(な) suitable, appropriate, proper
tokubetsu-na 特別(な) special, particular, exceptional
tokui-na 得意(な) strong (point of ability), in one's line
tōzen no 当然(の) natural, reasonable
yukai-na 愉快(な) pleasant, enjoyable
yūmei-na 有名(な) famous, well-known, noted
yūshū-na 優秀(な) excellent, superior
zettai no 絶対(の) absolute, unconditional
zeitaku-na ぜいたく(な) luxurious, extravagant

Borrowed (foreign) adjectives can also be dealt with as other Japanese adjectival nouns.

derikēto-na デリケート(な) delicate
gōjasu-na ゴージャス(な) gorgeous
hotto-na ホット(な) hot
hansamu-na ハンサム (な) handsome

ADJECTIVES (also known as *i*-adjectives)
I-adjectives are used to modify nouns which directly follow them, but are also used as predicates and thus can be conjugated. They conjugate depending on the word following and their function in the sentence.

Adjective Forms
Note that the adjective type of auxiliaries (*-tai*, *-nai*, and *-rashii*) conjugate in the same manner as *i*-adjectives.

1. DICTIONARY FORM
   • As non-past predicate
     (Adding *desu* at the end makes it polite.)
     *Kono ryōri wa taihen **oishii** desu.*
     This dish is very tasty.
     (Used as a present predicate in a quotation, *desu* does not follow.)

*Ano fuku wa **yasui** to omoimasu.*
I think that dress is cheap.
(In questions in direct speech, *desu* is used before *ka* or *ne*, while in questions in reported speech, *desu* is not used before [*no*] *ka*.)
*Raishū no nichiyōbi wa **isogashii desu** ka.*
Are you busy next Sunday?
*Kyō wa totemo **atsui desu** ne.*
It's very hot today, isn't it?
*Kanojo ni dore ga **ii** (no) ka tazuneyō.*
I will ask her which is good.

• As attributive adjective, modifying noun directly following
*Watashi wa totemo **takai kamera** o kaimashita.*
I bought a very expensive camera.

• As presumptive predicate, followed by *deshō/kamoshirenai*
*Ashita wa **samui deshō**.*
It will probably be cold tomorrow.
*Kono tabemono wa **furui kamoshirenai**.*
This food may be stale.

• Preceding the following words and phrases, dealt with in Part I:
aida, dake, deshō, desu, dokoro de (wa) nai, dokoroka, hazu desu, hazu ga nai, hō, hodo, kagiri, kamoshirenai, kara, keredo(mo), koto, mitai (2), mono, na, nagara, nara, ni chigai nai, ni mo kakawarazu, no, node, no desu, no ni, rashii, sō desu, to, toki ni, tokoro, to shitemo, to sureba, tsumori desu, uchi ni, wake, yō desu, yori

2. *KU*-FORM

This form is made by replacing the final *-i* with *-ku*. It is used in making the *te*-form and negative form, and functions in the various ways listed below.

DICT. FORM (MEANING)	*KU*-FORM	POLITE NEG. (NON-PAST)	POLITE NEG. (PAST)
isogashii (busy)	*isogashiku*	*isogashiku arimasen*	*isogashiku arimasen deshita**
tanoshii (fun)	*tanoshiku*	*tanoshiku arimasen*	*tanoshiku arimasen deshita*
hayai (early)	*hayaku*	*hayaku arimasen*	*hayaku arimasen deshita*
yoi (good)	*yoku*	*yoku arimasen*	*yoku arimasen deshita*
takai (tall)	*takaku*	*takaku arimasen*	*takaku arimasen deshita*
kowai (scary)	*kowaku*	*kowaku arimasen*	*kowaku arimasen deshita*

(**arimasen* is the polite negative of *aru* [to be], and *deshita* is the past form of *desu* [to be])

- As polite negative in predicate
  *Watashi no ie wa eki kara **tōku arimasen**.*
  My house is not far from the station.
  *Shiai no kekka wa **yoku arimasen deshita**.*
  The results of the game were not good.
  (*Wa* may be put between the *ku*-form and *arimasen* in order to express something in contrast with the preceding adjective.)
  *Kore wa **takaku wa arimasen** ga amari yoku arimasen.*
  This is not expensive, but it's not so good.

- As adverb
  *Kare wa itsumo **isogashiku** ugokimawatte imasu.*
  He is always busily moving about.
  *Watashi tachi wa kyō **tanoshiku** gogo o sugoshimashita.*
  We spent this afternoon pleasantly.

- Decribing the subject or object as a result of change
  *Kanojo wa **utsukushiku** narimashita.*
  She became beautiful.
  *Watashi o **kanashiku** sasenaide kudasai.*
  Please don't make me sad.

- Preceding the following words and phrases, dealt with in Part I:
  *arimasen, nai, nakereba ikenai, nakereba naranai, nakutemo
  yoi, naru, suru, te, temo ii*

3. *NAI*-FORM

   This form expresses the non-past negation. It is made by
   adding *-nai* to the *ku*-form. *Nai* in turn conjugates like an *i*-
   adjective.

DICT. FORM	*NAI*-FORM (PLAIN)	*NAI*-FORM (POLITE)
muzukashii	*muzukashiku nai*	*muzukashiku nai desu*
samui	*samuku nai*	*samuku nai desu*

- The functions are exactly the same as those of the dictionary
  form above, as *nai* is the dictionary form of the adjective *nai*.
  The *nai*-form can be followed by any words or phrases that
  follow the dictionary form.
  *Kyō wa amari **samuku nai** desu ne.*
  Today isn't very cold, is it?
  ***Waruku nai** to omoimasu.*
  I think it is not bad. (I don't think it is bad.)

*Amari **muzukashiku nai** hon o katta hō ga ii desu.*
It would be better for you to buy a book that is not very difficult.
*Kanojo no iū koto wa **tadashiku nai** deshō.*
Probably what she says is not right.

4. *TA*-FORM
This form expresses past states and states that have continued up to the time of speaking. It is made by replacing the final -*i* with -*katta* (affirmative) or by adding *nakatta* to the *ku*-form (negative).

DICT. FORM	PLAIN PAST (AFF.)	PLAIN PAST (NEG.)
yoi	*yokatta*	*yoku nakatta*
isogashii	*isogashikatta*	*isogashiku nakatta*

• As simple past predicate
(Adding *desu* after the adjectve makes it polite.)
*Watashi wa motto yukkuri shi**takatta desu**.*
I wanted to stay longer.
(In a quotation, *desu* is not used.)
*Kanojo wa **yoku nakatta** to itte imashita.*
She said it was not good.
(In questions in direct speech, *desu* is used before *ka* or *ne*, while in questions in reported speech, *desu* is not used before [*no*] *ka*.)
*Kyō wa totemo **samukatta desu ne**.*
It was very cold today, wasn't it?
*Kare ni nani ga **yokatta no ka** kikanakatta.*
I didn't ask him what was good (about it).

• Expressing state which has continued up to the time of speaking
*Nihongo wa watashi ni wa totemo oboe**nikukatta** desu.*
Japanese has been very difficult for me to learn.

- Modifying noun which directly follows
  Tanoshikatta omoide *wa wasuremasen.*
  I will never forget the pleasant memories.

- As presumptive predicate, followed by *deshō/kamoshirenai*
  *Kono mondai wa karera ni wa **muzukashikatta kamoshiremasen**.*
  This problem might have been difficult for them.

- Preceding the following words and phrases, dealt with in Part I:
  dake, dokoro ka, hazu desu, hazu ga nai, kara, kamoshirenai, keredo(mo), koto, mitai (2), mono, nara, ni chigainai, ni mo kakawarazu, no, node, no desu, no ni, rashii, sō desu (1), tame ni, toki ni, to shitemo, to sureba, tsumori desu, wake, yō desu

5. *TE*-FORM

This form expresses an unemphatical reason or cause, a condition, or contrastive qualities.

It is made by adding *-te* to the *ku*-form. The negative of the *te*-form can be made by adding *nakute* (*te*-form of *nai*) to the *ku*-form.

DICT. FORM	*TE*-FORM	NEG. OF *TE*-FORM
muzukashii	*muzukashikute*	*muzukashiku nakute*
atsui	*atsukute*	*atsuku nakute*

- Expressing unemphatic reason or cause
  *Kono mondai wa **muzukashikute** watashi ni wa dekimasen.*
  This problem is so difficult that I can't solve it.

- Expressing actual condition
  *Kyō wa **atsuku nakute** yokatta desu ne.*
  Fortunately today was not hot.

• See also *sore ni, te* in Part I

6. *BA*-FORM
This form expresses a present or past condition.

It is made by replacing the final *-i* with *-kereba*. The negative of the *ba*-form is made by adding *-nakereba* (*ba*-form of *nai*) to the *ku*-form. A future condition is expressed by the *ku*-form + *nareba*.

DICT. FORM	BA-FORM	NEG. OF BA-FORM
warui	*warukereba*	*waruku nakereba*
isogashii	*isogashikereba*	*isogashiku nakereba*

> *Tenki ga **warukereba** enki shimashō.*
> If the weather is bad, let's postpone it.
> *Anata no tasuke ga **nakereba** dekimasen deshita.*
> Without your help, I couldn't have done it.
> *Ima **isogashiku nakereba** o-hanashi shitai no desu ga.*
> If you are not busy now, I would like to talk with you.

• See also *ba, nara, tara, to* in Part I

7. *TARA*-FORM
This form expresses a present condition.

It is made by adding *-tara* to the stem of the *ta*-form. The negative of the *tara*-form is made by adding *-nakattara* (*tara*-form of *-nai*) to the *ku*-form. A past condition is expressed by the *ta*-form + *no nara*, and a future condition by the *ku*-form + *nattara*.

DICT. FORM	TARA-FORM	NEG. OF TARA-FORM
takai	*takakattara*	*takaku nakattara*
samui	*samukattara*	*samuku nakattara*

Takaku nakattara sore o kau kamoshiremasen.
If it is not expensive, I may buy it.

• See also *ba*, *nara*, *tara*, *to* in Part I

8. STEM
The stem is made by dropping the final *-i*.

It can be followed by *garu, sō desu,* and *sugiru,* included in Part I.

DICT. FORM	STEM
samui	*samu*
furui	*furu*

9. COMPARATIVE
The comparative is the same as the dictionary form, but using *hō* and *yori* makes it clear that the adjective is comparative.
Ano hō ga *kore yori takai* desu.
That is more expensive than this.
Kono hō ga *watashi ni wa ii* desu.
This is better for me.
Ano kuruma no hō ga *atarashii* desu.
That car is newer.

10. SUPERLATIVE
The superlative is made by putting *mottomo* or its informal equivalent, *ichiban*, before the positive form of the adjective. *De*, *no uchi de,* or *no naka de* are used to indicate which items are included in the comparison or the scope of comparison.
Nihon de ***mottomo takai*** *yama wa fuji-san desu.*
The highest mountain in Japan is Mt. Fuji.
Kenji ga ***san nin no uchi de ichiban wakai*** *desu.*

Kenji is the youngest of the three.
Kono naka de *dore ga* ***mottomo yoi*** *desu ka.*
Which is the best of them?

11. EQUIVALENT DEGREE COMPARISON

To onaji kurai/gurai, which literally means "to the extent of similarity," is used in the affirmative, and *hodo* in the negative.

Katakana wa ***hiragana to onaji kurai*** *oboeru no ga* ***muzukashii***.

Katakana is as difficult as hiragana to learn.

Watashi wa ***kare hodo kashikoku arimasen***.

I am not as clever as he.

- Comparison of adjectival nouns and adverbs is made in the same manner as above

- See also *hō, hodo, kurai, mottomo, yori* in Part I

List of Common Adjectives

abunai 危ない dangerous
akarui 明るい bright, cheerful
amai 甘い sweet, superficially optimistic, not strict
atarashii 新しい new, fresh, up-to-date
atatakai 暖かい warm
atsui 熱い, 暑い hot
buatsui 分厚い thick, bulky
chiisai 小さい small, low (of volume)
chikai 近い near, close
furui 古い old (not used of humans)
futoi 太い fat, bold
hayai 速い fast, quick, rapid, speedy, prompt
hayai 早い early
hazukashii 恥かしい shy, bashful

hiroi 広い wide, broad, spacious, vast
hosoi 細い thin, slender
ii いい good, nice, fine, right, suitable
isogashii 忙しい busy
itai 痛い painful, sore
kanashii 悲しい sad, sorrowful
karui 軽い light, slight (of illness)
kashikoi かしこい smart, clever, wise
katai かたい stiff, tight, hard
kawaii かわいい lovely, cute, tiny
kitanai 汚い dirty, foul, nasty
kowai 恐い afraid, fearful
kurai 暗い dark, gloomy
mijikai 短い short, brief
muzukashii むずかしい difficult, troublesome
nagai 長い long
nai ない there is not, does not exist
nemui 眠い sleepy, drowsy
nikui にくい hateful, hard (to do)
oishii おいしい tasty, delicious
okashii おかしい funny, crazy, improper
omoi 重い heavy, serious (of illness)
omoshiroi 面白い interesting, amusing, enjoyable
ōi 多い many, much, numerous, frequent
ōkii 大きい big, large, loud, tall
osoroshii 恐ろしい fearful, terrible, horrible
otonashii おとなしい obedient, tame, well-behaved, quiet
sabishii 寂しい lonely
samui 寒い chilly, cold (of the weather)
semai 狭い narrow, small
subarashii 素晴らしい wonderful, excellent, marvelous, splendid
sukunai 少ない a few, a little
suzushii 涼しい cool (of the weather)
tadashii 正しい correct, accurate, right

takai 高い tall, high, expensive
tanoshii 楽しい pleasant, delightful, enjoyable
tarinai 足りない lacking, insufficient, foolish
tōi 遠い distant, far
tsumaranai つまらない boring, dull, worthless
tsumetai 冷たい cold, icy
tsuyoi 強い strong, tough, powerful
umai うまい good (of technique), delicious
ureshii 嬉しい glad, happy
usui 薄い thin, light (of color)
utsukushii 美しい beautiful
yasashii やさしい easy, kind
yasui 安い cheap, easy (to do)
yoi 良い good, fine, sufficient
yoroshii よろしい all right, good, allowable
yowai 弱い weak, frail
wakai 若い young
warui 悪い bad, stale, sick

ADVERBS
Japanese adverbs are placed flexibly in any position in a sentence except at the end.

List of Common Adverbs
amari あまり (not) very much
ato de 後で later
chanto ちゃんと neatly, properly, punctually, correctly
chotto ちょっと a little, a bit, a moment
dōzo どうぞ please
hotondo ほとんど almost, hardly, seldom (with a negative)
korekkiri これっきり for this once, once and for all
māmā まあまあ so-so
mazu まず to begin with, first of all
mō もう already, (by) now, soon, yet (in questions)

sakki さっき a short while ago
shibaraku しばらく for a while, for the time being
shitagatte したがって accordingly
sukkari すっかり completely, perfectly
sukoshi 少し a little, a bit, a moment
sukoshimo 少しも (not) at all
susunde すすんで willingly, voluntarily
taihen たいへん very (much)
tatoe たとえ even, no matter
tokuni 特に especially, in particular
tonikaku とにかく anyhow, anyway, in any case
totemo とても very, really, (not) by any means
tsui つい unintentionally, by mistake
yagate やがて before long, soon
yoku よく often, well, hard
yukkuri ゆっくり slowly, without hurry
zehi ぜひ by all means
zuibun ずいぶん fairly, very much
zutto ずっと all the time

Nouns Used as Adverbs

asatte あさって day after tomorrow
ashita あした tomorrow
chōdo ちょうど just now, precisely
gūzen 偶然 by chance, by accident
ima 今 now, at present
itsumo いつも always, usually
kinō きのう yesterday
kondo 今度 next time, this time, some other time
kyō きょう today
ototoi おととい day before yesterday
rai(shū/getsu) 来（週／月） next week/month
saikin 最近 recently
tokubetsu 特別 especially, particularly

totsuzen 突然 suddenly, abruptly, unexpectedly
zenbu 全部 all
zenzen 全然 (not) at all, completely
(The above can be used as adjectives as well, by adding *no* before the noun they modify.)

Ku-form of Adjectives Used as Adverbs
hayaku はやく early, fast, quickly, rapidly
hidoku ひどく badly, severely, terribly
kuwashiku 詳しく in detail
mijikaku みじかく briefly
sugoku すごく terribly, awfully

Adjectival Nouns + *Ni*, Used as Adverbs
gutaiteki ni 具体的に concretely, definitely
hontō ni 本当に really, truly
jiyū ni 自由に freely
jōzu ni 上手に skillfully
kantan ni 簡単に easily
omo ni 主に chiefly, mainly

Onomatopoeic Words (+ *To*), Used as Adverbs
(The following are words that imitate sound or voice, called *giseigo*.)
dokidoki (to) どきどき（と） (heart beats) fast
gayagaya (to) がやがや（と） (talk) noisily
zāzā (to) ざあざあ（と） (rain) heavily

Mimicry Words (+ *To*), Used as Adverbs
(The following are words that imitate action or movement, called *gitaigo*.)
kotsukotsu (to) こつこつ（と） (work) steadily
nikoniko (to) にこにこ（と） smilingly
wakuwaku (to) わくわく（と） excitedly

CONJUNCTIONS
To Connect Nouns
1. *TO*
   - Between nouns: . . . and . . .
   *Watashi wa **tenisu to sukii** ga tokui desu.*
   I am good at tennis and skiing.

2. *YA*
   - Between nouns: . . . and . . .
   *Hima-na toki wa **shinbun ya zasshi** o yomimasu.*
   When I'm free, I read things such as newspapers and magazines.

3. *MO*
   - After each noun: . . . and (also) . . .
   *Kanojo wa **nihongo mo chūgokugo mo** hanashimasu.*
   She speaks Japanese and also Chinese (both Japanese and Chinese).

4. *KA*
   - Between nouns: . . . or . . .
   ***Kōhii ka o-cha** o nomitai.*
   I want to drink coffee or green tea.

To Connect Sentences
1. COMMON CONJUNCTIVE WORDS
   daga だが but, however (written language)
   dakara だから and so, therefore, that's why
   dewa では then, if so (informal form is *ja*)
   keredo(mo) けれども but (informal)
   shikashi しかし but (formal)
   sorekara それから and, and then, after that, since then
   soreni それに moreover, besides

soshite そして and, and then

2. USED BETWEEN SENTENCES

Gūzen michi de Tanaka-san ni aimashita. **Sorekara/Soshite** *issho ni shokuji o shimashita.*

I happened to meet Mr.Tanaka on the street. And then we had a meal together.

Kinō anata ni nando mo denwa o kakemashita. **Keredomo/ Shikashi** *demasen deshita.*

I telephoned you many times yesterday. But there was no answer.

To Connect Verbs/Adjectives/Adjectival Nouns

1. *TE*-FORM OF VERB CAN BE FOLLOWED BY ANOTHER VERB/ADJECTIVE/ADJECTIVAL NOUN:. . . AND . . .

*Ie e kaette **neta** hō ga ii.*

You had better go back home and sleep.

*Anata ni aete totemo **ureshii** desu.*

I met you and I am very glad. (I am very glad to meet you.)

*Kare wa hatarakisugite **byōki ni** natta.*

He overworked and became sick.

2. *TE*-FORM OF ADJECTIVE CAN BE FOLLOWED BY ANOTHER VERB/ADJECTIVE/ADJECTIVAL NOUN: . . . AND . . .

*Ano kuruma wa takakute **kaemasen**.*

That car is expensive, and so I can't buy it. (That car is too expensive for me to buy.)

*Kono sashimi wa atarashikute **oishii** desu yo.*

This raw fish is fresh and delicious.

*Kare wa se ga takakute **suteki** desu.*

He is tall and cute.

3. (ADJECTIVAL) NOUN + *DE* CAN BE FOLLOWED BY AN-

OTHER VERB/ADJECTIVE/ADJECTIVAL NOUN: . . . AND
. . .

> *Haha wa **byōki de nete** imasu.*
> My mother is sick and sleeping. (My mother is sick in bed.)
> *Kyō wa **ame de mushiatsui**.*
> Today is rainy and sultry.
> *Kare wa **reisei de kenmei-na** hito desu.*
> He is a calm and earnest man.

To Connect Clauses

1. *TE*-FORM OF VERB/ADJECTIVE, OR ADJECTIVAL NOUN
   + *DE*, CAN BE FOLLOWED BY ANOTHER STATEMENT

   > *Densha ni okure**te dō shita n desu ka**.*
   > What did you do after you missed the train?
   > *Takusan kanji o oboe**te yatto shinbun ga yomeru yō ni nari-mashita**.*
   > I learned many kanji, and so finally am able to read newspapers.

List of Common Conjunctive Words Used Between Clauses

aida (ni) 間(に) while (doing)
ato de 後で after (doing)
ga が but, though
ka (soretomo) か(それとも) or
kara から because, since, after (doing)
keredo(mo) けれど(も) although
made まで till
mae ni 前に before (doing)
nagara ながら while (doing)
nara なら if
nimo kakawarazu にもかかわらず in spite of the fact
node ので because
noni のに although, in spite of the fact
tabi ni 度に whenever, each time
to と when, if, after (doing)

toki (*ni*) 時 (に) when

COUNTERS
Japanese uses various counters, depending on the nature or shape of the object being counted.

List of Common Counters
bai 倍 times (multiplicative number)
ban 番 No. (number or ranking)
banme 番め (ordinal number)
dai 台 vehicles or machines
doru ドル dollars
en 円 yen
fun 分 minutes
gatsu 月 months (of the year)
hai 杯 cups or glasses
hiki 匹 small animals, fish, worms, or insects
hon 本 long objects like sticks, bottles, etc.
ji 時 o'clock
jikan 時間 hours
ka 日 days (of the month, from the second to the tenth)
kagetsu ヶ月 months (as the unit)
kai 回 times (frequency)
kiro キロ kilometers or kilograms
ko 個 objects of small, round, or non-specific shape
mai 枚 thin or flat objects, like paper, boards, slices, etc.
nen 年 years (as the date and unit)
nichi 日 days (for one day or more than ten days, or for days of the month after the tenth)
nin 人 persons
sai 才 years old
satsu 冊 books, volumes
shūkan 週間 weeks
wa 羽 birds

Usage of Counters

1. IN A SENTENCE, THE NUMBER + COUNTER IS GENER-
   ALLY PLACED AFTER THE NOUN (+ PARTICLE) TO
   WHICH IT REFERS

   *Ie no mae ni **kuruma ga ni dai** tomatte imasu.*
   Two cars are parked in front of the house.
   *Koko ni **pen ga ni hon** to **kami ga ni mai** arimasu.*
   Here are two pens and two sheets of paper.
   ***Kōhii o ni hai** nomimashita.*
   I drank two cups of coffee.
   *Eki made **takushii de ni juppun** kakarimasu.*
   It takes twenty minutes to the station by taxi.

2. WHEN PRECEDING A NOUN, THE NUMBER + COUNTER
   IS FOLLOWED BY *NO*

   ***San nin no seito** ga kesseki desu.*
   Three students are absent.
   *Migi kara **san banme no seki** ni suwatte kudasai.*
   Please sit down in the third seat from the right.

3. IN A QUESTION (HOW MANY/HOW MUCH), *NAN* +
   COUNTER IS USED

   *Isshūkan ni hon o **nan satsu** gurai yomimasu ka.*
   About how many books do you read in a week?
   *Hagaki o **nan mai** motte imasu ka.*
   How many postcards do you have?
   *Kyō wa **nan nichi** desu ka.*
   What day of the month is today?

   • Note the following euphonic changes after *nan* :

nan bon	何本	How many sticks
nan bai	何杯	How many cups
nan biki	何匹	How many animals
nan pun	何分	How many minutes

List of Counters With Euphonic Changes

Following are several of the most common counters in Japanese. Note the euphonic changes that occur when these counters are combined with a number.

1. MINUTES (*fun* 分)

1	*ippun*	6	*roppun*
2	*nifun*	7	*nanafun*
3	*sanpun*	8	*hachifun/happun*
4	*yonpun*	9	*kyūfun*
5	*gofun*	10	*juppun*

2. CUPS OR GLASSES (*hai* 杯)

1	*ippai*	6	*roppai*
2	*nihai*	7	*nanahai*
3	*sanbai*	8	*hachihai*
4	*yonhai*	9	*kyūhai*
5	*gohai*	10	*juppai*

3. SMALL ANIMALS (*hiki* 匹)

1	*ippiki*	6	*roppiki*
2	*nihiki*	7	*nanahiki*
3	*sanbiki*	8	*hachihiki/happiki*
4	*yonhiki*	9	*kyūhiki*
5	*gohiki*	10	*juppiki*

4. LONG OBJECTS LIKE STICKS, BOTTLES, ETC. (*hon* 本)

1	*ippon*	6	*roppon*
2	*nihon*	7	*nanahon*
3	*sanbon*	8	*hachihon/happon*
4	*yonhon*	9	*kyūhon*
5	*gohon*	10	*juppon*

5. DAYS (OF THE MONTH) (*ka* 日)

1	*tsuitachi*	6	*muika*
2	*futsuka*	7	*nanoka*
3	*mikka*	8	*yōka*
4	*yokka*	9	*kokonoka*
5	*itsuka*	10	*tōka*

6. DAYS (AS A UNIT) (*nichi, ka* 日)

1	*ichinichi*	6	*muika*
2	*futsuka*	7	*nanoka*
3	*mikka*	8	*yōka*
4	*yokka*	9	*kokonoka*
5	*itsuka*	10	*tōka*

7. MONTHS (AS A UNIT) (*kagetsu* カ月)

1	*ikkagetsu*	6	*rokkagetsu*
2	*nikagetsu*	7	*nanakagetsu*
3	*sankagetsu*	8	*hachikagetsu*
4	*yonkagetsu*	9	*kyūkagetsu*
5	*gokagetsu*	10	*jukkagetsu*

8. KILOGRAMS OR KILOMETERS (*kiro* キロ)

1	*ichikiro*	6	*rokkiro*
2	*nikiro*	7	*nanakiro*
3	*sankiro*	8	*hachikiro*
4	*yonkiro*	9	*kyūkiro*
5	*gokiro*	10	*jukkiro*

9. SMALL, ROUND, OR NON-SPECIFIC OBJECTS (*ko* 個)

1	*ikko*	6	*rokko*
2	*niko*	7	*nanako*
3	*sanko*	8	*hachiko*
4	*yonko*	9	*kyūko*
5	*goko*	10	*jukko*

10. PERSONS (*nin* 人)

1	*hitori*	6	*rokunin*
2	*futari*	7	*nananin/shichinin*
3	*sannin*	8	*hachinin*
4	*yonin*	9	*kyūnin/kunin*
5	*gonin*	10	*jūnin*

11. BOOKS, VOLUMES (*satsu* 冊)

1	*issatsu*	6	*rokusatsu*
2	*nisatsu*	7	*nanasatsu*
3	*sansatsu*	8	*hassatsu*
4	*yonsatsu*	9	*kyūsatsu*
5	*gosatsu*	10	*jussatsu*

12. BIRDS (*wa* 羽)

1	*ichiwa*	6	*rokuwa*
2	*niwa*	7	*nanawa*
3	*sanba*	8	*hachiwa*
4	*yonwa*	9	*kyūwa*
5	*gowa*	10	*juppa*

13. YEARS OLD (*sai* 才)

1	*issai*	6	*rokusai*
2	*nisai*	7	*nanasai*
3	*sansai*	8	*hassai*
4	*yonsai*	9	*kyūsai*
5	*gosai*	6	*jussai*

EUPHONIC CHANGES

Only the consonant-stem verbs have euphonic changes, and these occur only when the *te-*, *ta-*, or *tara-* form of the verb is made. There are three types of euphonic changes: the *i*-sound change, the gemi-

nated consonant change, and the syllabic nasal consonant change.
See also *te* in Part I and Verb Forms in Part II.

I-Sound Change

When the dictionary form of the verb ends with the syllable -*ku* or
-*gu*, replace it with -*i*. When -*gu* is replaced with -*i*, *te* and *ta* after the
-*i* become *de* and *da* respectively.

DICT. FORM	*TE*-FORM	*TA*-FORM
hataraku (to work)	*hataraite*	*hataraita*
kaku (to write)	*kaite*	*kaita*
nugu (to take off)	*nuide*	*nuida*
oyogu (to swim)	*oyoide*	*oyoida*

    Iku (to go) is an exception which is dealt with below.

Geminated Consonant Change

When the dictionary form ends with the syllable -*u*, -*ru*, or -*tsu*,
replace it with the geminated consonant -*tt*, resulting in -*tte* and -*tta* in
the -*te* and *ta*-forms. This double consonant sound is expressed by the
reduced *kana* っ.

DICT. FORM	*TE*-FORM	*TA*-FORM
iku (to go)	*itte*	*itta*
iū (to say)	*itte*	*itta*
kau (to buy)	*katte*	*katta*
matsu (to wait)	*matte*	*matta*
motsu (to hold)	*motte*	*motta*
noru (to ride)	*notte*	*notta*
owaru (to end)	*owatte*	*owatta*

Syllabic Nasal Consonant Change

When the dictionary form ends with the syllable -*bu*, -*mu*, or -*nu*, replace it with *-n*. The following *te* and *ta* become *de* and *da* respectively.

DICT. FORM	*TE*-FORM	*TA*-FORM
asobu (to play)	*asonde*	*asonda*
manabu (to learn)	*manande*	*mananda*
nomu (to drink)	*nonde*	*nonda*
shinu (to die)	*shinde*	*shinda*
yomu (to read)	*yonde*	*yonda*

INTRANSITIVE AND TRANSITIVE VERBS

Verbs which do not or cannot take a direct object are called intransitive verbs. Verbs which can take a direct object are called transitive verbs. The objects are mainly followed by the particles *o*, *wa*, *ni*, or *ga*. However, the object before any Japanese transitive verb can be freely dropped.

"*Akari o keshimasu ka.*" "*Kesanaide kudasai.*"
"Shall I turn off the light?" "Please don't turn (it) off."
"*Kinō pōru ni aimashita ka.*" "*Aimasen deshita.*"
"Did you meet Paul yesterday?" "I didn't meet (him)."
"*Watashi wa gorufu ga dekimasen.*" "*Watashi mo dekimasen.*"
"I cannot play golf." "I can't play (it), either."

List of Pairs of Intransitive and Transitive Verbs

Pairs of intransitive and transitive verbs are listed below, but as explained above, the transitive verbs of these pairs do not necessarily take a direct object.

INTRANSITIVE	TRANSITIVE
agaru 上がる (to go up)	*ageru* 上げる (to raise)
aku 開く (to open)	*akeru* 開ける (to open)
ataru 当たる (to hit)	*ateru* 当てる (to hit)

butsukaru ぶつかる (to bump)

butsukeru ぶつける (to bump)

deru 出る (to go out)

dasu 出す (to let out)

fueru 増える (to increase)

fuyasu 増やす (to increase)

hairu 入る (to go in)

ireru 入れる (to put in)

hajimaru 始まる (to begin)

hajimeru 始める (to begin)

hanareru 離れる (to separate)

hanasu 離す (to let go)

hazureru 外れる (to come off)

hazusu 外す (to remove)

hieru 冷える (to grow cold)

hiyasu 冷やす (to cool)

hirogaru 広がる (to spread)

hirogeru 広げる (to spread)

kaeru 帰る (to go back)

kaesu 帰す (to let go back)

kakureru 隠れる (to be hidden)

kakusu 隠す (to hide)

kawaru 変わる (to change)

kaeru 変える (to change)

kieru 消える (to be put out)

kesu 消す (to put out)

kimaru 決まる (to be decided)

kimeru 決める (to decide)

kireru 切れる (to be cut)

kiru 切る (to cut)

koboreru こぼれる (to spill)

kobosu こぼす (to spill)

kowareru 壊れる (to break down)

kowasu 壊す (to break)

magaru 曲がる (to bend)

mageru 曲げる (to bend)

matomaru まとまる (to be united/arranged)

matomeru まとめる (to unite/arrange)

mawaru 回る (to rotate)

mawasu 回す (to rotate)

mazaru 混ざる (to be mixed)

mazeru 混ぜる (to mix)

michiru 満ちる (to become full)

mitasu 満たす (to fill)

mitsukaru 見つかる (to be found)

mitsukeru 見つける (to find)

moreru もれる (to leak)

morasu もらす (to let leak)

mukeru むける (to peel)

muku むく (to peel)

muku 向く (to face)

mukeru 向ける (to turn)

nakunaru なくなる (to be lost)

nakusu なくす (to lose)

narabu 並ぶ (to be lined up)

naraberu 並べる (to line up)

nokoru 残る (to be left over)

nokosu 残す (to leave)

nobiru 伸びる (to grow long)

nobasu 伸ばす (to lengthen)

nobiru 延びる (to be postponed)

nobasu 延ばす (to postpone)

noru 乗る (to ride/get on)

noseru 乗せる (to give a ride)

nukeru 抜ける (to fall out)

nuku 抜く (to pull out)

ochiru 落ちる (to fall)

otosu 落とす (to drop)

okiru 起きる (to get up)

okosu 起こす (to wake up)

oreru 折れる (to break in two)

oru 折る (to break off/fold)

oriru 降りる (to get down)

orosu 降ろす (to take down)

owaru 終わる (to be over)

oeru 終える (to finish)

sagaru 下がる (to go down/off)

sageru 下げる (to lower)

sameru さめる (to get cold)

samasu さます (to cool)

shimaru 閉まる (to close)

shimeru 閉める (to close)

tamaru 貯まる (to be saved up)

tameru 貯める (to save up)

tasukaru 助かる (to be rescued)

tasukeru 助ける (to rescue)

tatsu 立つ (to stand up)

tateru 立てる (to stand)

tokeru 溶ける (to melt)

tokasu 溶かす (to melt)

tomaru 止まる (to stop)

tomeru 止める (to stop)

toreru 取れる (to come off)

toru 取る (to remove)

tsuzuku 続く (to continue)

tsuzukeru 続ける (to continue)

tsuku 点く (to be lighted)

tsukeru 点ける (to light)

tsumaru 詰まる (to be packed)

tsumeru 詰める (to pack)

tsunagaru つながる (to connect)

tsunagu つなぐ (to connect)

tsutawaru 伝わる (to spread)

tsutaeru 伝える (to tell)

umareru 生まれる (to be born)

umu 生む (to give birth to)

yakeru 焼ける (to bake)

yaku 焼く (to bake)

yasumu 休む (to take a rest)

yasumeru 休める (to rest)

waku 沸く (to boil)

wakasu 沸かす (to boil)

wareru 割れる (to crack)

waru 割る (to crack)

NOUNS

Japanese nouns have no gender or cases in themselves. Case is indicated by a particle. There is also no distinction between singular and plural nouns. However, certain suffixes such as *tachi* may be added after a pronoun to indicate the plural.

Types of Nouns

1. CONJUNCTIVE FORM AS NOUN

There are several verbs whose conjunctive forms can be dealt with as nouns.

DICT. FORM OF VERB	CONJUNCTIVE FORM AS NOUN
hajimeru (to begin)	*hajime* (the beginning)
hareru (to clear up)	*hare* (good weather)
kangaeru (to think)	*kangae* (a thought/idea/ opinion)
kotaeru (to answer)	*kotae* (an answer)
odoroku (to be surprised)	*odoroki* (a surprise)
owaru (to end)	*owari* (an end)
tasukeru (to help)	*tasuke* (a help)

2. ADJECTIVE STEM AS NOUN

There are several adjectives whose stems can be dealt with as nouns, though some require a specific suffix.

DICT. FORM OF ADJECTIVE	STEM AS NOUN
akai (be red)	*aka* (the color red)
shiroi (be white)	*shiro* (the color white)
takai (be high)	*taka-sa* (height)
tanoshii (be pleasant)	*tanoshi-mi* (pleasure)

3. COMPOUND NOUNS
 • Noun + noun
  kyūkō ressha express train
  gijutsu kakushin technological innovation
 • Conjunctive form of verb + noun

wasure-mono forgotten item
de-guchi exit, way out

- Stem of adjective + noun
  chika-michi shortcut
- Noun + conjunctive form of verb
  hana-mi flower viewing
- Conjunctive form of verb + conjunctive form of another verb
  hiki-dashi drawer
- Stem of adjective + conjunctive form of verb
  yasu-uri bargain sale
- Noun + stem of adjective
  ki-naga leisurely attitude
- Stem of adjective + stem of another adjective
  hoso-naga slenderness
- Double noun
  hito-bito people

POLITE LANGUAGE

In Japanese two kinds of polite language are very commonly used. Respectful language shows respect toward a person to whom or about whom the speaker is talking, and humble language indicates the speaker's humbleness. Caution is advised regarding the overuse of polite language, as it can create a sense of distance between the speaker and those being addressed.

Prefixes and Suffixes

1. *O-*

   Noun prefix, mainly for words of Japanese origin.

o-kāsan	mother (of the other person)
o-miyage	a souvenir
o-namae	the name (of the other person)
o-shigoto	the work (of the other person)
o-tenki	the weather
o-tōsan	father (of the other person)

2. *GO-*
   Noun prefix, mainly for nouns of Chinese origin.

go-jitaku	home (of the other person)
go-kurō	hardship (of the other person)
go-seikō	success (of the other person)
go-jūsho	address (of the other person)
go-shujin	husband (of the other person)

3. *-SAN*
   Suffix added to family or first names, or nouns expressing relation, status, or condition.

Tanaka-san	Mr. (Ms.) Tanaka
Tarō-san	Taro
oji-san	uncle or an oldish gentleman
oba-san	aunt or an oldish lady
kachō-san	the chief of a section
o-tsukare-san*/ *go-kurō-san**	tiredness (You worked hard, thank you.)

   (*set phrases for thanking somebody after finishing a job)

4. *-SAMA*
   A suffix used in the same way as *-san*, but more respectful and formal.

Yamada-sama	Mr. (Ms.) Yamada
o-kyaku-sama	customer or visitor
dochira-sama/ donata-sama	who

Polite Auxiliary Verbs

1. *DESU*
   The polite equivalent of the auxiliary verb *da*.

2. *-MASU*
   The polite auxiliary verb used for making the *masu*-form of verbs.

3. *-REMASU*

A respectful and polite auxiliary verb. It conjugates just like *masu* and is used with consonant-stem verbs or the irregular *suru*.

- Consonant-stem verbs: added to the stem of *nai*-form
  iku → *ikaremasu*
  iū → *iwaremasu*
- Irregular verb: *suru*
  suru → *saremasu*

4. *-RAREMASU*

A respectful and polite auxiliary verb. It conjugates just like *masu* and is used with *iru*- and *eru*-verbs or the irregular *kuru*.

- *Iru*- and *eru*-verbs: added to the stem of *nai*-form
  miru → *miraremasu*
  taberu → *taberaremasu*
- Irregular verb: *kuru*
  kuru → *koraremasu*

Patterns Indicating Speaker's Humility

1. *O* + CONJUNCTIVE FORM OF VERB + *SHIMASU/ITASHI-MASU*

   (*Itashimasu* is more humble than *shimasu*.)
   *Denwa o **o-kari itashimasu**.*
   I'd like to use your telephone.

2. *GO/O* + NOUN + *SHIMASU/ITASHIMASU*

   (*Itashimasu* is more humble than *shimasu*.)
   ***Go-kyōryoku shimasu**.*
   I'm pleased to cooperate with you.
   *Sukoshi **go-shitsumon itashimasu**.*
   I'd like to ask you something.

Patterns Showing Respect and Politeness to Another

1. *GO/O* + NOUN OF ACTION + *NASAIMASU*

*Kono kippu o **go-riyō nasaimasu** ka.*
Will you make use of this ticket?

2. *GO/O* + NOUN OF OBJECT + *NI NASAIMASU*
   ***O-shokuji ni nasaimasu** ka.*
   Will you be having a meal?

3. *O* + CONJUNCTIVE FORM OF VERB + *NI NARIMASU*
   ***O-yobi ni narimashita** ka.*
   Did you call me?

4. *GO/O* + NOUN OF ACTION/STATE + *NI NARIMASU*
   *Tanaka sensei ga **go-tōchaku ni narimashita**.*
   Dr. Tanaka has just arrived.

Respectful Verbs

RESPECTFUL VERB	PLAIN FORM	MEANING
de gozaimasu	*da*	to be
gozonji desu	*shitte iru*	to know
irasshaimasu	*iru*	to be/stay/come/go
meshiagarimasu	*taberu*	to eat
nasaimasu/ saremasu	*suru*	to do
osshaimasu	*iū*	to say

Humble Verbs

HUMBLE VERB	PLAIN FORM	MEANING
itadakimasu	*taberu*	to drink/eat/receive
itashimasu	*suru*	to do
mairimasu	*iku/kuru*	to go/come
mōshiagemasu	*iū*	to say
sashiagemasu	*ageru*	to give
ukagaimasu	*iku/kuru/tazuneru*	to go/come/ask
haiken suru	*miru*	to look at/inspect

Dochira

This is the polite equivalent of *doko* (where), *dore* (which), and *dare* (who). Which meaning it carries must be determined by context (and can at times be confusing).

PREPOSITIONS

Common English prepositions are generally expressed by post-positional particles or phrases in Japanese. When a post-positional phrase using particles precedes a noun and is used to modify it, as a rule the *ni* or *de* in the phrase is replaced with *no*. If *made* or *kara* are used in the phrase, they must be followed by *no*.

Compare the following two sentences:

*Sono hon wa **kaban no naka ni** iremashita.*
I put that book in the bag.
***Kaban no naka no hon** o nakushimashita.*
I lost the book that was in the bag.

(*no naka ni* becomes *no naka no* as it is used to modify the noun [*hon*] which follows)

English Prepositions Expressed in Japanese

1. ABOVE
   - *no ue de/ni*: higher than
     *Ima **kumo no ue ni** imasu.*
     We are above the clouds now.
   - *ijō*: to a greater degree than
     *Tesuto no ten wa **heikin ijō** desu.*
     My test scores are above average.

2. ACROSS
   - *o yokogitte*: crossing from one side to the other side of
     *Obāsan ga **dōro o yokogitte** aruite imasu yo.*

An old woman is walking across the road.

- *no mukō ni*: on the opposite side of
  *Shiyakusho wa ano **ginkō no mukō ni** arimasu.*
  The city office is on the other side of that bank.

3. AFTER
   - *(no) ato de/ni*: the time that follows
     ***Shigoto no ato de** o-cha o nomō.*
     Let's have tea after work.
     *Kaimono o **shita ato de** eiga o miyō.*
     Let's see a movie after doing the shopping.
     ***Anata no ato de** kekkō desu.*
     After you is fine.

4. ALONG
   - *ni sotte* or *o*: parallel to the length of
     *Tokidoki **kaigan ni sotte** sanpo shimasu.*
     I sometimes take a walk along the beach.
   - *o*: from one end to the other end of
     *Kono **tōri o** iku to kōen ga aru.*
     If you go along this street, you will find a park.

5. AMONG
   - *no naka de/ni*: in the middle of/being one of
     ***San satsu no naka de** kore ga ichiban suki desu.*
     I like this best among the three (books).
   - *no aida de/ni*: in the group of
     *Sore wa **karera no aida de** sude ni giron sareta.*
     It was already discussed among them.

6. AT
   - *ni*: time
     ***San ji ni** aimashō.*

Let's meet at three.
- *ni*: place of existence
  *Nichiyōbi wa **ie ni** imasu.*
  I stay at home on Sundays.
- *ni*: cause of some feeling
  *Ano **jiko ni** wa odoroita.*
  I was surprised at that accident.
- *ni*: arriving point
  *Ima **eki ni** tsukimashita.*
  I arrived at the station just now.
- *de*: place where an action is performed
  *Kore wa ano **mise de** kaimashita.*
  I bought this at that store.
- *de*: place where an event is held
  *Kare no **ie de** pātii ga arimasu.*
  There will be a party at his house.

7. AROUND
- *no mawari de/ni*: on all sides of
  ***Eki no mawari ni** mise ga takusan arimasu.*
  There are a lot of stores around the station.

8. BEFORE
- *(no) mae ni*: the time that precedes
  ***Chōshoku no mae ni** sanpo o shimasu.*
  I take a walk before breakfast.
  ***Iku mae ni** suru koto ga arimasu.*
  I have something to do before I go.
- *no mae de/ni*: in front of
  ***Ōzei no mae de** hanasu no wa suki de nai.*
  I don't like speaking before many people.

9. BEHIND
- *no ushiro de/ni*: in the back of

*Kiiroi **sen no ushiro ni** sagatte kudasai.*
Please step back behind the yellow line.
- *no ura de/ni*: at the back of
  *Chūshajō wa **tatemono no ura ni** arimasu.*
  The parking lot is behind the building.
- *yori okurete*: later than
  *Hikōki wa **yotei yori okurete** tsukimashita.*
  The airplane arrived behind schedule.

10. BELOW
    - *no shita de/ni*: in/on a lower place than
      *Tsuki ga **chiheisen no shita ni** shizunda.*
      The moon went below the horizon.
    - *ika de/ni*: less than
      *Kion wa **go do ika ni** naru deshō.*
      The temperature will go below five degrees.

11. BESIDE
    - *no soba de/ni:* near
      ***Ie no soba ni** kōen ga arimasu.*
      There is a park beside my house.

12. BESIDES
    - *ni kuwaete*: in addition to
      ***Jishin ni kuwaete** kaji mo okotta.*
      Besides the earthquake, fires also occurred.
    - *no hoka ni*: except
      ***Kore no hoka ni** o-kane wa arimasen.*
      I have no money besides this.

13. BETWEEN
    - *. . . to . . . no aida de/ni*: in the space
      *Yūbinkyoku wa **ginkō to kōban no aida ni** aru.*
      The post office is between the bank and the police box.

• *. . . kara . . . no aida de/ni*: in the time
Ni ji kara san ji no aida ni *kite kudasai.*
Please come between two and three o'clock.

14. BY

• *de*: method or means
Takushii de *ikimashō.*
Let's go by taxi.
• *made ni*: limit of time/deadline
Go ji made ni *modorimasu.*
I'll be back by five.
• *no soba de/ni*: near
Toire wa **deguchi no soba ni** *arimasu.*
The rest room is by the exit.
• *ni (yotte)*: the agent of a passive verb
Demo wa **guntai ni yotte osaerareta.**
The demonstration was suppressed by the army.

15. DURING

• *no aida* or *jū:* throughout the whole period of
Natsu **yasumi no aida** *gaikoku ni imasu.*
I'll be abroad during the vacation.
• *no aida ni*: at some time within a period of
Rusu no aida ni *dareka kimashita ka.*
Did anyone call on me during my absence?

16. EXCEPT

• *igai wa/ni*: but
Ame no **hi igai wa** *aruite ikimasu.*
I walk there except on rainy days.

17. FOR

• *ni*: indirect object
Kanojo ni *nani o katte agemashita ka.*

What did you buy for her?

- *ni*: purpose
  *Mai asa **sanpo ni** ikimasu.*
  I go for a walk every morning.
- *ni*: occasion
  ***Tanjōbi ni** kore o moratta.*
  I was given this for my birthday.
- *kan* or *no aida*: period of time
  ***Ni nen kan** nihon ni imashita.*
  I was in Japan for two years.
- *no tame ni* (modifies verbs): benefit of someone/thing
  ***Kanojo no tame ni** pātii o shimasu.*
  We'll give a party for her.
- *e* or *ni*: destination or direction
  *Asu **tōkyō e** dekakemasu.*
  I'm leaving for Tokyo tomorrow.
- *ni totte*: semantic subject of verb in the infinitive
  *Kanji o oboeru no wa **watashi ni totte** muzukashii.*
  It is difficult for me to learn kanji.
- *ni wa*: someone for whom some state is excessive
  *Kore wa **watashi ni wa** takasugiru.*
  This is too expensive for me.
- *de*: price
  *Kore o **sen en de** kaimashita.*
  I bought this for one thousand yen.

18. FROM
    - *kara*: starting point
      *Shinkansen wa kono **eki kara** demasu.*
      The shinkansen starts from this station.
    - *kara*: point in time something starts
      *Mise wa **ku ji kara** aite iru.*
      The store is open from nine o'clock.
    - *kara*: material

*Sake wa **kome kara** tsukurareru.*
Sake is made from rice.
- *de*: cause
*Ojiisan wa **gan de** shinimashita.*
My grandfather died of cancer.

19. IN
- *ni*: at some time during
Go gatsu ni *kare wa nihon ni kimasu.*
He'll come to Japan in May.
- *ni*: place of existence
*Ani wa **kyōto ni** sunde imasu.*
My brother lives in Kyoto.
- *de*: place where an action is performed
*Kare wa **heya de** nete iru.*
He is sleeping in his room.
- *de*: place where an event is held
*Konsāto wa ano **hōru de** arimasu.*
The concert is given in that hall.
- *no naka de/ni*: within an enclosed space
*Kamera wa **kaban no naka ni** aru.*
The camera is in the bag.
- *de*: method or means
Nihongo de *hanasemasu ka.*
Can you speak in Japanese?
- *ni*: direction toward which an action is directed
*Karera wa ano **hōkō ni** itta.*
They went in that direction.

20. INTO
- *no naka e*: toward the inside of
*Inu ga **heya no naka e** haitte kita.*
A dog came into the room.
- *ni*: result of a change

Kore o **nihongo ni** *naoshite kudasai.*
Please put this into Japanese.

21. NEAR
 • *no chikaku de/ni*: close to
 Eki no chikaku ni *yasui hoteru wa arimasu ka.*
 Is there a cheap hotel near the station?

22. OF
 • *no*: belonging or in relation to
 Kuruma no taiya ga panku shita.
 My car has a flat tire.
 • *no*: semantic object/subject of a noun expressing action
 Sono **imi no setsumei** *wa muzukashisugiru.*
 The explanation of the meaning is too difficult.
 • *no*: apposition
 Watashi wa **kōbe no machi** *ga suki desu.*
 I like the city of Kobe.

23. ON
 • *ni*: at the time of
 Nan **yōbi ni** *koraremasu ka.*
 On what day can you come?
 • *ni/de*: on the surface of
 Kabe ni *kirei-na e ga aru.*
 There is a beautiful picture on the wall.
 • *no ue de/ni*: on the horizontal surface of
 Jisho wa **tsukue no ue ni** *aru.*
 The dictionary is on the desk.

24. ONTO
 • *no ue e/ni*: toward the surface of
 Neko ga **tēburu no ue e** *tobiagatta.*
 A cat jumped onto the table.

25. OVER

- *no ue de/ni*: in a higher position
  *Sono **kaikyō no ue ni** hashi ga dekita.*
  A bridge was built over the strait.
- *yori takaku*: higher than
  *Ano kikyū wa **kumo yori** takaku tonde iru.*
  That balloon is flying over the clouds.
- *o koete*: to the far side of
  *Neko ga **hei o koete** nigeta.*
  A cat ran away over the fence.
- *no mukō de/ni:* on the other side of
  *Kanojo wa kono **dōro no mukō ni** sunde imasu.*
  She lives on the other side of this road.
- *ijō:* more than
  ***Hyaku mai ijō** shii dii o motte imasu.*
  I have over one hundred CDs.

26. SINCE

- *kara* or *irai*: from a point in past time
  *Senshū no **nichiyōbi kara** byōki desu.*
  I've been sick since last Sunday.
  *Kanojo to **saigo ni atte kara** ni nen ni narimasu.*
  It is two years since I saw her last.
- *no toki kara*: from a point in past time
  *Watashi tachi wa **gakusei no toki kara** tomodachi desu.*
  We've been friends since we were students.

27. THROUGH

- *o tōtte*: in one side and out the other side of
  *Densha ga nagai **tonneru o tōtte** kita.*
  The train came through the long tunnel.
- *no aida*: from the beginning to the end of
  ***Fuyu no aida** shinshū de sukii o shimasu.*
  I'll ski in Shinshū through the winter.

• *made*: up to and including
*Getsuyōbi kara **kin'yōbi made** hatarakimasu.*
I work from Monday through Friday.

28. THROUGHOUT
    • *no aida (zutto)* or *jū*: from start to finish
    ***Gakusei jidai no aida zutto** arubaito o shita.*
    I worked part-time throughout my school days.

29. TO
    • *ni*: indirect object
    ***Anata ni** sore o agemasu.*
    I'll give that to you.
    • *ni* or *e* or *made*: destination/direction
    ***Tōkyō ni** ikimasu.*
    I'm going to Tokyo.
    • *made*: time when an action is stopped
    *Jū ji kara **go ji made** hatarakimasu.*
    I work from ten to five.

30. TOWARD
    • *no hō e:* direction
    *Kare wa **eki no hō e** ikimashita.*
    He went toward the station.

31. UNDER
    • *no shita de/ni*: in/to a lower place than
    ***Tēburu no shita ni** inu ga imasu.*
    A dog is under the table.
    • *miman* or *ika de/ni*: less than
    ***Jū hassai miman no** hito wa hairemasen.*
    People under eighteen may not enter.
    (As explained above, when the phrase is used to modify a
    noun immmediately following it, *no* is used in place of *ni*.)

32. UNTIL
- *made*: up to
  Asa made *hon o yonde imashita.*
  I was reading books till morning.

33. WITH
- *to issho ni*: accompanied by
  Anata to issho ni *ikitai desu.*
  I want to go with you.
- *de* or *o tsukatte*: means or method
  Enpitsu o tsukatte *kudasai.*
  Please use a pencil.
- *de*: cause
  Kinō wa **kaze de** *nete imashita.*
  I was in bed with a cold yesterday.
- *no aru*: character of
  Kare wa **yūmoa no aru** *hito desu.*
  He is a man with a sense of humor.
- *no tsuita*: attached, possessing
  Akai **raberu no tsuita** *shōhin ga bāgen desu.*
  The items with red labels are bargains.
- *de*: material for covering
  Fuji-san wa **yuki de** *ōwarete iru.*
  Mt. Fuji is covered with snow.

PRONOUNS
Personal Pronouns
Japanese personal pronouns are frequently omitted except when it is not easy to guess who is being referred to. In general, the name of a person or his/her position or occupation followed by the polite suffix *-san* is commonly used instead of a personal pronoun. Case is given to the personal pronoun by adding specific particles *wa*, *ga*, *o*, *ni*, or *no*.

I	*watashi, boku/ore* (male)
we	*watashi tachi, boku/ore tachi* (male)
you (sing.)	*anata, kimi* (informal)
you (pl.)	*anata tachi, kimi tachi* (informal)
he	*kare, kono/sono/ano hito*
she	*kanojo, kono/sono/ano hito*
they	*karera, kono/sono/ano hito tachi*

Demonstrative Nouns

These pronouns become *kono*, *sono*, and *ano* respectively before nouns they modify.

this, these	*kore, kochira* (polite)
it, they, that, those	*sore, sochira* (polite)
that, those (over there)	*are, achira* (polite)

The following are used for expressing place and direction (combined with the particles *ni*, *de*, *e*, *kara*, or *made*).

this place, here	*koko*
that place, there	*soko*
that place, over there	*asoko*
this way (direction/side)	*kochira*
that way (direction/side)	*sochira*
that way over there (direction/side)	*achira*
which way (direction/side)	*dochira*

• See also *are, kore, sore* in Part I

VERBS

Japanese verbs change form not according to person or the number of the subject, but according to the verbs, auxiliaries, particles, or other function words which follow the verb. There are three types of regular verbs and two irregular verbs. The dictionary form of all verbs ends with -*u*.

Iru-Verbs
The dictionary form always ends with -*iru*. The verbs listed below look like *iru*-verbs but actually conjugate as consonant-stem verbs.

hairu 入る to enter
hashiru 走る to run
kiru 切る to cut
shiru 知る to know
iru 要る to need

List of Common *Iru*-Verbs
dekiru できる can (do), to complete
kariru 借りる to borrow
miru 見る to see, look, watch
okiru 起きる to get up, wake up
ochiru 落ちる to fall, come down, crash
shinjiru 信じる to believe (in), trust

Eru-Verbs
The dictionary form always ends with -*eru*. The verbs listed below look like *eru*-verbs but actually conjugate as consonant-stem verbs.

keru 蹴る to kick
shaberu しゃべる to speak, chat
suberu すべる to slip, slide
kaeru 帰る to go back, come back
neru 練る to elaborate, knead

List of Common *Eru*-Verbs
ageru あげる to give, raise, do (something) for others

akeru 開ける to open
akirameru あきらめる to give up
dekakeru 出かける to go out, set out
deru 出る to go out, come out, leave, graduate, appear
hareru 晴れる to clear up
ireru 入れる to put in, insert
kikoeru 聞こえる to be heard, be audible
kotaeru 答える to answer
kowareru 壊れる to break down, get out of order
kureru くれる to be given, get a profit by an action
mieru 見える to be seen, be visible, appear (come)
miseru 見せる to show, let (somebody) see
neru 寝る to sleep, go to bed
noberu 述べる to describe
oboeru 覚える to memorize, learn (by heart)
oeru 終える to finish
okureru 遅れる to be late, be delayed
oshieru 教える to teach, tell
tasukeru 助ける to help
tazuneru 尋ねる to ask, visit, call on
tomeru 止める to stop, park
tsukareru 疲れる to get tired
tsukeru つける to turn on, light, attach
umareru 生まれる to be born
wasureru 忘れる to forget, leave (something) behind
yameru やめる to quit, stop, retire

Consonant-Stem Verbs

The dictionary form ends in *-ru*, *-u*, *-ku*, *-gu*, *-su*, *-tsu*, *-nu*, *-bu*, or *-mu*. The second to last syllable may be any consonant + any vowel, or just a vowel.

List of Common Consonant-Stem Verbs

aru ある to exist

aruku 歩く to walk

asobu 遊ぶ to play, amuse oneself

au 会う to meet, see (a person)

chigau 違う to differ, be wrong

dasu 出す to let out, take out, post, hand in, pay

furu 降る to fall (of rain or snow)

ganbaru がんばる to do one's best, hold on, try hard

hanasu 話す to speak, talk, tell

harau 払う to pay

hataraku 働く to work

hiku 引く to pull, draw, minus, reduce a price

iku 行く to go

iū 言う to say, tell

kaku 書く to write

kasu 貸す to lend

kau 買う to buy

kesu 消す to turn off, erase, extinguish

kiku 聞く to hear, listen, ask

magaru 曲がる to turn (a corner), curve, bend

ma ni au 間に合う to be in time, catch (a train, bus, etc.)

matsu 待つ to wait

morau もらう to be given, receive

motsu 持つ to hold, have, possess

naku 泣く to cry, weep

nakunaru なくなる to be gone, run out, pass away

nakusu なくす to lose

narau 習う to take lessons, learn

naru なる to become

nomu 飲む to drink, eat (soup), take (medicine)

noru 乗る to ride, get on, board

odoroku 驚く to be surprised

okonau 行う to do, perform (an action)

oku 置く to put, place

okuru 送る to send, see off

oru おる to be, stay
osu 押す to push, press
owaru 終わる to be over, end
shimaru 閉まる to be closed, be shut
shinu 死ぬ to die
sumu 住む to live, reside
suwaru 座る to sit down, be seated
tatsu 立つ to stand up, leave
tomaru 止まる to come to a stop, run down
tomaru 泊まる to stay (overnight)
toru 取る to take, take off, remove
tsuzuku 続く to continue, follow
tsukau 使う to use, handle, spend (money)
tsuku 着く to arrive, get to
tsukuru 作る to make, cook, manufacture
utau 歌う to sing
wakaru わかる to understand, know, recognize
warau 笑う to laugh, giggle, grin, chuckle
yaru やる to do, give (informal)
yasumu 休む to take a rest, be absent
yomu 読む to read

Irregular Verbs
kuru 来る to come
suru する to do, perform various actions, be in some state

Verb Forms
1. DICTIONARY FORM

This refers to the plain form found in the dictionary and always ends with *-u*.

• This form is used at the end of a relative clause which modifies a noun placed directly after it, or in other types of subordinate clauses such as noun clauses. The *masu*-form cannot be used in such clauses. Also note that the use of the *masu*-form to end sentences in conversation is more polite.

Anata ga susumete kureru jisho *o kaimashō.*
I'll buy the dictionary that you recommend to me.
Kare ga chūgoku ni iku koto *o shitte imasu ka.*
Do you know that he is going to China?

- This form is also used at the end of an appositive clause which precedes specific nouns, such as *yōsu* (sign/look), *nozomi* (hope), *yakusoku* (promise/appointment), *jijitsu* (fact), etc.

  *Kare wa **akirameru yōsu** ga nai.*
  He shows no sign of giving up.
  *San ji ni **tomodachi to au yakusoku** ga aru n desu ga.*
  Sorry, I have an appointment to meet my friend at three.
  *Kare ga **seikō suru nozomi** wa nai.*
  There is no hope that he will succeed.

- The dictionary form can also precede the following words and phrases, dealt with in Part I: *bakari, beki, bun, dake, deshō, dokoro de (wa) nai, dokoro ka, hazu desu, hazu ga nai, hō, hodo, hō ga ii, hoka nai, igai, kagiri, kamoshirenai, kara, kawari ni, keredo(mo), koto, koto ga aru, koto ga dekiru, koto ni naru, koto ni natte iru, koto ni shite iru, koto ni suru, kurai, made, made ni, mae, mitai (2), mono, na, nara, ni chigai nai, ni mo kakawarazu, ni tsurete, ni wa, no, node, no desu, no ni, rashii, shika, sō desu (1), tabi ni, tame ni, to, toka, toki ni, tokoro, to shitemo, to sureba, tsuide ni, tsumori desu, tte, uchi ni, wake, ya, yō desu, yō ni, yō ni suru, yō ni iū, yori*

2. *NAI*-FORM

This form expresses plain negation.

- This form is made as follows:
  Consonant-stem verbs: Replace the final *-u* with *-a* and add *nai*. When the final *-u* is preceded by another single vowel, as in *iū* or *kau*, replace the *u* with *wa* and add *nai*.

Iru-verbs and *eru*-verbs: Delete the final *-ru* and add *nai*.
Irregular verbs: *kuru* → *konai, suru* → *shinai*

- *Nai* is an *i*-adjective, thus the *nai*-form conjugates just like an *i*-adjective. The *ta*-form, *te*-form, *ba*-form and *tara*-form of the *nai*-form are *-nakatta, -nakute, -nakereba,* and *-nakattara* respectively.

DICT. FORM	NAI-FORM	TA-FORM OF NAI-FORM
	•	•
	TE-FORM OF NAI-FORM	BA-FORM OF NAI-FORM
miru	*minai*	*minakatta*
	minakute	*minakereba*
deru	*denai*	*denakatta*
	denakute	*denakereba*
iku	*ikanai*	*ikanakatta*
	ikanakute	*ikanakereba*
kau	*kawanai*	*kawanakatta*
	kawanakute	*kawanakereba*
suru	*shinai*	*shinakatta*
	shinakute	*shinakereba*
kuru	*konai*	*konakatta*
	konakute	*konakereba*
iū	*iwanai*	*iwanakatta*
	iwanakute	*iwanakereba*

- This form is used at the end of a relative or other type of clause which modifies a noun placed directly after it. It can also be used at the end of a sentence, but the negative form of *masu* is more polite.

Yomanai hon *ga takusan arimasu.*
There are many books that I don't read.
Kanojo wa **sore o shiranai** *to omoimasu.*
I think she doesn't know that. (I don't think she knows that.)

- Like the dictionary form, the *nai*-form can be used at the end of an appositive clause which precedes specific nouns, such as *yōsu* (sign/look), *yakusoku* (promise/appointment), *jijitsu* (fact), etc.
  *Dare ni mo **iwanai yakusoku** desu yo.*
  That's a promise not to tell it to anybody, all right?

- The *nai*-form can also precede the following words and phrases, dealt with in Part I: *bun, dake, deshō, dokoro ka, hazu desu, hazu ga nai, hō, hodo, hō ga ii, kagiri, kamoshirenai, kara, kawari ni, keredo(mo), koto, koto ga aru, koto ga dekiru, koto ni shite iru, koto ni suru, kurai, mitai (2), nara, ni chigai nai, ni mo kakawarazu, no, node, no desu, no ni, rashii, sō desu (1), tame ni, to, to shitemo, to sureba, tsumori desu, uchi ni, wake, yō desu, yō ni, yō ni suru, yō ni iū, yori*

- See also *nai, nai uchi ni, nakereba ikenai, nakereba naranai, nakutemo yoi* in Part I

3. CONJUNCTIVE FORM
   This form can be conjoined with *-masu, -te, -ta, -tara* and other various function words.
   - This form is made as follows:
     Consonant-stem verbs: Replace the final *-u* with *-i*.
     Iru-verbs and *eru*-verbs: Delete the final *-ru*.
     Irregular verbs: *kuru* → *ki, suru* → *shi*

   - The conjunctive form can precede the following words and phrases, dealt with in Part I: *au, dasu, hajimeru, kata, masu, na, nagara, nasai, ni, nikui, sō desu (2), sō ni natta, sugiru, tai, te, yasui*

4. *MASU*-FORM
   This is the polite affirmative form, which is made by adding

masu to the conjunctive form of the verb.

This form cannot be used in relative clauses. It is commonly used at the end of a sentence or certain subordinate clauses.

- *Masu* can be replaced with the following variations of *masu* to express the meanings on the right respectively:

masen	Polite non-past negative
mashita	Polite past affirmative
masen deshita	Polite past negative
mashō	Polite volitional

DICT. FORM	*MASU*-FORM	NON-PAST (NEG.) • PAST (NEG.)	PAST (AFF.) • VOLITIONAL
miru	*mimasu*	*mimasen*	*mimashita*
		mimasen deshita	*mimashō*
deru	*demasu*	*demasen*	*demashita*
		demasen deshita	*demashō*
iku	*ikimasu*	*ikimasen*	*ikimashita*
		ikimasen deshita	*ikimashō*
suru	*shimasu*	*shimasen*	*shimashita*
		shimasen deshita	*shimashō*
kuru	*kimasu*	*kimasen*	*kimashita*
		kimasen deshita	*kimashō*

- Used to express an invitation
  *Ashita wa eiga o mi ni **ikimasen** ka.*
  Would you like to go see a movie tomorrow?
  *Watashi no atarashii kuruma de doraibu ni **ikimashō**.*
  Let's go for a drive in my new car.

- Used to express habitual action
  *Sumimasen ga, watashi wa nama no tabemono wa zenzen **tabemasen**.*
  I'm sorry, but I don't eat raw food at all.

- Used to express a suggestion
  *O-cha demo **nomimashō** ka.*
  Shall we have tea or something?

- Used to express present action
  *Kono natsu yasumi wa dokoka e **ikimasu** ka.*
  Are you going anywhere during this summer vacation?

- Used to express past perfect action
  *Sono eiga wa mō **mimashita**.*
  I've already seen that movie.

- Used to express volition
  *Watashi ga kawari ni sore o **shimashō**.*
  I will do it in place of you.

- See also *masu* in Part I

5. *TE*-FORM
   This form expresses actions in succession, an unemphatical reason or cause, a process of action, contrastive actions, or a condition.
   - This form is made by adding *-te* to the conjunctive form. However, the *-te* of *te*-form becomes *-de* after the conjunctive form of a consonant-stem verb whose dictionary form ends with *-bu*, *-gu*, *-mu*, or *-nu*. The last syllable of the conjunctive form of a consonant-stem verb whose dictionary form ends with the following syllables is also euphonically changed before *-te* as follows. See also Euphonic Changes in Part II.

     -ku, -gu → *-i-* (*-ite/-ide*)
     -u, -tsu, -ru → *-t-* (*-tte*)
     -bu, -mu, -nu → *-n-* (*-nde*)

DICT. FORM	TE-FORM
asobu	*asonde*
iku*	*itte*
oyogu	*oyoide*
kaku	*kaite*
kuru	*kite*
shimaru	*shimatte*
shinu	*shinde*
suru	*shite*
taberu	*tabete*
nomu	*nonde*
matsu	*matte*
miru	*mite*
iū	*itte*

(*iku is an exception)

- The *te*-form can precede the following words and phrases, dealt with in Part I: *ageru, aru, bakari, hoshii, irai, iru, itadaku, kara, kudasai, kureru, mitai (1), morau, oru, sorekara, soshite, yoroshii*
  See also *te hoshii, te iku, te kuru, te miru, te oku, temasu, te shimau*

- See also Euphonic Changes in Part II

6. *TA*-FORM

This form expresses past actions or events, completion of an action or movement, lasting state as the result of an action, or movement and experiences at some undefined time.

- This form is simply made by replacing -*te* of *te*-form with -*ta*.

DICT. FORM	TA-FORM
iku	*itta*

304 • GRAMMATICAL EXPLANATIONS

kaku	*kaita*
kuru	*kita*
suru	*shita*
taberu	*tabeta*
miru	*mita*
iū	*itta*

- This form is used in a relative clause which modifies a noun, or in other types of subordinate clauses. It can also end a sentence, but in conversation it is more polite to use *-mashita*.
  *Watashi wa **kinō katta hon** o mō yomimashita.*
  I've already read the book that I bought yesterday.

- Like the dictionary form, this form can be used at the end of an appositive clause which precedes specific nouns, such as *yōsu* (sign/look), *jijitsu* (fact), etc.
  *Kanojo wa **yoku natta yōsu** ga nai.*
  She shows no sign of having gotten better.
  *Kare ga **misu o okashita jijitsu** wa hitei dekinai.*
  The fact that he made a mistake cannot be denied.

- The *ta*-form of several verbs may be used as an attributive adjectival which can be used to modify a noun immediately following it.

DICT. FORM	*TA*-FORM
hanareru (to stay away)	*hanareta* (distant)
kawaru (to differ)	*kawatta* (peculiar/unusual)
komaru (to have difficulty)	*komatta* (difficult/embarrasing)
machigau (to make an error)	*machigatta* (wrong/incorrect)
megumareru (to be blessed)	*megumareta* (blessed/comfortable)

- The *ta*-form can precede the following words and phrases, dealt with in Part I: *ato de, bakari, bun, dake, dokoro ka, hazu desu, hazu ga nai, hō, hodo, hō ga ii, kamoshirenai, kara, kawari ni, keredo(mo), koto, koto ga aru, mitai (2), mono, na, nara, ni chigai nai, ni mo kakawarazu, no, node, no desu, no ni, rashii, sō desu (1), tame ni, toki ni, tokoro, tokoro ga, to shitemo, to sureba, tsuide ni, tsumori desu, tte, wake, yō desu, yori*

7. *BA*-FORM

This form expresses a non-past condition.

- This form is made as follows:
  Iru- and *eru*-verbs: Replace the final *-ru* with *-re*, and add *ba*.
  Consonant-stem verbs: Replace the last vowel with *-e*, and add *ba*.
  Irregular verbs: *suru* → *sureba*, *kuru* → *kureba*

DICT. FORM	*BA*-FORM	NEG. CONDITIONAL
iku	*ikeba*	*ikanakereba*
miru	*mireba*	*minakereba*
taberu	*tabereba*	*tabenakereba*

- See also *ba*, *nara*, *tara*, *to* in Part I

8. *TARA*-FORM

This form is a conditional that means "if," "when," "after (doing)," and so forth. It implies the completion of an individual action.

- This form is made by adding *-tara* to the stem of the *te*-form. Note that *tara*-form of the copula verb *da* is *dattara*.

DICT. FORM	*TARA*-FORM	NEG. FORM
iku	*ittara*	*ikanakattara*
miru	*mitara*	*minakattara*
taberu	*tabetara*	*tabenakattara*

- See also *ba*, *nara*, *tara*, *to* in Part I

9. POTENTIAL FORM

This form expresses potential and ability.

- This form is made as follows:

  Consonant-stem verbs: Replace the final *-u* with *-areru*. When the final *-u* is preceded by another vowel, as in *iū* or *kau*, replace it with *-wareru*. To be more informal, replace the final *-u* with *-eru*.

  Iru- and *eru*-verbs: Replace the final *-ru* with *-rareru*, or replace the final *-ru* with *-reru*. (The latter is ungrammatical but commonly used.)

  Irregular verbs: *suru* → *dekiru* (*iru*-verb), *kuru* → *korareru/ koreru* (The latter is ungrammatical but commonly used.)

- All verbs in the potential form made by the rules above, except *dekiru*, are dealt with as *eru*-verbs. Refer to the explanation of *eru*-verb conjugation in the entries above.

DICT. FORM	PLAIN POTENTIAL (FORMAL/INFORMAL) POLITE POTENTIAL (FORMAL/INFORMAL)
iku	*ikareru/ikeru* *ikaremasu/ikemasu*
taberu	*taberareru/tabereru* *taberaremasu/taberemasu*
hanasu	*hanasareru/hanaseru* *hanasaremasu/hanasemasu*
matsu	*matareru/materu* *mataremasu/matemasu*
miru	*mirareru/mireru* *miraremasu/miremasu*

- The direct object of potential verbs is indicated by *ga* or *o*. *Kanojo wa nihongo **ga/o hanasemasu** ka.* Can she speak Japanese?

• See also *koto ga dekiru* in Part I

10. PASSIVE FORM

This form expresses the passive.

 • This form is made as follows:
   Consonant-stem verbs: Replace the final -*u* with -*areru*.
   When the final -*u* is preceded by another vowel, as in *iū* or
   kau, replace it with -*wareru*.
   Iru- and *eru*-verbs: Replace the final -*ru* with -*rareru*.
   Irregular verbs: *suru* → *sareru*, *kuru* → *korareru*

 • Verbs in the passive form are dealt with as an *eru*-verbs. Refer
   to the explanation of *eru*-verb conjugation in the entries
   above.

DICT. FORM	PASSIVE (PLAIN)	PASSIVE (POLITE)	TE-FORM
kowasu	*kowasareru*	*kowasaremasu*	*kowasarete*
nusumu	*nusumareru*	*nusumaremasu*	*nusumarete*

 • Usually transitive verbs that describe an action toward a
   direct object can be formed into the passive.
   *Densha no naka de saifu ga/o **nusumaremashita**.*
   My wallet was stolen (I had my wallet stolen) in the train.

 • In Japanese a few intransitive verbs that do not take an object,
   such as *kuru* or *furu*, can be formed into the passive to express
   an action that is inconvenient for the speaker. The agent of the
   passive verb may be indicated by *ni*.
   *Isogashii toki ni mata **o-kyaku-san ni korareta**.*
   A visitor came again when I was busy.
   *Kaeru tochū de **ame ni furaremashita**.*
   I was caught in the rain on my way home.

 • See also *ni, ni yotte* in Part I and honorific form below

11. HONORIFIC FORM

This form is used for showing the speaker's respect toward the subject of the verb.

- This form is made in the same manner as the passive form. Therefore, whether the form is passive or honorific must be determined from the context. A verb in the honorific form is dealt with as an *eru*-verb.

  *Anata mo **ikaremasu** ka.*

  Will you go, too?

  Sensei wa kyō wa koraremasen.

  The teacher isn't coming today.

- See also Polite Language in Part II

12. COMMAND FORM

This form expresses a strong, emphatic command. Its use in conversation is not advised unless the speaker wants to sound abrupt. It is used when a superior orders something to be done, or when spectators cheer a team.

- This form is made as follows:

  Consonant-stem verbs: Replace the final *-u* with *-e*.

  Iru- and *eru*-verbs: Replace the final *-ru* with *-ro*.

  Irregular verbs: *suru* → *shiro*, *kuru* → *koi*

- The negative command form is the dictionary form + *na*.

- The sentence-ending particle *yo* may be added, especially when speaking to a friend, in order to soften the command.

  *Chanto **shiro yo.***

  Do it right, okay?

- See also *ka, kudasai, kureru, masen, morau, nasai* in Part I

13. PRESUMPTIVE FORM

This form expresses the speaker's uncertainty concerning future, present, or past actions, events, or states.

- This form is expressed by adding *deshō, mitai, rashii, sō desu,* or *yō desu* to the dictionary form of verbs.

- See also *deshō, mitai, rashii, sō desu, yō desu* in Part I

14. VOLITIONAL FORM

This form expresses the speaker's volition in making a suggestion, similar to the English expression "I will/let's."

- This form is made as follows:

    Consonant-stem verbs: Replace the final *-u* with *-ō.*

    Iru- and *eru*-verbs: Replace the final *-ru* with *-yō.*

    Irregular verbs: *suru → shiyō, kuru → koyō*

DICT. FORM	PLAIN VOLITIONAL	POLITE VOLITIONAL
iku	*ikō*	*ikimashō*
iru	*iyō*	*imashō*
miru	*miyō*	*mimashō*
oku	*okō*	*okimashō*
yameru	*yameyō*	*yamemashō*

- This form can be used to express invitations, offers, or suggestions. However, as it is used rather informally, it is better to use *mashō* (the volitional form of *masu*) in polite speech.

    *Eiga o mi ni **ikō** yo.*

    Let's go and see a movie.

    *Kūrā o **tsukemashō** ka.*

    Shall I turn on the air conditioner?

    *Koko de kaimono o **shimashō** ka.*

    Let's do our shopping here, shall we?

- The negative of this form is as follows:

  Nai-form + *de* + *iyō/imashō*: Let's keep ourselves from (doing).

  Nai-form + *de* + *okō/okimashō*: Let's leave as it is unperformed.

  Dictionary form + *no o* + *yameyō/yamemashō*: Let's give up (doing).

  *Amari **nomanai de okimashō**.*

  Let's not drink too much.

  *Ame na node doraibu ni **iku no o yameyō**.*

  Let's not go for a drive because it is rainy.

- See also *masu*-form in Part II

15. CAUSATIVE FORM

This form expresses the idea that the subject person makes or permits somebody or something to perform an action. In Japanese inanimate things are rarely used for the subject of the verb in the causative form. A verb in the causative form is dealt with as an *eru*-verb.

- This form is made as follows:

  Consonant-stem verbs: Replace the final *-u* with *-a*, and add *-seru*. When the final *-u* is preceded by a vowel, as in *iū* or *kau*, replace it with *-wa* and add *-seru*.

  Iru- and *eru*-verbs: Replace the final *-ru* with *-saseru*.

  Irregular verbs: *suru* → *saseru*, *kuru* → *kosaseru*

DICT. FORM	CAUSATIVE (PLAIN)	CAUSATIVE *NAI*-FORM	CAUSATIVE *TA*-FORM
iku	*ikaseru*	*ikasenai*	*ikaseta*
tsukau	*tsukawaseru*	*tsukawasenai*	*tsukawaseta*
miru	*misaseru*	*misasenai*	*misaseta*
nomu	*nomaseru*	*nomasenai*	*nomaseta*

neru   *nesaseru*   *nesasenai*   *nesaseta*
  (*miseru* [to show, let see] is widely used instead of *misaseru*)

- Some verbs may be changed into causative form by the following rules and conjugate as consonant-stem verbs. These verbs
  then become transitive verbs and must take an object (either
  stated or implied).
  Consonant-stem verbs: Replace the final *-u* with *-asu*. When
  the final syllable is *u*, as in *iū* or *kau*, replace it with *-wasu*.
  Iru- and *eru*-verbs: Replace the final *-ru* with *-sasu*.
  Irregular verbs: *suru* → *sasu*, *kuru* → *kosasu*

DICT. FORM	CAUSATIVE (PLAIN)	CAUSATIVE *NAI*-FORM	CAUSATIVE *TA*-FORM
hataraku	*hatarakasu*	*hatarakasanai*	*hatarakashita*
naku	*nakasu*	*nakasanai*	*nakashita*
hashiru	*hashirasu*	*hashirasanai*	*hashirashita*
ugoku	*ugokasu*	*ugokasanai*	*ugokashita*
tobu	*tobasu*	*tobasanai*	*tobashita*
kawaku	*kawakasu*	*kawakasanai*	*kawakashita*

  *Kuruma o sukoshi mae e **ugokashite** kudasai.*
  Please move your car a little forward.

- Use of *ni* with the causative
  The person or thing which is made or let to perform an
  action is followed by *ni* or *o*. *Ni* is used to indicate the
  person made to do something when the verb takes a direct
  object with *o*, or when the person is permitted to do
  something.
    ***Kodomo ni** motto **yasai o** tabesaseta hō ga ii.*
    It is better to make children eat more vegetables.
    ***Watashi ni** soko e ikasete kudasai.*

Please let me go there.
Watashi no buka ni tori ni ikaseru.
I'll have my assistant go and get it.

- Use of *o* with the causative
  This is used when the person or thing is made to do something (with transitive verb), the person is made to have some emotion, or the person is permitted to do something on the subject person's own responsibility (transitive or intransitive verb).
    *Hayaku **kodomo o nekaseta** hō ga ii.*
    It's better to make the child go to bed early.
    ***Josei o nakasete** wa ikenai.*
    You should not make a lady cry.
    Kodomo tachi o** suki-na yō ni **asobaseta.
    I let the children to play as they pleased.

- *Ageru* and *kureru* may be used after *te*-form of the causative in order to express permission in a declarative sentence, or a request in a question.
    *Anata ni watashi no suki-na uta o **kikasete agemasu**.*
    I will let you listen to my favorite songs.
    *Chotto kopii o **tsukawasete kuremasen ka.***
    Will you let me use the copy machine for a while?

16. CAUSATIVE PASSIVE FORM

This form means "to be made to (do)," or "be permitted to (do)."
- This form is made as follows:
  Consonant-stem verbs: Replace the final *-u* with *-a* and add *sareru* or *serareru*. When the last syllable is *-u* as in *iū* or *kau*, replace it with *-wa* and add *sareru* or *serareru*.
  Iru- and *eru*-verbs: Replace the final *-ru* with *-saserareru*.
  Irregular verbs: *suru* → *saserareru*, *kuru* → *kosaserareru*

• *Serareru/saserareru* is made by combining the causative ending *-seru/-saseru* with the passive ending *-rareru*. *Sareru* is the abbreviated form of *serareru*. (The former is more commonly used than the latter.)

• A verb in the causative passive form conjugates as an *eru*-verb.

DICT. FORM	CAUSATIVE PASSIVE FORM
iku	*ikasareru/ikaserareru*
kau	*kawasareru/kawaserareru*
shinjiru	*shinjisaserareru*
akirameru	*akiramesaserareru*

*Watashi wa tokidoki nichiyōbi mo **hatarakasaremasu.***
I am made to work even on Sundays at times.
*Takai mono o **kawasarete** komatte imasu.*
I am distressed because I was forced to buy something expensive.

Election Night of November, 1864

On November 8th, election day, I went over to the War Department about half past eight o'clock in the evening, and found the President and Mr. Stanton together in the Secretary's office . . . . Presently there came a lull in the returns, and Mr. Lincoln called me to a place by his side.

"Dana," said he, "have you ever read any of the writings of Petroleum V. Naseby?"

"No, sir," I said; "I have only looked at some of them and they seemed to be quite funny."

"Well," said he, "let me read you a specimen"; and, pulling out a thin yellow-covered pamphlet from his breast pocket, he began to read aloud. Mr. Stanton viewed these proceedings with great impatience. . . . He could not understand, apparently, that it was by the relief which these jests afforded to the strain of mind under which Lincoln had so long been living, and to the natural gloom of a melancholy and desponding temperament—this was Mr. Lincoln's prevailing characteristic—that the safety and sanity of his intelligence were maintained and preserved.

THE COLLIER BOOKS CIVIL WAR CLASSICS

EARL SCHENCK MIERS, *General Editor*

Noah Brooks
Washington, D. C., in Lincoln's Time
Edited, with an Introduction, by Herbert Mitgang

Charles A. Dana
Recollections of the Civil War
Introduction by Paul M. Angle

Jefferson Davis
The Rise and Fall of the Confederate Government
Foreword by Earl Schenck Miers

Thomas C. DeLeon
Four Years in Rebel Capitals
Introduction by E. B. Long

Those Who Knew Lincoln
Edited by Lloyd Dunlap

Ulysses S. Grant
Grant's Civil War
Edited, with a Foreword, by Earl Schenck Miers

Hinton Rowan Helper
Impending Crisis of the South
Introduction by Earl Schenck Miers

Thomas Wentworth Higginson
Army Life in a Black Regiment
Introduction by Howard N. Meyer

The Official Story of the Decisive Battles of the Civil War
Edited, with a Foreword, by Earl Schenck Miers

William T. Sherman
Sherman's Civil War
Edited, with a Foreword, by Earl Schenck Miers

Sam R. Watkins
"Co. Aytch," A Side Show of the Big Show
Introduction by Roy Basler